The Man Who Made
the Jailhouse Rock

ALSO BY MARK KNOWLES
AND FROM MCFARLAND

The Tap Dance Dictionary (1998; paperback 2012)

*The Wicked Waltz and Other Scandalous Dances:
Outrage at Couple Dancing in the 19th
and Early 20th Centuries* (2009)

Tap Roots: The Early History of Tap Dancing (2002)

The Man Who Made the Jailhouse Rock

Alex Romero, Hollywood Choreographer

MARK KNOWLES

McFarland & Company, Inc., Publishers
Jefferson, North Carolina, and London

LIBRARY OF CONGRESS CATALOGUING-IN-PUBLICATION DATA

Knowles, Mark, 1954–
    The man who made the jailhouse rock : Alex Romero, Hollywood choreographer / Mark Knowles.
        p.   cm.
    Includes bibliographical references and index.

    ISBN 978-0-7864-7594-0
    softcover : acid free paper ∞

    1. Romero, Alex. 2. Choreographers—United States—Biography. 3. Mexican Americans—Biography. I. Title.
GV1785.R584K66 2013
792.8'2092—dc23
[B]   2013026685

BRITISH LIBRARY CATALOGUING DATA ARE AVAILABLE

© 2013 Mark Knowles. All rights reserved

No part of this book may be reproduced or transmitted in any form or by any means, electronic or mechanical, including photocopying or recording, or by any information storage and retrieval system, without permission in writing from the publisher.

On the cover: *inset* Alex Romero, 1959 (Twentieth Century–Fox Film Corporation/Photofest; background (Hemera/Thinkstock)

Manufactured in the United States of America

McFarland & Company, Inc., Publishers
   Box 611, Jefferson, North Carolina 28640
     www.mcfarlandpub.com

For Alex

"[Alex was] the most loved person in the business. I mean it. The most loved. You never heard a bad thing about him. Incredible human being. And talent, incredible. The greatest talent. If they had treated him right at MGM, he would have been as big as any of them, if they had been fair. They were not fair. Not even a credit on the Presley thing, for God's sake! It's horrible. How can they allow you do something as brilliant as that and not give you credit?"

— Jack Mattis, dancer
February 29, 2000

Table of Contents

Acknowledgments ix
Preface 1
  1. Beginnings (1913–1914) 7
  2. Early Life (1914–1929) 12
  3. Vaudeville (1929–1938) 20
  4. Dancing in the Movies (1938–1944) 32
  5. Dancing for Jack Cole (1944–1947) 38
  6. *Words and Music* to *On the Town* (1947–1949) 50
  7. *The Red Danube* to *Two Weeks with Love* (1949–1950) 63
  8. *An American in Paris* to *The Band Wagon* (1950–1953) 72
  9. *Seven Brides for Seven Brothers* to
     The Eddie Fisher Show (1954–1957) 84
10. *Jailhouse Rock* (1957) 97
11. *tom thumb* to "The Goulash" (1958–1962) 108
12. *The Stripper* to *Hustle* (1963–1975) 123
13. Endings (1976–2007) 133
Filmography 143
Television Shows 155
The Theater 158
Chapter Notes 161
Bibliography 197
Index 201

vii

Acknowledgments

Many people have generously supported me in the writing of this book.

First, I would like to thank Bill and Debbie Bartlett. The three of us decided to preserve Alex's stories, and the taped interviews we did provided the groundwork for this biography. Their hard work, determination, and insight was the stepping-off point for this book, and I treasure the memories of being with Bill and Debbie as we sat transfixed while Alex told us about his life.

Bill, Debbie, and I also recorded interviews with Alex in the company of some of his old friends, in particular, Jack Mattis, Alex Ruiz, Sally Whalen, and Lance LeGault. I thank these dancers for their insights about Alex.

As I was writing this book, I tried to find a recording of Alex's memorial service. Although I attended the event and remembered much of it, I wanted to accurately document the tributes that were made during this celebration. Unfortunately, I was unable to find one. However, in the process of looking for the tape, I learned that Dora Kranning had a videotaped interview of Alex. Recorded on July 20, 2004, at the Motion Picture Home in Woodland Hills, California, the interview was one of Alex's last, and I had not seen it before. It was conducted by Aimee Harvey, Caroline Rattray, and Grace Crawford as part of their senior research project for the Aukland University of Technology, Faculty of Health, Bachelor of Dance degree. Ms. Kranning had been one of the project supervisors, along with Dr. Alice Knappstein and Jennifer Nikolai. Kranning's husband, Dr. Pasquale Moscatello, filmed and edited the interview. I thank all of these people for the use of this information and especially Dora and Pasquale for lending me the DVD.

Acknowledgments

I spoke with the following people who knew and loved Alex, and I thank them for their stories: Brian Byers, Gregory Gast, Nancy Gregory, Richard Kuller, Suzanne Collins Kuller, Ruta Lee, Patti Nestor Cox Maser, Russ Tamblyn, and especially Ted Klein and his wife Lysa Baugher Klein. On July 2, 2012, Ted and Lysa hosted a dinner party with some of Alex's friends. Together we reminisced, and I recorded their memories.

That evening, Gregory Gast, Richard Kuller, and I recalled visiting Alex in the Alzheimer's unit at the Motion Picture Home shortly before he died. Alex was in a wheelchair by then and Richard said, "Hey, Alex, let's trade eights." Richard did a short tap step. Greg did a short tap step. Alex, with a huge smile on his face, took his feet off the metal supports at the bottom of his wheelchair and did a tap step. Alex looked at me to do a step. I managed to do a tap step, then had to leave the room for a while, overcome with joy and sadness. I thank Richard and Greg for giving Alex that pleasure.

Richard and Gregory were also responsible for the mini-documentary of Alex's career that was first shown at the Jazz Dance LA "Tribute to Alex Romero" held on October 13, 2001, at the Harriet and Charles Luckman Fine Arts Complex at California State University, Los Angeles. They are talented men and I am grateful for their friendship and for their inspiration.

I received assistance in translating Spanish documents from three of my colleagues at La Salle High School in Pasadena: Maria Santana, Brother de Salles, and Arnold Roche. I thank them for their help.

I also would like to thank my colleagues at the American Academy of Dramatic Arts for continuing to encourage me to grow creatively and to share my own stories with younger generations of artists.

A special thank you to the Huntington Library in San Marino where I was given access to the Fanchon and Marco archives, and to the UCLA Library, Performing Arts Special Collections, for helping me as I explored the Jack Cole papers. I also received help from the librarians at the Margaret Herrick Library at the Academy of Motion Picture Arts and Sciences.

Alex's niece Alix Bainbridge was a great joy. I loved talking with her on the phone and she was always enthusiastically proactive about digging through her mementoes and sending me copies of pictures and

Acknowledgments

documents. Many of these helped me unravel some of the mysteries of the Quiroga family. Alex's nephew John Romero, Jr., also provided important information to me. I am deeply grateful to both of them.

I would especially like to thank Alex's daughters Melinda and Judy, who not only shared their memories of their father and mother, but also gave me unlimited access to family documents and photos. Without their kindness, enthusiasm, and support, this biography would never have been possible. They treated me as if I were one of the family, and I hope I have honored their father's legacy.

My best friend, Tom Robinson, truly is the best. He has helped me in more ways than I could ever say. Thank you, Tom.

My sister Anne has always been there for me. Anne is an accomplished writer and, as with my other books, she proofread the manuscript and gave me advice. My other siblings, Nancy, Rex, and Trudy, have always encouraged me. I am blessed to have them in my life.

My partner, William Holmes, is my proudest supporter, and I thank him for his love, companionship, and excellent cooking. Charlie the cat slept on the desk and kept me company for the writing of this book, and our dog Ruth reminded me to take things easy once in a while. Thanks, family!

Lastly I would like to thank Alex Romero. Once, I was having lunch with Alex and his wife, Faun, at their home. Faun was a great cook and was always trying to fatten me up. She set a second helping of cake on the table in front of me and said, "You are like the son we never had." Alex said, "Yes you are."

Thank you, Alex, for sharing your heart, your family, and your wonderful stories with me. I love you.

Preface

I first met Alex Romero when I worked for him as a dancer on an episode of the television show *Hart to Hart*. He hired me sight unseen upon the recommendation of another dancer. The first day of rehearsal, I was impressed with his complex yet accessible choreography. It was challenging but really fun to do. I also noticed his meticulous preparation and his attention to detail.

What struck me the most, however, was that Alex was such a gentleman. He was kind and courteous to everyone on the set; he was never condescending or mean; and he shared his creativity, enthusiasm, and passion with openness and honesty.

When correcting a dancer, he put his arm around him or her and whispered the note. It was done with gentleness and respect. When it happened to me, I felt such admiration for him that I wanted to do anything I could to make my own performance as good as possible. Other dancers had the same response.

During breaks the other dancers often left to get food or do errands. I stayed on the set to watch Alex. I was fascinated with how he communicated camera angles to the director and cameraman, how he suggested an idea for lighting, and how he worked with his stars, teaching them the moves and putting them at ease.

Alex and I became friends on the project and later he made a special effort to show support for me whenever I was working on other shows. He came and saw almost everything I did. We also met regularly to tap dance together. His footwork was challenging, and his Jack Cole–style arms were nearly impossible for me to do. Alex was patient. He kept working with me. I did not know Alex Romero's movie credits during this time, but I recognized that I was working with a master.

Preface

Alex introduced me to two other performers he thought I should meet, Bill and Debbie Bartlett. The Bartletts are lovely people, and as we spent more and more time together with Alex, we began to learn about his rich life. Every time we were with Alex, we asked him questions about this or that movie. Eventually Bill and Debbie and I approached Alex about making a documentary about his life and work. Alex was excited about the idea, and we started recording interviews with him.

Alex had a lot to tell. His memories of the events in his life were abundant. He had an amazing mind for details, even remembering the names of the crew members and chorus dancers he had worked with on a film.

Alex spoke to us honestly. He was not the type of man to exaggerate things or zealously defend his point of view. I never heard him brag or mislead. In each interview we conducted, he took great pains to correct anything that might be misinterpreted, and when we checked details with him, he let us know if we had misunderstood something. That is not to say that Alex didn't enjoy telling a good story. He worked in the movies, and he knew how to make a story interesting. I suspect that at times he embellished his stories.

Alex was the quintessential gentleman. He was hesitant to tell tales that might shed a negative light on someone. Occasionally, he could be coaxed into opening up, but there were stories that he asked not to be included, out of respect for others' reputations. I have honored his wishes.

Alex was humble. When he told stories about assisting other choreographers and being given full control of numbers, he always ended the story by restating that he was only the assistant. He had respect for the choreographers he helped. He always gave them credit and spoke of them with gratitude. He was pleased to be telling his stories, but he accepted with grace the fact that he did not get credit for many of his contributions. He always said that he was just happy to be doing what he loved.

As Alex grew older, his hearing became progressively compromised. Out of courtesy to others, Alex sometimes just smiled and agreed, so I suspect there were times when we misunderstood what he was saying. As a result, we asked him to recount his memories over and over again. Debbie was especially adept at figuring out that a certain story was probably related to an event he had described to us previously. When we asked, Alex was usually able to clarify and confirm it.

Preface

The stories in this biography are taken from the interviews that the Bartletts and I conducted with Alex and his family and friends, and from interviews I did with others after his death. When the words are Alex's, I have put them in quotes. I have not footnoted them because over the course of many interviews, he often repeated stories, or clarified events, so specifying the date and time of the quote would be impossible.

The longer I knew Alex, the more opportunity I had to meet some of the other people in Alex's life — his wonderful wife Faun, his daughters and his grandchildren, other members of his family, his longtime assistant Alex Ruiz, celebrities such as Russ Tamblyn and Betty Garrett, and many dancers who worked with Alex. One such dancer was Jack Mattis. In February of 2000, he told me that Alex was "the most loved person in the business.... The most loved. You never heard a bad thing about him. Incredible human being and talent ... incredible ... the greatest talent."

Every person I spoke with and every letter I read reaffirmed Alex's kind, positive personality. That was certainly my experience with him. His daughter Melinda told me that he never raised his voice to them and never struck them. Dancers I spoke with said he was always charming, always kind, and was the man every dancer wanted to work with.

That is not to say that Alex did not take his work seriously or expect his dancers to do the same. His rehearsals were fun, but could be grueling. He once told me that he had to get his dancers to remind him to take union breaks because if they didn't, he would make them work right through. Alex never sat down during those breaks. Many people told me he always stayed on his feet and kept working.

His longtime assistant, Alex Ruiz, said in an interview with Roy Palmer in *Dance Magazine* in January 1962, p. 44,

> Alex loves people. When he meets someone for the first time, he gives his undivided attention. He is interested in understanding the person. His concentration is completely sincere and honest. Even though he may have problems, or an immediate problem on his mind, when he is with you he seems to forget everything but you. As a result, even on first meeting, he wins your confidence. In a rehearsal hall or studio set, his manner of working creates a relaxed feeling. The result is a maximum of response from the dancers and the stars, too.

Alex did have a temper although he had learned how to keep it in check. When he got mad, he started to stutter. If pushed the wrong way, he was willing to fight, and he was a good fighter. His older brothers, especially John, a professional boxer, had taught him to fight to win. If someone threatened his family, he was not hesitant to raise his fists if needed.

Russ Tamblyn said in a filmed statement made for Alex's memorial, held at the Dance Theater at Glendale Community College on November 10, 2007:

> We took trips together when we were in London [during the filming of *tom thumb*]. We flew to Paris to see the sights and walk around. We would breakfast together and lunch and dinner, and he was just a beautiful, beautiful guy. Never got out of line — never got mad.... Just once. Once he had a glass of wine with us and he never forgot it, right up until the last time I saw him — his ninety-second or ninety-third birthday or something. I said, "Yeah, one time I saw you..." I talked him into having a glass of wine, you know, 'cause he doesn't drink. And he saw these guys and he said, "Those guys... There's a gang over there. I'm gonna go over and punch them." And I said, "Alex! Chill out. Just cool it!" And he still remembered it to this day. He said, "I remember those guys." He still remembered them all this time. That's the only time I ever even saw him get a little mad. He never got mad, never got out of line. It was tremendous.

Some people who worked with Alex and loved him deeply said that Alex's sweet temperament was actually his biggest flaw. At a dinner with some of Alex's friends on July 2, 2012, Lysa Baugher Klein said to me, "He was so sweet that people walked all over him." Patti Nestor Cox Maser told me on March 3, 2012, "Alex's only fault was that he was soft-spoken ... if you could call that a fault. And every dancer that has ever worked with him has loved him to pieces ... literally, loved him to pieces."

Working on this book, I discovered inconsistencies and contradictions about certain stories and facts. Some things I was able to sort out, but others, such as Alex's actual birth date, remain a mystery. I have tried to supplement Alex's remembrances with supporting research; however, this book remains Alex's stories the way he told them.

It was an impossible task to list all the films on which Alex worked. As staff choreographer and as an assistant, he was not only assigned to big musicals, he was also frequently called in to set a single number on a film. Alex himself told me that he couldn't remember the names of all the films he did because if a picture needed some choreography or staging, he just did it and then moved onto another project the next day. Near the end of his life, I sometimes sat with Alex and we would look through coffee table books on the movies. Often he would see a photograph of a film and say, "Oh, I worked on that." I then asked him questions to elaborate. For example, he saw a picture of Alice Faye in the 1962 film *State Fair*. He told me he didn't choreograph the movie, but was called in to set a number for Faye. Another time, he saw a picture of Cyd Charisse doing the scarf dance from *Singin' in the Rain* and said he helped on the number. I quizzed him over and over again and finally said to him, "You told me you didn't assist on *Singin' in the Rain*." He answered, "I didn't. I was only helping out my friends."

Alex worked on so many films simultaneously that it is next to impossible to determine what project he was doing at any given time. Many productions overlapped, and rehearsal times and filming varied from movie to movie. Unless he told me specifically about going from one certain project to another, I have put the films he worked on in order of release date.

Alex primarily worked in the visual medium of film. To truly appreciate his work, it has to be seen. Choreography has to be experienced, so I urge anyone who reads this book to watch Alex's films. You will be amazed at the energy, creativity, and athleticism of his work. It's my hope that by reading his stories you will also come to know the gentle individual who played such a vital part of moving in the movies.

1
Beginnings (1913–1914)

Alex Romero, a slender, muscular man in his eighties, sat on the couch in his Woodland Hills home and told his story. Images of Fred Astaire, Gene Kelly, Judy Garland, and Debbie Reynolds glistened in his eyes as the Southern California sun reflected off the autographed pictures that hung on the wall across the room from where he sat. His voice was soft yet intense as he remembered. He began in Mexico.

A little after midnight on October 23, 1913, his father, General don Miguel Quiroga,[1] was preparing to ride out with his troops to meet the revolutionary forces of Jesus Carranza and Pablo Gonzalez, who were threatening to attack Monterrey. Alex's mother,[2] who was three months pregnant with him at the time, stood on the steps of their home,[3] located in the most beautiful residential district in Monterrey. She had come outside to wish her husband good luck.

Miguel Quiroga was 42 years old at the time, a dashing, dark-haired man with a full moustache. As a personal friend and confidante of Mexico's president, Victoriano Huerta, Quiroga was part of Mexico's political elite.[4] He had been commissioned by Huerta to command a group of irregulars, known as the *Brigada Quiroga,* which had been entrusted with defending Northern Mexico against rebel forces. Quiroga planned to confront the insurgents, who were moving towards the city, in the nearby mountains, so that Monterrey, which many believed was even more beautiful than the capitol, would not be ruined by rebel cannon-fire.

Quiroga kissed his wife and mounted his horse, but as soon as he was in the saddle "they started shooting." Alex explained that during the night, the rebel forces had snuck into the city to ambush the general and his troops: "Just like you see in the movies, they climbed the rooftops...."

Several of the soldiers in Quiroga's brigade fell before they could even draw their weapons. As Alex told the story, his soft voice grew even quieter. "My mother said she heard somebody shout, 'The general is my target.'"

Alex paused and said, "So, he was shot, and he fell."[5] He explained, "He was supposed to have been hit with a dum-dum bullet ... a tiny hole like this when it goes in ... but when it goes out, well, it goes...." Alex opened his hands in an elegant gesture that mimed an explosion. His long fingers moved with the self-assurance of a man who had staged the most famous names in Hollywood. He closed his hands, lowered them, stood up and walked to the wall on the other side of the room. His father's sword and sword belt hung there next to a grouping of signed photos and studio shots from Alex's many movies. The pictures ran up the full length of the staircase to his practice studio where he still danced every day.

Alex took the sword and belt off the wall and held them out. A small

Left: General don Miguel Quiroga Cantu, Alex's father. *Right:* Soledad Chapa Quiroga, Alex's mother.

1. Beginnings (1913–1914)

Casa de Quiroga, the family home in Monterrey, Mexico, after it was attacked by Revolutionary forces.

bullet hole was visible at the front of the belt, close to the buckle. "It came out the back. His back just split wide open."

He returned to the couch and explained that his father's officers feared that if their commander's body was captured, he would be decapitated — his head put on a pike on public display. Two or three of the general's lieutenants jumped off their horses and dragged Quiroga up the stairs to the mansion. "Before they climbed four or five steps ... he died.... And my mother was right there." They dragged the general into the house and in the front hallway a large carpet was pulled back. The body was hidden in an underground cistern to prevent the revolutionaries from finding it.[6]

"And all this while, bullets were coming in through the windows and killing people ... and there were a lot of the smaller children that got killed...." Outside, the governmental troops were also riddled with bullets. Señora Quiroga saw several of her older sons, who served in their father's brigade, fall as they were shot.[7] That night, 13 of Alex's brothers were killed.

In the midst of the chaos, Quiroga's men shouted for someone to get the general's wife out of the house before she was also killed. A young girl named Norma, one of the family's maidservants, pulled her mistress away from the windows and began stripping off her dressing gown, replacing it with servant clothes.

Miguel and Soledad Quiroga had 22 sons and one daughter.[8] In the chaos, only four-year-old Judith was rescued with her mother. The little girl, the maid Norma, and Señora Quiroga, disguised as a peasant and pregnant with her last son Alejandro, were spirited out of Casa de Quiroga. The remaining 21 boys, one as young as two years old, were either killed that day or were left to fend for themselves.

This is the family history that was passed down from Soledad Quiroga to her son Alejandro. Although there are inconsistencies regarding some of the narrative's facts, the story always remained the same when Miguel Quiroga's widow related the events again and again to her son throughout the years. Alejandro, whom everyone called Alex, remembered his mother's stories about his father. Alex was proud to be

Alex's birth certificate.

1. Beginnings (1913–1914)

the son of Miguel Quiroga, a great general and one of Mexico's most powerful politicians. Alex also was proud to be Mexican, and his Latino heritage defined a large part of who he was.

Alejandro Bernardo Quiroga, later known as Alex Romero in his professional life, was born on August 20, 1913, in San Antonio, Texas, or so he was told.[9] According to his mother, she escaped the revolutionary forces at the battle of Monterrey during the Mexican Revolution and, disguised as a peasant, she had fled the city with her daughter Judith and her maid Norma.[10]

"This little maid actually saved my mother's life," Alex said. "It took them a long time and a lot of fighting along the way because she was traveling on one of those flat cars that Pancho Villa always traveled on ... and they didn't know where they were going." With her maid and daughter as companions, Señora Quiroga traveled briefly around Mexico with the camp followers of the same revolutionary forces that had murdered her husband and several of her children. She and the others rode on flatbed railroad cars until the train neared Laredo, Texas, where the trio slipped across the border into the United States.[11]

In Laredo, "they hoofed it." Alex smiled at his choice of words. He was a tap dancer. He had hoofed it with the best on the silver screen and helped create choreography for the greatest tap stars.

Alex explained that his mother, his sister, and Norma had set out from Laredo to San Antonio on foot. A stranger offered them a lift in his cart for a brief time, but for most of the trip they walked. When they reached San Antonio, "they went to this place, and it was a small room ... about twelve by twelve. It was a mud hut." There, Soledad Quiroga gave birth to Alejandro Bernardo Quiroga, who would later choreograph Elvis Presley in *Jailhouse Rock*—a choreographer who became "the last link to the Golden Age of movie musicals," and who "moved movie choreography into the next generation."[12]

2

Early Life (1914–1929)

Alex Romero's earliest memories were of being left in the mud hut with his sister Judith, while his mother and Norma took jobs cleaning houses to support the family.[1] He remembered his only toys—chicken bones. He liked pretending they were soldiers, lining them up and moving them around in formations, just as he would later move dancers around a soundstage. "You know, a kid doesn't know if you're poor or not—I wasn't unhappy."[2]

As the Revolution in Mexico raged on, Señora Quiroga held out hope that some of her other children had survived. During the first two years in San Antonio, she was able to get messages to Monterrey with the help of Norma, who sent notes to other servants in the city. The message was always the same: "If you see any of the Quiroga boys, tell them we are safe and where we are."

Eventually, six survivors did show up in San Antonio: Alfonso, Humberto, Jeronimo, Juan, Oscar, and Mario. The Quiroga boys looked for work, shining shoes and selling newspapers to help feed the family. All shared the tiny hut with their mother and the two little ones—nine people living together in the 12 by 12 foot mud hut.[3]

Around 1919, Jeronimo, later known by his stage name Carlos, hit upon the idea of forming a dance act with his 10-year-old sister Judy. "[He] refused to work like the other boys. He was gonna be a dancer," Alex said of his older brother. In Monterrey, their father had been the owner of the *Teatro Independencia* and Carlos often hung around during performances, watching the Spanish dance acts and hoping to meet the pretty young chorines.

After several attempts at trying to teach Judith some routines, Carlos realized that she was too young. Through a friend, he found another

2. Early Life (1914–1928)

young woman who was interested in forming an act with him. The two practiced and began doing small charity events.[4] Alex recalled

> They got a couple of paying jobs. I don't think it was very much, but certainly much more than the boys were making. And then one fellow saw them and said, "Hey, you two are very good. You ought to go to Hollywood because that's where the movies are and they're using dancers there. You'll get good money — real money there."

Carlos took the advice and told his mother that he wanted to go to Hollywood. If things worked out as he hoped, he could make good money there and eventually send for the rest of the family. His mother agreed, and after saving enough for his trip, Carlos moved to Los Angeles while little Alex, Judith, and the others stayed behind in San Antonio.

In Hollywood, Carlos enrolled in a few tap and ballet classes, and eventually got a dancing job when he was hired to perform in *The Mission Play* in San Gabriel.[5] Encouraged, he worked up a dance act with a young woman named Ginette Vallon. The two started dancing in various nightclubs and performing on the Paramount and Orpheum Vaudeville Circuits.[6] They specialized in dancing the Apache. The two took advantage of the scandalous nature of violent dance and in each performance Carlos dragged Vallon across the stage by her hair.

By 1920, the large-scale fighting of the Mexican Revolution had ended, although it was still a dangerous place. In the early months of 1921, Señora Quiroga decided to leave San Antonio briefly to face the hazards of a trip into Mexico to see if she could recover some of her husband's lands and business interests. According to family legend, she somehow arranged to meet Pancho Villa on his private train car. After being escorted through a coterie of armed guards, the 46-year-old, 5'5" Soledad approached Villa, who towered over her, and demanded that Villa return all of the Quiroga family holdings. Villa laughed at her request. An irate Soledad Quiroga slapped the revolutionary leader across the face. Pancho Villa got very serious and ordered Señora Quiroga off the train, shouting at her that he should have shot her then and there but admired her courage.[7]

That same year, the family heard that Carlos had enough money to rent a small house in Los Angeles. Carlos first sent for Judith to join him, and shortly afterwards, had saved enough to bring the rest of his family. Mamacita, Juan, Oscar, Mario, and eight-year-old Alex took a train to Los Angeles. Norma, the maid who had helped them survive, also went with the family to help them settle in their new home.[8] The remaining Quiroga brothers decided to take off on their own, some returning to Mexico.[9]

Meanwhile, Carlos made the rounds of the various film studios. In 1922, he got work as a dancer in silent films at Pathé Studios and in some Buster Keaton shorts for Eddie Kline Productions. In 1923, he appeared in Universal Pictures' *Dancing Cheat* and in *Lights Out,* performing a tango that earned him the nickname "The Second Valentino." His popularity as a dancer in Hollywood was growing. The following year, Carlos did the Independent Production of Finis Fox's *A Woman Who Sinned,* Paramount's *Her Sister from Paris* with Constance Talmadge, and *Thief in Paradise* with Ronald Colman. He also did several films at MGM. The same year, he was hired to dance in the prologue of Charlie Chaplin's film *A Woman of Paris.* A young actress in the film, who was under contract to Chaplin at the time, was 15-year-old Malvina Polo.[10] Carlos and Malvina fell in love during filming and in 1924 were married.

The Quiroga family lived at 3861 Second Avenue in Los Angeles in an area that Alex later described as "a poor Mexican neighborhood."[11] Despite Carlos' earnings in the silent movies,[12] they struggled financially. Everyone in the family was expected to work. At age six, Alex got his first official job, selling newspapers on the corner of Western Avenue. It was a tough task for a kid. He often had to defend his territory against the other newsboys. His older brothers taught him how to fight. He was also a fast runner if he needed to get away.

One of the ways the younger boys earned extra money was by stealing golf balls at a nearby golf course. Alex and his brother Mario were masters at it. Because Mario was weakened by tuberculosis at the time and Alex was healthy, Alex would grab a golf ball, even if it was in play, and throw it to Mario, who was hiding in the bushes. Alex then ran off to distract the golfers while Mario stuck the balls in his pockets and snuck away. Mario later sold the golf balls, telling Alex, "Don't tell Mamacita what we did."

Mamacita urged her sons to chase the neighbors' chickens into their own yard so she could catch them for dinner. Sometimes she made them steal eggs at the market, telling her boys that she would give them a licking if they got caught.

Eventually, Alex was expected to go to school. It was his first experience with formal education. The family was too poor to afford shoes

2. Early Life (1914–1928)

for Alex, but his mother saved up to buy him a coat. He hated it. It was covered in long fur. "I looked like a goat, just like a goat. I wasn't about to go with that." Ashamed of being seen in the coat, every morning Alex pretended to start off for school, but slipped into an alley behind the house and hid. He also hid the coat, preferring to shiver in the cold. "I kept hiding it ... behind the garage ... in an alley. I hid it over the fence.... I put it somewhere."

Mamacita finally discovered him, as he put it, "just sitting around spending time," and he was ordered to go to school. Alex refused, telling Mamacita that he would not go if he had to wear the coat. Both were strong-willed. Mamacita was a fierce woman, but Alex would not give in. They finally compromised. Alex went to school, barefooted and without the coat.

Even without the goat-hair coat, Alex was often teased. He was shy and he had a lisp. He was also Mexican, and as he said later, "The American kids hated the Mexicans. I mean, *hated* them."[13] His brother Mario used to accompany him to school to defend him. If a kid laughed at Alex or bothered him, Mario punched him in the face. "He was always for me," Alex said.

Alex was miserable at school. At home he only spoke Spanish. He had trouble understanding English and at first could not write his ABCs. He also was used to taking a siesta every day between one and three P.M. "You know when I was a kid everybody took siestas. They put me in this screen porch and I slept there on this mattress until three o'clock, and I got used to that, and so when I got to school, I'd put my head down and go to sleep on the desk ... and the teacher would shake me and I was a mess."

His name also presented a problem. The teacher Anglicized it, changing it from Alejandro to Alexander. Alex didn't mind that, but there were two other students who were also named Alexander in the class. During roll call, students were required to stand up and say, "Present." Whenever she called out "Alexander," the two African American Alexanders, and Alex all stood up at the same time. The others in the class pointed at them and laughed. The teacher solved the problem by adding the three Alexanders' middle initial to the "A" of their first name. Alexander Bernard became "AB." That made it worse for Alex. The other students laughed even harder at him because it sounded like the new Mexican boy had the Jewish name Abie.

The Man Who Made the Jailhouse Rock

While Alex continued to struggle in school academically,[14] a coach at his elementary school on the corner of Olympic Boulevard and Western Avenue recognized that he had athletic potential. He began to mentor him, and gave Alex exercises to help correct his pigeon-toed stance. He also taught him how to run properly. He made Alex lean over at the waist until he began to fall forward and then told him to imagine his feet catching up. As Alex's family remembered, eventually he "could run like the wind."

As Alex grew stronger, his brother Mario's tuberculosis worsened. When Mario was 10 or 11, he passed away. Alex was devastated. "I didn't know what to do then. Mario was my favorite."

As the family adjusted to its life in Los Angeles, Juan, who began to call himself John, and Oscar took a hint from Carlos and began to look for jobs in the entertainment industry. They worked up dance routines and comedy skits.

Carlos continued as the main breadwinner of the family. In addition to his work in films, he worked for the vaudeville producing team of Fanchon and Marco, performing and eventually staging numbers for the organization. He brought his wife Malvina into the shows as a pianist and enlisted his sister Judith as one of his dance partners. Seeing the opportunity to make more money for the family, he also drafted his brothers John and Oscar into the act. Concerned that people might mispronounce the name Quiroga, Carlos and his family decided to bill themselves as "The Romeros."

The new family act gained notice and worked regularly for the Fanchon and Marco organization. One show called "Dance Paintings" was reviewed in the *Ogden Standard-Examiner*:

> Carlos Romero and his dancing partner, Dorothy Crocker, have been featured dancers of Fanchon and Marco shows along the Pacific coast for four years.... The Fanchon and Marco program has been developed as a studio scene in which an artist, portrayed by Romero, presents the dances of the nations, his partners being the "inspiration" of paintings hung about the stage. With Malvina Polo at the piano, his first partner is Judith Romero in the Spanish dance, then Alma Ortega in the Argentine tango, and later Dorothy Crocker in the American sweetheart waltz.[15]

In December of 1928, Fanchon and Marco's "Artists Idea" show was reviewed in *The Salt Lake Tribune*:

2. Early Life (1914–1928)

Publicity shot of The Romeros. The family's Spanish dance act appeared in vaudeville, primarily on the Fanchon and Marco circuit. From left to right: Judith, John, Carlos, Malvina (in dip), Oscar, and Alma Ortega.

> The Romeros comprise a dance act of three brothers and three sisters, offering a variety of interpretive Spanish dances in a decidedly new form.[16]

The three brothers listed in the review were Carlos, John, and Oscar. The three sisters were Judith, John's wife Sydney[17] (whom he had met and married that year), and Carlos' wife Malvina, who danced as well as played the piano. Another review of the same time reads:

> For the stage production, Fanchon & Marco have provided one of their most elaborate and colorful acts. "Artists Idea" has two headliners of unusual merit, Art Hadley, the nationally famous cartoonist, and the Romeros, a family of Spanish dancers, three brothers and three sisters, who are unusually light on their feet. The Romeros give a series of Spanish dances which are pleasingly beautiful.[18]

In 1929, Judith developed tuberculosis and grew weaker until she was unable to dance.[19] She told her brothers that she wanted to go home to be with her mother in Los Angeles as she died. Alex and his mother moved from downtown Los Angeles to the countryside in Tujunga to prepare for her arrival so that Judith could be in clean country air. Alex was 15 or 16 years old at the time.

The coach,[20] who had taught Alex how to "run like the wind" in grammar school, came out to Tujunga to help the family. He built a small shack in the yard behind the house. Nothing more than a glorified chicken coop, the shack became Alex's living quarters, and allowed him to be isolated from Judith while she was cared for by her mother in the main house. Alex said that the coach probably "saved his life" by building the shelter for him. Although Alex remained isolated from Judith when she was ill, he went into the house when she was dying and held her in his arms as she succumbed to tuberculosis at the age of 19 or 20.

When Judith died, Alex's mother was so distraught, she ran out of the house screaming, threatening to kill herself. The death of her daughter was the final straw in a long line of losses—her husband, her other children, her homeland, and now her only daughter. She beat her head against a telephone pole and then a wall, until she was completely covered in blood. Alex wrapped his mother's head in towels as best he could and finally was able to calm her down. He ran next door to get help but, as he remembered, the neighbors hated Mexicans and only "laughed at the crazy Mexican lady." Alex begged, "Can you read something for me? My sister has died and I need to read." What Alex needed help reading was the vaudeville performance schedule so that he could contact his brothers. Finally, he was able to convince one woman to help him. She followed Alex back to his house to

Fifteen-year-old Alex on the day he got his first pair of shoes. He is with his dog, Branded. This picture was taken shortly before his sister Judith died at the home in Tujunga.

2. Early Life (1914–1928)

read the schedule. Eventually another neighbor let Alex use his telephone to call Carlos, who was in Illinois performing with John and Oscar at the Chicago Theater. Carlos immediately flew to Los Angeles on a mail plane.

When he got home, Carlos realized that his mother could no longer be left alone in Los Angeles with Alex expected to care for her. It was decided that both would join the rest of the family and travel with them as they toured in vaudeville.

3

Vaudeville (1929–1938)

Alex had no training in dance, and when he and his mother joined the others on the road after his sister's death, he did not perform with his family. "Pup," as he was nicknamed, simply watched his brothers from the wings every night.[1]

One day while the Romeros were performing on the Fanchon and Marco Vaudeville Orpheum Circuit, Alex's brother John arrived at the State-Lake Theater in Chicago and heard someone tap dancing on the stage. He knew there were no other dancers on the bill and, curious, he snuck up to the stage and discovered that it was Alex. John secretly watched his brother for a while then stepped out of hiding and asked a startled Alex where he had learned to tap. Alex replied that he wasn't really tap dancing. He was just making up his own steps. He explained to John that after watching other vaudeville dancers, he wanted to try it himself. John asked Alex if he could repeat the step he had just done. Alex did. Then John took off his coat and ordered Alex to teach him the step.

That night, John showed Carlos the various tap steps Alex had taught him that afternoon. He convinced Carlos to draft their youngest brother into the act and to put Alex in charge of teaching the others his own unique version of American tap. Carlos agreed. The Romeros began experimenting with adding some American tap to their Spanish dance act. Alex didn't hesitate to show his brothers the steps he created. Whenever he made a choreographic suggestion that Carlos liked, his oldest brother picked him up and repeatedly threw him up in the air.

In December of 1930, the publicity department of Fanchon and Marco productions issued the following press release:

> THE ROMEROS. Four brothers and one sister ... a family of remarkable dancers ... headed by Carlos, the elder brother are well-known on the Fan-

3. Vaudeville (1929–1938)

chon & Marco circuit having appeared in "Artists," "Fiesta," and "Manila Bound" Idea.... Alexander, the younger brother, is the newest member of the troupe, this tour marking his first appearance in the act.[2]

This was Alex Romero's first performing job, dancing with his brothers Carlos, John, and Oscar, and Carlos' wife, Malvina, for Fanchon and Marco on the vaudeville circuit.[3] The publicity paper described the act:

> For the opening, a piano is on center stage with Malvina playing Drigo's "Serenade" ... and the 12 Sunkist Beauties grouped around the piano. The girls come forward and offer a very unusual ballet number, attired in striking long costumes. Then they bring on huge flower-twined hoops and offer a colorful routine while Carlos and Malvina are featured in an effective waltz number ... working in and out of the hoops. The three younger Romeros are next with a splendid novelty rhythm dance ... performed to Shubert's "Serenade."[4]

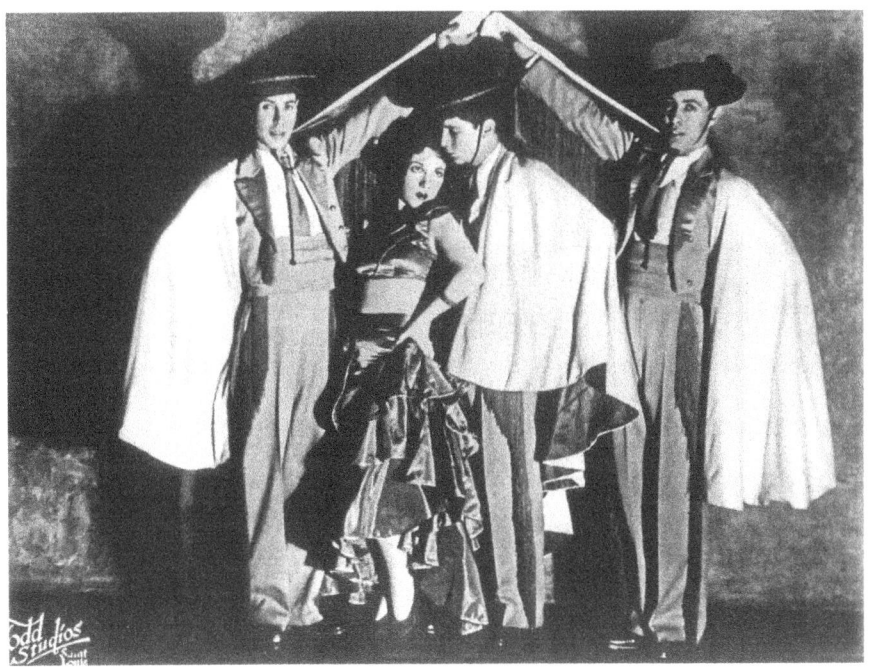

The family vaudeville act after Alex had joined them on the road. From left to right: Oscar, John's wife Sydney, Alex, and John.

And later in the press release:

> Next billed is the "International episode" ... featuring Carlos wooing the girls of various lands with a dance instead of a song.... Carlos also works with Malvina and Alexander in an unusually novel toy number which is followed by a lightning-fast tap featuring John and Oscar Romero.[5]

Alex continued to dance with his brothers on the Fanchon and Marco circuit. They were billed as "The Aristocrats of Dance." Vaudeville provided an excellent training ground for Alex. He had the opportunity to observe many types of acts and to absorb many styles of dance. He performed on the bill with many of the top vaudeville entertainers of the day including Donald O'Connor and his family, and the Gumm Sisters. Frances Gumm, who eventually changed her name to Judy Garland, later became great friends with Alex when they were both working at MGM.

Alex remembered, "My brothers would stay up all night and wouldn't get up 'til show time. I'd get up and go see vaudeville." He remembered seeing some of the great tap dancers of the period, such as Tom Patricola and Pat Rooney. Alex recalled that Rooney wore a bowler and danced with his hands in his pockets. He was short and stocky, and could jump in the air to do a bell kick, and click his heels together three or four times before landing. Alex said, "This little fat guy was so graceful, I can't tell ya!"

Alex especially loved watching African American tap dancers.[6] "That started me," he said. Later in life, when he was interviewed by Rose Eichenbaum for the book *Masters of Movement*, he explained how the black vaudeville tappers inspired him:

> One day while we were in Chicago, I wandered into a neighboring theater and sat down in the third row. Out on the stage came three black performers. They called themselves King, King, and King. They started tap-dancing—hoofing. I'll tell you, I had never seen anything like it. That night I couldn't get it out of my mind. I came back the next day and secretly memorized their rhythms—*ta-ca-ta-ca-ta-ca-ti-ca-ti-ca-ti*. Then I started to make up steps to match those rhythmic taps.[7]

Alex vividly remembered seeing the tap trio for the first time. He said that at the top of the act, they pushed a piano out onto the stage and then began "slipping and sliding." He memorized King, King, and King's rhythms by singing them over and over to himself in his head. Later in life, whenever Alex talked about tap choreography, he'd break into a rhythmic patter song similar to rapping. Once he had the sounds firmly in his head, he'd make up steps to match the rhythms. Then he practiced and practiced, a lifelong habit with him.

"I'd get there [to the theater] before anyone." Other acts often came in and saw him up on the stage practicing his made-up tap steps over and over again. They'd ask, "Hey, Alex, would you show us some of that?" A generous boy, he'd always agree. "Sure, I'd be glad to, if you show me some acrobatic tricks." Alex traded tap steps and practiced the new acrobatic tricks he got in return. "The first thing I learned was walking on my hands. Then I got to do a round-off and a back flip, and falls...." "Athleticism, stunts, and gymnastics later became hallmarks of Alex Romero's movie choreography. Whenever Alex put an acrobatic trick in a film, he always tried it himself first. When asked if learning acrobatics proved useful in creating choreography for films, Alex replied, "Yeah, especially with Russ Tamblyn."

The Romeros changed their family act regularly. Carlos was always trying out new ideas. The act included Spanish dancing, tap, and acrobatics, and the members of the troupe often had to underdress their costumes in order to make all the quick changes.

Alex remembered one time when Carlos approached his brothers and said, "You know, we ought to do what would be different ... play violins!" Used to Carlos' schemes, the boys went along and Carlos worked up a dance routine that featured the four boys playing instruments while they danced.

Because none of the brothers played violin, they mimed bowing their prop fiddles as the instrumentalists in the pit provided the music. One day the Romero boys came out onto the stage ready to dance, but when they raised the bows to the strings of their violins, no violin music came from the pit. They had forgotten it was Sunday. The violin players in the pit refused to play on the Lord's Day.

The violin section of the Romeros' act also provided Alex with one of his most embarrassing memories. The boys were rushing to get into their violin player costumes. Alex grabbed his prop violin, but forgot to put on his trousers.[8] He recalled, "I was plumb naked!" He remembered that "the Aristocrats of Dance" got more applause that night than usual. Alex said the audience wouldn't stop clapping until he came out for a bow.

One night John checked out the stage before their performance and noticed a hole in the floor on stage right, left open by workmen who had been making some repairs. He spoke to Alex and warned him to be careful on his entrance. Ready to go on, the brothers and their partners entered from opposite sides of the stage. The dance number had begun when John whispered to the others, "Good God! Where's Alex?" The Romeros finished the number without him. "When the curtain closed they rushed to the hole, stage right. Sure enough, Alex was looking up at them. He had stepped right into the hole on his entrance."[9]

Vaudeville was an interesting but tough life. Moving from town to town, the Romeros performed their act in front of all kinds of audiences. Alex recalled that in one theater the boys were dancing when three men in the audience began to heckle them. The Romeros kept dancing until John, who had studied boxing, jumped off the stage. He grabbed the men and pummeled them. The three hecklers begged for mercy and limped out of the theater as the audience applauded.

Between tours on the road, the family returned to their home base in Los Angeles. They often performed their vaudeville act in theaters around the area. On one occasion, a couple of Alex's friends invited him to dinner and asked him if he wanted to join them after his shows at a club that featured black dancers.[10] Eager to learn some new rhythms, Alex quickly agreed. When they stopped to pick up a couple of girls they had also invited, Alex was introduced to a young blond woman named Frances Fleury Driscoll, known to her friends as Faun.[11] Struck by Faun's beautiful blue eyes, he fell hard and fast. His friends couldn't help but notice. Alex blushed as he remembered, "I kept looking at her and they kept looking at me."

That night, Alex's friends urged him to get up on the dance floor to show them some of his own tap steps. When he did, Faun fell for Alex as well.

After his friends dropped Alex off at his hotel that night, he received a phone call from one of them informing him that Faun really liked him. He suggested that Alex call her the next day and maybe go out and meet her family.

The next morning, Alex called Faun and asked her if he could come out to her house for a visit. When Faun asked her father if she could have a caller, Mr. Driscoll asked her, "Who is he?"

Faun replied, "He's a Mexican fellow."

The Romero boys in costume for the violin number "Drigo's Serenade." This photo was a publicity shot taken for a show entitled *The Vanities of 1933*. From left to right: John, Alex, and Oscar.

"Stop right there. Stop right there," her father said. "You know what they do? You see that couch we have over there? When everybody goes to bed, they just step in there and start in making love. No!"

Despite Mr. Driscoll's objections, Faun convinced her father to meet him, so Alex put on his good necktie and went for a visit. It was not the ideal date he had hoped for. He sat uncomfortably on the couch with Faun on one side of him and her father glaring at him on the other. Faun's father didn't like Alex at all. He was not only worried that Alex was a Mexican, but he also found out that day that Alex was an entertainer. To complicate matters, Faun was already engaged to Gordie Jenkins, son of the president of Prudential Life Insurance Company.[12] But that didn't deter Alex, who kept visiting Faun.

Eventually Alex proposed, and Faun broke off her engagement to the millionaire's son. When she informed her family that she intended to marry Alex, her father was still reticent. He asked his daughter, "Has he got any money?"

Faun replied, "He gets money all the time for dancing...."

Her father refused to relent and would not give his blessing. Finally Alex begged his mother to speak with Mr. Driscoll. Mrs. Quiroga agreed, and even though she could not speak English, the two hit it off famously. Mr. Driscoll figured that any son of the charming Mrs. Quiroga must be suitable. Permission was given, and Alex and Faun were officially engaged.

Frances Fleury Driscoll, "Faun."

In the fall of 1933, feeling that there was not enough work in the States because of the Great Depression, John and his wife Sydney decided to try their own vaudeville act in Europe and Asia.[13] They left the family act in the States and performed as a duo in Shanghai and other Chinese cities, Java, Sumatra, and finally in Calcutta, India. From India, they went to Italy for about six months.[14]

Finding success abroad, John and Sydney encouraged other members of the Romeros to join them. When John and Sydney reached Italy, Alex and Oscar came over from the States. A new dancing act was

3. Vaudeville (1929–1938)

The Two Californians, the vaudeville act, in Europe. Alex is on the left and his brother John is on the box.

formed. Carlos elected to stay in New York where he was working as a choreographer at the Roxy.

John, Oscar, and Alex were first booked in a casino in Monte Carlo, "a fancy place," as Alex remembered it. For several months they performed in Paris, where Oscar met a ballerina whose stage name was Madame Gobri. After debating with his brothers, Oscar decided to leave the act and stay in Paris with his new love. John and Alex reformulated the act, billing themselves as "The Californians" or sometimes as "The Two Californians," and continued touring in France, Luxembourg, Switzerland, Germany, Czechoslovakia, Poland, Hungary, Rumania, Sweden, Denmark, and Norway.[15]

Alex enjoyed working in the act but missed Faun. When he arrived in Norway,[16] Alex wrote to Faun's father and asked if his fiancée could travel to Europe so they could be wed. The father was hesitant, but when Alex's mother told him she would accompany Faun on the ocean voyage as her chaperone, Mr. Driscoll agreed. Alex arranged for his bride-to-be and his mother to take an Norwegian America Line ship, the S.S. *Stavangerfjord*, from New York to Oslo on April 25, 1936.[17]

On May 20, 1936, Alex and Faun were married in Oslo, Norway. The service was in Norwegian and, because neither could speak the language, they spent a large part of the ceremony trying to suppress their laughter. They couldn't understand a word that was said. The humor was compounded when Alex gave Faun a gold wedding ring and matching cross. He had asked the jeweler to engrave on the inside of the ring "Love me." When Faun first looked at the engraving, at Alex's prompting, she read, "Lose me." The engraver had made a mistake. Faun put on the ring and wore it until she died.

The newlyweds continued to travel throughout Europe with John and Sydney.[18] John and Alex usually performed the act as a duet. When they needed a woman to do a walk-on for a new skit they were trying out, John talked Faun into doing it. The part required the woman to hit John. For some reason, Faun got mad at John during the show and when it came time to punch him, she socked him as hard as she could. John flew across the stage. The audience went wild. Alex recalled with a chuckle, "We really raked in the money that night."

In the summer of 1936, John and Alex played Berlin, where the summer games of the XI Olympiad were being held. News reports fea-

3. Vaudeville (1929–1938)

A photograph taken after Alex's marriage to Faun in Oslo, Norway. From left to right: Alex, Faun, John, Alex's mother, and John's wife Sydney.

tured stories about the new German leader. Two years later, while performing in Munich, John and Alex were summoned to perform their comedy dance act at a command performance for Hitler. The German Führer came backstage after the show and met each member of the cast. John remarked later that Hitler's "eyes were those of a madman."

In 1938, the Romero brothers performed in Poland. In a restaurant one afternoon, John, Alex and their wives looked out the window and saw a large dark mass moving down the street towards them. They initially thought it was a dust cloud or a swarm of insects, but as the mass moved closer they realized that it was a group of people. Jews were being herded through town by the Nazis. Horrified, the two couples quickly paid their bill and left the restaurant. Across the street, they saw that the German soldiers had stopped the group and were warning others to keep moving and not to talk to the Jews. Alex remembers walking by the prisoners while holding Faun's hand and seeing children who eyes were caked with flies. He didn't know what to do. When he noticed that the guards were not looking, he gave them the rolls from his restaurant meal and all the money he had in his pockets.

Although John and Alex continued to perform, things deteriorated rapidly in Poland. One night they were on stage doing a comedy dance in one of the city's better nightclubs when a drunken man wearing a German general's uniform entered the club. He pointed to Alex and John on the stage and shouted, "They're Americans. I don't like Americans." The club owner tried to calm the general but he became more and more irate. The Nazi then pointed directly at Alex and shouted, "He looks like a Jew, and I'm going to kill him." The club owner said, "He's not Jewish. I even have his passport here to prove it." He showed the passport to the Nazi and the Nazi said, "It's a fake." He pulled out his pistol, pointed it at Alex, and fired. The club owner bumped the man and the shot missed, but not by much. Alex felt the bullet whiz over his head. Faun, who was watching from offstage, screamed. The two brothers hurried off the stage, quickly dressed, and left the club with their terrified wives.

Alex was especially concerned because Faun was pregnant at the time with their first child. He decided that it was too dangerous to remain in Europe with the growing power of Hitler's Nazis. He wanted Faun to be safe, and he wanted his first child to be born in the United States. John tried to convince him to stay longer because they were making good money. Finally John looked at Alex and demanded, "Are you going home?"

Alex simply said, "I just got shot at."

Arrangements were made to leave Poland as soon as possible. Alex and Faun returned to the U.S. sailing from Cherborg, France, on the *Hamburg*. Alex was 24 years old and Faun was 22. John's wife Sydney remained with her husband for a while, but as things worsened and war was finally declared on Germany, she came back to the States in 1939,

3. Vaudeville (1929–1938)

followed shortly by John. Oscar stayed in Paris, where he joined the French resistance.[19]

Alex and Faun finally arrived in New York. They had saved lots of money while performing abroad. Since Faun had never seen the Big Apple, Alex decided to show her the town. He took her to a fancy restaurant. During dinner they kept laughing. One of the other patrons in the restaurant stopped by their table and, winking at Alex, said, "I know what you are. You're show people!"

Faun looked at the man and said, "No, we're just husband and wife."

4
Dancing in the Movies (1938–1944)

Alex and Faun returned to Los Angeles where, on September 8, 1938, their first daughter Melinda was born at the Queen of Angels Hospital. Although the parents' last name was Quiroga, when Faun was asked by the staff for her new baby's name, she accidentally gave them Alex's stage name. Their daughter was officially "Melinda Maria Romero."

Alex decided to develop his own solo act to support his growing family. "It was all I knew how to do at the time," he later recalled. But the family's savings were rapidly disappearing, and the expense of musical charts, costumes, and publicity photographs made Alex abandon the idea.

He heard through a friend that an engraver had an opening at his shop. Originally hired as a shipping clerk, Alex was approached by the owner after he had been working only a short while. The man told him that his cameraman needed an apprentice, and the job paid more money. Alex said he was interested.

The business specialized in engraving posters, magazines, and commercial ads. Their biggest customer was the Tournament of Roses association. The shop made its own film, a dangerous process. It required pouring liquid cyanide onto a large piece of glass. The glass, held in one hand, had to be moved constantly, swirling the liquid until it was level over glass and did not drip off. Hot lights were then directed onto the glass to burn the image. The owner told Alex, "The first thing you gotta learn is don't open your mouth. Close your lips real tight. Because if one drop ... it has happened ... we've had people killed." He warned him that when the cyanide hit the glass it bounced, and if it bounced up onto his

4. Dancing in the Movies (1938–1944)

lips and he licked his lips, it could be fatal. Alex recalled, "So, I really shut my mouth."

Alex continued working at the shop, and his family continued to grow. On February 18, 1941, Faun and Alex had another daughter. They planned to name her after Alex's sister Judith, but were concerned that there might be negative connotations associated with the name since Judith had died so young from tuberculosis. They compromised and officially christened her Judy Ann Romero, continuing the tradition of using Alex's stage name instead of Quiroga.

That same year the army called, and Alex was ordered to report for a physical. He got his 1A status. When he asked the sergeant how much time he had before he would be called up, Alex was told he had about a week. He waited, but the army never called.

Anxious to return to show business, Alex kept looking for opportunities to leave the engraving shop and get back to performing. A friend suggested registering with Central Casting. Alex did, and shortly after signing up with the agency, he received a call.

It was about 5:00 A.M. and pitch black, when the phone rang. Alex answered, and the voice on the other end asked, "Are you Alex Romero?" When Alex replied, "Yes," the voice asked, "Can you do toe dancing?" He knew the man meant ballet, and although Alex had no real ballet training, he wanted the job. Besides, he reasoned, he had learned a couple of steps in vaudeville. He answered, "Yes." The caller told Alex to take his rehearsal clothes and be at Warner Brothers Studios before 10:00 A.M. LeRoy Prinz was looking for 12 male dancers for a film.

Without a car, Alex had to take the electric rail red car into Los Angeles, then catch the trolley into Hollywood and wait for a bus to take him over the Cahuenga Pass into the Valley to Warner Brothers. The trip took almost four hours. He arrived just before the audition.

At the studio, Alex was taken into a small rehearsal room where 10 other dancers were waiting. As the 11th, Alex thought he might have a chance since Central Casting had said Prinz needed 12 men for the movie.

At 10 o'clock, a short, husky man smoking a cigar entered the room, "a real tough guy," as Alex remembered him. LeRoy Prinz[1] barked, "Spread out, will ya?" He looked the boys over. They were all different heights and sizes. At the end of the line was one effeminate boy who was thin as a rail.

In a gruff voice, Prinz asked, "You guys do ballet?" The boys answered, "Yes. Yes sir." Prinz replied, "Well, come with me," and led them out of the room to the soundstage where he was filming. On the set was a theater stage. He led the boys up onto the stage and shouted out: "I'll tell you what you're gonna do. You're gonna just introduce in dance the two opera singers. You two, you enter from over there, and you two from over there, and you two come from the other side, and two from there." Alex was left with the remaining three boys. "You four … two come from this side of the stage and two from the other." With that, Prinz turned and walked down the stairs.

Then the effeminate dancer, who was standing right next to Alex, squeaked with a lisp, "Mithter Printhe?"

Prinz turned back and barked, "Yeah?"

"What thtep do we do?"

Prinz ran back up the stairs, grabbed the boy by his shirt, and literally lifted him off the ground, leaving the poor kid's feet dangling in the air. Prinz growled, "You do ballet, don't you?" "Y-y-y-yeth, thir." Prinz tossed him away and said, "Well, do a ballet step." He turned, walked down the stairs, and climbed onto the boom.

The dancers looked at each other. Alex whispered, "Listen, why don't we all enter like that, but all do the same thing." To the last group of three, he said, "It would be funny if two of us came from one side and only one from the other, so why don't all three of us come out together."

Prinz was already looking through the camera. He shouted, "Get on out, willya? Come on!"

Alex spoke up for the others: "Wait a minute. You didn't give us a dance step. We gotta make one up and it takes a little time."

"Well, hurry it up."

The dancers talked about what step to do.

Prinz shouted, "What's keepin' ya?"

Finally Alex whispered to the others, "The hell with him. Let's try it twice and make sure it works."

The sound man hit the playback and the dancers did their hastily improvised combination, running onstage into an assemblé, throwing in a grand jeté, and eventually ending with a single pirouette down into a kneel.

4. Dancing in the Movies (1938–1944)

Prinz said, "That's fine, but it needs work. You guys practice that. We shoot in an hour."

Years later, with a sly smile on his face, Alex recalled, "He came back, and we did the damn thing."[2] It was Alex's first dancing job in the movies.

Finding that he was able to support his family by working as a dancer in the movies, Alex continued to audition and was next hired for a film at Columbia, *The Heat's On* starring Mae West. Then he was called to do a film at Universal.[3] On his first day at Universal, he arrived on the soundstage and saw a huge mountain that had been constructed for part of the set. Choreographer Lester Horton gathered the dancers around him and said, "First, is anybody here afraid of heights?" He pointed to the top of the mountain set.

Most of the dancers raised their hands. "Anyone not afraid of heights?" Alex raised his hand. Horton explained that he needed some dancers on the top of the mountain, so Alex volunteered.

The choreographer said, "This is kinda dangerous, but it pays more." Another fellow with blonde hair and green eyes raised his hand.

Horton said, "Well, I'll take you two." Together the three of them climbed to the top of the 60-foot-high set. A little platform of wood about three or four feet deep was at the top. There was a dead drop off the outside edge to the stage floor below.

They carefully stepped onto the platform and the choreographer said, "I want you both to do a double air tour to the knee. Don't do it now. You guys practice a while." Then he left.

The other dancer, Alexander Goudavich, immediately did a perfectly executed double tour to the knee, then repeated it.[4]

Alex didn't do anything at first, then tried one. He made a good attempt, but nearly fell off the back of the set. After a few more not-so-great tries, Goudavich, whom Alex came to call Sasha, gave him a few pointers in his heavily accented English: "Jump higher, and make sure you go straight up."

Alex improved under his new friend's guidance. Eventually Sasha climbed back down the mountain, leaving Alex on top to continue practicing. During a break, Alex discovered that the director didn't plan to film the number until three days later, so he knew he had more time to perfect his air tours.

The Man Who Made the Jailhouse Rock

To save money, Alex always brought a brown bag lunch. He went outside, away from the sound stages, to the backlot near some empty hills by Deanna Durbin's bungalow. There he had his lunch, and after eating, he practiced his air tours on the grass. The tours were getting easier and better all the time.

Some other fellows came out to the grassy area to play touch football that day. Alex stopped practicing and was getting ready to leave when one of the men asked him he if he wanted to join in the game. Alex loved athletics and agreed. Any time someone missed a pass and had to chase after the football, Alex practiced his air tours. Soon he was doing them in between every play.

Halfway through the game, a balding man walked up, leaned against a tree, and began to watch. Alex figured he was an extra in the movies because he was wearing makeup.

Alex called to him, "Hey, ya wanna get in?"

"Yeah, I'd love to," the man replied. He jumped right into the game and proved to be quite athletic, running fast and always catching the ball. In between each play, Alex practiced his tours. The new man finally asked him what he was doing.

Alex replied, "I gotta learn this. I got a movie over there and I gotta do two turns without falling off. But I'll get it."

The man studied him for a while, and then asked, "How do you do that?"

Alex said, "Well, the guy that taught me said that you just ... " and he explained the move.

The man tried it. But after he went up in the air, he fell flat on his butt. Alex remembered that the man fell "hard!"

Alex said, "Great! Great!"

"What do you mean, great? I fell on my ass, didn't I?"

"Yeah, but that's the first time. My God, you got it almost."

The man tried again. And again he fell on his backside. Alex encouraged him to try it again, but the man left. The game ended shortly afterwards, and they all returned to the various movie sets.

That next weekend, Alex took Faun to see a new movie called *Cover Girl* starring Gene Kelly. They were in the middle of the film when Alex saw Kelly execute a wonderful dance move. It dawned on him that the man on the screen was the same balding men he had been trying to teach

4. Dancing in the Movies (1938–1944)

air tours during the football game the day before. He sank down in his seat and covered his face with his hand, thinking, "Oh my God, that's the guy I was trying to teach ... the greatest dancer in the world." Years later, when Kelly and Alex became close friends, working together on several films, they laughed about that day.[5]

Alex continued to work in films. In *Ali Baba and the Forty Thieves* he did a dance with scimitars with his new friend, Sasha Goudavich. In 1944, he danced in *Four Jills in a Jeep*, and also did *The Merry Monahans*, on which his brother Carlos was one of the choreographers.

Also in 1944, Alex appeared in *Follow the Boys*. The Universal film starred Vera Zorina and George Raft. The dances were to be staged by a new choreographer fresh from New York who didn't know anything about choreographing for the movies. His assistant was running the audition, and asked the dancers, "You all do tap dancing?"

Some of the group said they didn't. In those days, Alex explained, the ballet dancers traditionally didn't do tap and the tap dancers didn't do ballet, "and they kind of hated each other. And the ballet dancers got more money!"

The assistant asked again for tap dancers, and Alex raised his hand. She asked him to do a time-step. Although Alex usually did his own steps, he had learned how to do traditional time-steps in vaudeville. He went into it and the woman ran over and actually threw her arms around him. She said, "You got the job. Do you know any other tap dancers?"

Alex said, "No, I don't know a soul," then hesitated and added, "Well, gee, I do know my brother. I got a brother.... But I don't think he's got a card. He was not gonna do movies."

"Will you call him anyway. I'll see he gets in."

So Alex called his brother John, who was hired for the project. During filming, because John and Alex were the same height, and also the same height as George Raft, the choreographer put the two Romero brothers on either side of the star in the center. It was Alex's first time tapping in the movies.

5
Dancing for Jack Cole (1944–1947)

At the end of the summer of 1944, Alex got a call for an audition at MGM, where dance director Robert Alton was doing a film called *The Ziegfeld Follies*.[1] Alton had an assistant from New York, who was running the audition. According to Alex, he was a "wild tap dancer." Although Alex had tapped in vaudeville and in the film *Follow the Boys* at Universal earlier that same year, he was still insecure about his tap dancing talents. He had had no formal training and still felt that when it really came down to it, he could "only do a time-step."

But Alton's assistant liked Alex, recommended him to Alton, and Alton cast Alex in the film. He danced in several numbers including "The Great Lady Has an Interview," which featured Judy Garland, and "Limehouse Blues" with Fred Astaire.

During rehearsals, whenever the dancers were given a break, Alex snuck into Soundstage 30 to work on tap steps at the back of the building. He was practicing there one day when he heard two other men dancing—but they were doing nothing that Alex recognized from *The Ziegfeld Follies*. One of the men called to Alex and asked him, "Hey, you want to learn this?" Alex answered, "Sure."

The men were doing a ballet combination consisting of "glissade, assemblé, and then a double turn." Alex didn't know the terminology then, but he watched the men a couple of times and was able to do the steps. As he explained, "I can pick up things pretty fast." Alex also reversed the routine so he had it mastered on each side. He remembered later, "That's all I learned."

A few days later, Alex was getting ready to have his brown bag lunch

5. Dancing for Jack Cole (1944–1947)

when he ran into the same two dancers. They told him they were looking for a way to get to an audition over at Columbia Studios. "We have an appointment with Jack Cole," they told him. Alex had heard Cole's name before. He was the hot new choreographer in Hollywood, with his innovative, unique, theatrical blend of ethnic, ballet, and jazz.

Alex had recently bought a 1923 Cabriolet Ford for $20[2] and offered to drive the boys from MGM to the audition. During the trip, the dancers explained that Cole was holding the appointment-only audition to hire six boys and six girls to form a new dance department at Columbia Pictures.

Upon arriving at the Columbia lot, the two men went into the soundstage for their audition with Cole, and Alex sat down outside the building to eat his lunch. It was a hot August day, and the loading dock door of the soundstage was open. Alex heard a drum pounding and became intrigued. He remembered thinking, "What kind of dancing is that?" He put down his lunch and leaned over towards the open door, but from where he was sitting he couldn't see anything. He got up and approached the edge of the door. From that angle he couldn't see any of the dancers but he did see a man standing there. His head was clean-shaven, and he had a big nose, broad shoulders, and a small waist. He was the one pounding on a drum.

Just then, the man looked over his shoulder. Alex ducked behind the door, afraid the man had seen him. The drum kept beating. He waited a while and, curious about the audition, snuck up to the door again. He stuck his head around the corner of the door and found himself staring straight into the face of the man pounding the drum. Years later Alex recalled, "It was just timed so beautifully. It was like dancers' counts."

Realizing he was caught, Alex froze. The man kept on beating the drum, looking Alex up and down. Then he asked, "Are you a dancer?"

"Yeah."

"You want to audition?"

"Okay."

"Just go right around there and come around in."

Alex thought, "Oh my God. What a mistake. He's doing something with a drum. I can't do that." He entered the studio rehearsal hall. Jack Cole was holding the drum and, after Alex was inside, Cole asked all the male dancers to line up in staggered rows. He said, "I want you to glissade, assemble, point, prepare, then double turn.... Then to the left." It was the same combination that Alex had learned from the two men he had driven to the audition.[3] Cole counted the dancers off and the men went into the routine. Alex had already practiced the combination over at MGM the week before. He knew that he nailed it on the first try.

Next, Cole had the boys do big assemblés moving forwards and backwards. Alex was an athletic young man and easily kept up with the others. Then Cole went into some West Indian movements and taught them a mambo and rhumba.

Cole demonstrated the combination he wanted in front of the group but didn't break the quick, rhythmic movements down. None of the auditioners could get them. Cole kept repeating the movements, waiting until someone got the complicated routine. Over and over again he did the dance until he was sweating heavily.

After a few minutes of watching Cole dance, Alex thought to himself, "He's doing rhythms. Why don't I just sing these rhythms to myself. Maybe I'll pick up some of the accents." This was how Alex originally had learned to tap — by singing the rhythms to himself. So, as Cole repeated the dance, Alex sang the rhythms to himself, doing the movements he saw Cole demonstrate until they matched the song in his head.

After a few minutes, Cole looked back at Alex and said, "You got it!" Alex responded, "I don't think so." But Cole had the whole group do the combination again and then shouted at Alex, "You got it. You do it. Now you stand up front and do it." Alex recalled later that he thought it was that moment "that saved his neck."

At the end of the audition, Cole announced that three of the men had gotten the job. Alex was one of them. The other two were the dancers Alex had driven to the audition, Rod Alexander and Charles Lunard.[4]

All three were doing *The Ziegfeld Follies* at MGM and told Cole that they were not able to start working with him at Columbia until they had finished the production number on the film in about a week. Cole told them that that would be fine. He informed them, "Nobody does extra work. You're just gonna dance from morning 'til night." He also told them, "It pays $125 a week ... and you're gonna earn it."[5]

The next week, Alex and the other dancers reported to Columbia's Stage 10, which producer Harry Cohn had converted to a dance studio for Cole. There were 12 original members in the troupe: six men (George

5. Dancing for Jack Cole (1944–1947)

Martin, Rod Alexander, Alex Romero, Paul Steffan, Bob Hamilton, and Charles Lunard); and six women (Ethel Martin, Francine Ames, Gloria Maginetti, Ruth Godfrey, Nita Bieber, and Patricia Cummings). The dancers worked from nine in the morning until five in the afternoon, often with Cole forgetting to give them regular breaks to rest. The work was brutally intense.

Cole's pliés were very slow, important to his style because it built such strength, but exhausting for the dancers. He also did lots of isolations and knee slides.[6] Alex recalled the first time he saw Cole's infamous knee slides. "Cole told the dancers, 'Line up. Line up. Just line up and do as I do.' And all of a sudden ... and barefooted and no knee pads ... he took off and he did this leap and down to his knees and laid almost back...." Then Cole had his dancers try it. When asked if it hurt, Alex said, "Oh God, we were bleeding ... and he hates blood, and he got mad at us."

Rod Alexander recalled, "Every day we studied body mechanics for about two hours, then ballet for two hours, then lunch, after which we studied different ethnic forms of dance, including some tap. That was the general regimen."[7]

The dancers usually rehearsed to Cole beating a drum, and sometimes with a piano. The choreographer was an intense, moody individual. If he was not happy with the way his dancers were working, "he would beat the drum harder and harder until the soft end of the drumstick came off and flew through the air. Then he'd throw away the stick and beat time with his hand. Finally he'd walk away in disgust."[8]

The dancers rehearsed barefooted and often their feet bled. Alex remembered, "Our feet were all cut up for a while. Jack told us to soak them in hot salt water every night.... It toughened the skin ... and it helped."[9]

During one rehearsal, Ruth Godfrey fainted from exhaustion during the plié section. Alex was standing next to her and went to help her, but Cole hit him, elbowing him in the side. He shouted at Alex, "Get back. Get back." Alex reluctantly got back into his place and Cole left Godfrey passed out on the floor. The terrified dancers continued working around her, until finally Cole motioned to the prop man, who dragged her out of the room.[10]

When asked why the dancers put up with Cole's cruel behavior,

Alex explained that all of them recognized that they were working with a creative master, someone unlike any other person they had met. As Alex put it, "I think he's the only one who can be called a genius." But, that didn't mean it was easy or pleasant.

Alex remembered, "The first year we worked for Jack, he didn't talk to anybody — not anybody — not anybody — not even the kids he hired two months before that." Since his mother had taught him to be polite to others, Cole's behavior was disconcerting to Alex.[11]

> I'd drive that little Ford. I was always kinda late, always. At nine o'clock you had to be dressed and barefooted and on the floor ready to go, and so I'd leave early so I'd be sure to make it. And, for the longest time I'd come in and I don't know why, I guess I was coming in at the same time, [Cole] always was coming right across the room ... right for me ... and I go up to him and I'd say, "Good morning, Jack." And he'd go whoosh — right past me. And every morning it was the same thing — whoosh. And after about three weeks [I thought,] "It's embarrassing. I'm not gonna say 'good morning' to that guy." And sure enough I'd get there and I'd chicken out and say "good morning." ... and that went on forever. Then, one time I was pretty late and I had to go to the bathroom so bad I didn't think I was gonna make it to the stage ... and I ran for the bathroom door and I went to get the door and it opens and there's Jack ... and he smiled, and he said, "Oh, good morning Alex" and walked right by me. And I said, "Good morning, Jack," and I went into the bathroom and I couldn't go to the bathroom.... I couldn't do it.... It was just like God had spoken.

Cole's troupe was kept busy dancing in movies at Columbia.[12] In 1945 they appeared in *Eadie Was a Lady,* backing up tap dancer Ann Miller. Miller was, as Alex put it, "flabbergasted by Cole's choreography." He remembered that she always came to the set early and sat with the chorus kids. "She was so real. She wasn't putting on any airs. She was just excited about dancing. Didn't consider herself a big star, but boy could she dance!" Miller danced in a number entitled "I'm Gonna See My Baby," partnered on screen by Cole himself, and she also tapped in the title song. A Grecian style ballet in the film featured Miller tapping while backed up by Cole's boys doing jazz, and Cole's girls dancing with cymbals attached to their knees.

Also in 1945, Cole's dancers appeared in *Tonight and Every Night* with Rita Hayworth. In 1946 they worked in four films, *Meet Me on Broadway, The Jolson Story, Tars and Spars,* and *The Thrill of Brazil.* Alex remembered that in *Tars and Spars,* Cole had him hang upside down by

5. Dancing for Jack Cole (1944–1947)

his knees on a moving merry-go-round for the carnival number.

For *The Thrill of Brazil* Cole choreographed a big voodoo dance that featured Janet Collins, a soloist from Katherine Dunham's dance troupe. The cast also included Ann Miller.[13] Choreographer Nick Castle was called in to provide tap steps for Miller and Cole's dancers on the film, since Cole himself could not tap. After Castle had set the number, Cole decided he wanted to add arm movements to it. He called the boy dancers in on a weekend and worked two full eight-hour days on just eight bars of music. Alex recalled that Cole was "intense in everything ... down to the last finger." As hard as the dancers tried, they couldn't seem to satisfy Cole, whose style didn't jive with Castle's tap steps.

During the second day of the grueling rehearsal, Cole began screaming at Rod Alexander, who was standing on the end of the line. Alex was next to him and, embarrassed at the shouting, he slightly turned his face away. Cole swung his arm and hit Alex across the face and shouted, "You. You. I'm talking to you!" What Alex had forgotten was that when Cole got mad, he went cross-eyed. Alex thought Cole was shouting at Alexander because he was facing him, but he was actually looking at Alex from the side of his crossed eye. He had been shouting at Alex.

At the end of the two-day rehearsal, Cole was still not satisfied with his attempt at adding Afro-Cuban arm movements to Castle's complicated tap steps. He finally gave up trying to change the number and it reverted back to Castle's original choreography.

On the home front, Alex's and Faun's two daughters continued to grow. For Melinda's first year of school, Faun took her on the trolley to a private Catholic school, but then her parents decided she would be happier if she transferred to the local public school in El Sereno. While in the second grade, seven-year-old Melinda learned a new word, "nigger." She came home one day and told her father about someone whom she identified by the epithet. Alex immediately sat her down and gave her a long lecture about how words hurt and how racism was cruel and unfair. He told her about how he and his own brothers experienced prejudice when they first lived in Los Angeles.

Alex told her that one hot day he and his brother Mario wanted to go swimming at the Bimini Baths swimming pool at the corner of Third Street and Vermont Avenue. The guards at the pool stopped the boys before they entered. They looked them up and down and then said that

The Man Who Made the Jailhouse Rock

Dancing with Ann Miller in *The Thrill of Brazil,* choreographed by Jack Cole. Miller is center and Alex is on her left.

Alex could come inside the gate to swim, but Mario was not allowed in because his skin was too dark.[14] They said that Mexicans were only allowed in on the day before the water in the pool was going to be changed, when it was too dirty for whites to swim in.

Alex looked at his seven-year-old daughter sitting on the edge of the bed and asked her what she would feel like if someone was mean to her because of her skin color. She started to cry a little, and he asked her if she understood now what it meant to use a hurtful word, like the one she used. Little Melinda nodded and promised that she'd never use the

5. Dancing for Jack Cole (1944–1947)

word again.

In 1947, Cole used his dancers in another Rita Hayworth film, *Down to Earth*. When speaking of his time on that movie, Alex recalled,

> Almost every movie that we did, there was an element of danger. For instance, in this one you had this huge hill and [Hayworth] was coming from the stars ... and we were dressed kinda strange.[15] [Cole] wanted us to jump out of the hill, and didn't know how to do it, so what he did was make, like, diving boards. But the studio, they didn't use diving boards. They used planks and they shaved 'em.... These were kinda loose. And so what we had to do, we had to run up and hit the very tip of it and glide over the mountain and land ... and this was all done barefoot ... and then land there and do a knee spin. We practiced that a while!

Before the actual filming of the number, word of the stunt had spread around the lot. Stunt men who were working next door on another stage showed up to watch rehearsals. One of the stuntmen asked Alex, "How much you get for doing that?"

Alex replied, "A hundred and a quarter."

Alex in a staged studio shot for *Down to Earth*. The costume was designed by Jack Cole.

"A hundred and a quarter?"
"Yeah."
"How come?"
"That's our salary."
"That's your salary! You do that ... besides your salary? The stuntman looked at Alex and said, "You know, I wouldn't do that for six hundred dollars a day."[16]

Alex was making more money as a part of Cole's Columbia Dance Troupe than he had been before working independently as a dancer in films, but he looked for ways to supplement his income. He came up with the idea of opening his own dance studio. He found a space in El Sereno on Eastern Avenue at the North Drive on the second floor of a building next to the Riverside Furniture Company. He called it the Dance Art Studio, and offered classes in Tap, Soft Shoe, and Ballet. Whenever he wasn't rehearsing or performing for Cole at Columbia, Alex taught jazz classes there. He hired a few other teachers and invited fellow Cole dancer Charles Lunard to teach.[17]

Around this time, Alex's brother Oscar returned from Paris. When he left the family vaudeville act in Paris in the mid-1930s, Oscar remained in France during World War II and served in the French underground. He had maintained his Mexican citizenship. Because Germany had not declared war on Mexico, he was able to use his neutral status for a while to move under the radar and help in the resistance. He was eventually exposed and fled to the mountains where he contracted tuberculosis. By the end of the war, Oscar's health had so deteriorated he knew he did not have much longer to live. He returned to Los Angeles so that he could see his mother one last time. Shortly after he arrived, Madame Gobri, the woman Oscar had left the act for in Paris, joined him. The two were penniless and Alex offered to take them into his home on Topaz Drive in El Sereno to care for Oscar.

Although Faun loved Oscar, she feared that her daughters might contract tuberculosis from her brother-in-law. She followed Oscar around the house with a bottle of bleach, disinfecting everything he touched. She argued with Alex constantly, insisting that he must get his brother out of the house and away from the girls as soon as possible. Alex understood her concern but would not put his ailing brother out. Oscar stayed with the family for five weeks until Alex was finally able to

5. Dancing for Jack Cole (1944–1947)

find a sanitarium for him. Oscar died shortly after entering the facility on May 23, 1947.[18]

Alex continued to dance with Cole, but after the completion of *Down to Earth*, no more movies were on the horizon because of a protracted strike by IATSE film technicians against Columbia Studios. Cole became increasingly frustrated with the process of making movies and especially with Columbia. He asked his group of dancers if they would be willing to tour with his nightclub act. Some declined, but George and Ethel Martin, Carol Haney, Anita Beaver, Rod Alexander, Bob Hamilton, Ruth Godfrey, and Alex took him up on the offer.

Alex was on the road with Cole's act for about a year and a half. For a while, the members of the touring troupe were still drawing their $125 salary from Columbia. Alex was able to send most of that money home to support his family.[19]

In January 1947, Cole's act was booked into Chez Paris in Chicago for two weeks. The show as so popular, it was extended for 20. A reviewer said, "Their artistry is incomparable; their dancing a delight. Got a dictionary handy? Look up all the adjectives meaning wonderful — they apply to Jack Cole and his troupe."[20] Another simply said that Cole's dancers were "sensational."[21]

While in Chicago, Cole created a seven-minute killer of a number to Benny Goodman's "Sing, Sing, Sing," a quintessential Cole showstopper with knee-slides and jumps. It became synonymous with Cole's distinctive jazz stylings and athleticism.

"Sing, Sing, Sing" premiered at the Latin Quarter in New York City. Cole's dancers received raves. One reviewer wrote, "Some of the best ensemble dancing ever seen in a night club is to be found at the Latin Quarter where Jack Cole and his dancers opened Sunday night."[22] Again the run was extended.

The act then went to Slapsie Maxie's[23] in Hollywood. Lena Horne was also featured on the bill, and Desi Arnaz led the orchestra. The troupe played the club for 20 weeks, and everyone from the movie studios flocked to see the show. A review in the *Los Angeles-Herald Express* read,

> The Cole dancers are the finest dancing act I have seen in a nightclub. To see them send the audience into an excited, applauding crowd resembling a mass of frenzied Ballet Russe balletomanes, is something I never expected to see. Their work is modern. Their technique combines the best in Martha

Graham, the Ballet Theater, Katherine Dunham, Jood Ballet, and [Agnes] De Mille's *Oklahoma*. No story or ideas in their numbers, but they bring the patrons off their seats by the sheer drama of their performance. Timing, choreography, costumes and style are extraordinary.[24]

Another review said,

> Like poets who have found effective use of disconnected words to convey expression, these dancers have absorbed the varied rhythms of jive, folk dancing, African, East Indian and Caribbean dance patterns. They make pictures with body movements—exciting and picturesque. Some are as colorfully hot as a Gauguin canvas. Their first number exhibits a Harlem, Deep-South spiritual and primitive jungle influence. With the steady beat of bonga [sic] drums, the finale has a touch of Cuba, a splash of Tahiti and a dab of the Orient. Ranging in age from 19 to 24 (Cole himself is an old-timer of 32) the troupe, male and female, is destined for fame. They are also likely to revitalize the contemporary field of the dance.[25]

A young Arthur Laurents was in the audience on opening night and recalled,

> There is such a thing as cabaret history and it was made at Slapsie's in one night. Everybody lucky enough to be there (I was one of them: the Kelly group went to support Lena) saw fireworks explode twice. First from the heat of Jack Cole and His Dancers: three highly sexual males, three highly sexual females, dancing unlike any dancers anyone had seen anyplace before. The first number, "Spy," set to Benny Goodman's "Sing, Sing, Sing," fixed the tone—intense and erotic—and the style—angular, slashing, knee slides, tipping hats, twisting torsos and pelvises. That tone, that style, the moves and the steps themselves, unseen until then, became a permanent part of the choreographic language of the Broadway musical.[26]

Alex remembered that each night they performed at Slapsie Maxie's, "The house went crazy."[27]

In the middle of the Los Angeles engagement, Cole informed the dancers that after finishing their run at the L.A. nightclub, he planned to take the act on the road again. He told them, "Listen, from here on in, when we leave here we're gonna be gone at least a year and a half, possibly two." When Alex told Faun the news, she told him, "Honey, you can't do that. If something happens now ... you quit, or he lets you go, or the act stops, what are we going to do? We haven't got a cent, not a penny."

With the money he was sending back while on the road, Faun could

5. Dancing for Jack Cole (1944–1947)

only afford to buy one pound of ground beef a week, in addition to food for the girls. Money was so tight, the couple didn't even have a checking or savings account.

Alex loved dancing with Cole, and it was a tough decision to make. After two weeks of thinking about it, Alex decided he had to leave the act. He approached Cole and said, "Jack, I have to talk with you. I'm sorry but I'm gonna have to leave. I'm not trying to get more money out of you, but Faun said she just can't make it, and we haven't got any money in the bank." Cole responded, "I want to talk with her." He did, trying to convince Alex's wife that her husband should stay in the act, but as Alex put it, "He didn't get to first base with her."[28]

So, without any job prospects, Alex quit Cole's troupe.[29] About three weeks after leaving Cole, Alex got a phone call from MGM.

6

Words and Music to *On the Town* (1947–1949)

Three weeks after leaving Cole's Dance Troupe, Alex received a phone call from Robert Alton at MGM. Alex had worked for Alton as a dancer in the "Limehouse Blues" number in *The Ziegfeld Follies*, but as Alex recalled, "Now he doesn't know me [from] before, when I worked as a chorus boy. He just knows me as a Jack Cole dancer." Alton said to Alex, "I hear that you're leaving the act and I was wondering.... I want an assistant choreographer. Would you be interested in that?" Alex answered, "Absolutely."

Thinking that he was going to have to audition for Alton, Alex met the choreographer at MGM ready to dance. They went into a rehearsal hall, but when Alex asked about auditioning, Alton said, "No, you don't have to dance for me. I want to put you under contract right now." Alton called the front office to have them draw up the paperwork immediately. When Gene Kelly walked into the rehearsal room, Alton said, "Gene, come on over here. I want you to meet Alex Romero. He's one of Jack Cole's dancers." Kelly introduced himself and said, "God, you guys are great." Alton explained that Alex had just been hired to work as a staff assistant. Kelly immediately asked, "Bob, may I borrow him for a few minutes? I want to show him the 'Slaughter on Tenth Avenue' set."

Kelly and Alex walked to another hall where the number was being rehearsed. The set was a rough, unpainted mock-up of the one that would eventually be used in the movie. Kelly asked Alex, "You see that bar over there? First off, I want you to choreograph my number and part of Vera-Ellen's. She does part of the dance with me, and I do part of it

6. Words and Music *to* On the Town *(1947–1949)*

alone. Get me up on that bar and give me nothing but Jack Cole stuff." Alex, a bit terrified, replied, "Okay."

Kelly gave Alex a small tape recorder. "Here's the music. I'll be back in an hour and a half." And then the movie star left.

Ten minutes earlier, Alex had thought he was going to be auditioning for Robert Alton. Now, he was already at work in his new official capacity as staff choreographic assistant. He put on the music that Kelly had left with him, pondered how he could utilize the set, and after about 15 minutes of playing around, he had come up with some choreography. He remembered, "I just got onto the bar with a big slide of his, of Jack's, and when I slid, then I grabbed the other end of the bar, the back end, and twisted myself, and did a fanny spin for about three revolutions ... and came out of it and went into a knee drop. Then up, and I danced up and down the bar."

When Kelly returned, Alex showed him the choreography. Kelly loved the moves and the two collaborated on finessing the routine.[1] Rehearsals for "Slaughter on Tenth Avenue" ended up lasting a total of six weeks, and it took three weeks to shoot the 10-minute dance.[2] The collaboration with Kelly on "Slaughter on Tenth Avenue" was pivotal in Alex's career and secured him a steady working relationship with the star. Alex said, "And that's the way I got in with Kelly, and from then on he used me, probably more than Bob [Alton]."

The "Slaughter on Tenth Avenue" number was part of the movie musical *Words and Music*, a film based loosely on the lives of composers Richard Rodgers and Lorenz Hart. *Words and Music* had so many musical numbers that, in addition to Alton and the work contributed by Kelly, six other choreographers worked simultaneously on the film, Eugene Loring and Nick Castle among them. Alex recalled, "They were all busy. All the halls were busy."

Although Alex was only under contract to work as an assistant, Alton, as lead dance director on the film, approached Alex one day and said, "Listen, I can't do 'Thou Swell.' It's got the Blackburn Twins. They're tap dancers and I want you to do that. Do that number for me because I just don't have time." Alex eagerly accepted the assignment and began working out steps for the routine. In the number, the Blackburn Twins, Royce and Ramon, were to flank popular MGM leading lady June Allyson. Alex recalled working with Allyson, "She was great, and I liked the guys. We got along great. And it turned out to be a good number."[3] Although he was not credited, "Thou Swell" was Alex's first solo work as a choreographer in the movies.

After hearing of his contribution to Kelly's "Slaughter on Tenth Avenue" and seeing the witty and rhythmic dance moves in Allyson's "Thou Swell," Lena Horne, who was also in the film, asked to meet the young man who had worked on the numbers. Horne had already been assigned a choreographer to set her number, but after talking with Alex she felt that his youth, energy and modern sense of rhythm would suit her better. She approached Alton and requested that Alex stage her song. Alton agreed. Alex's second piece of solo staging in the movies was "The Lady Is a Tramp." Alex's elegant, understated staging on the song made it a classic, and the number became one of Horne's signature pieces.

Although Alex used his knowledge of the Jack Cole style to collaborate with Kelly on "Slaughter on Tenth Avenue," Alex made a conscious decision not to limit himself to Cole's style when asked to assist other choreographers or when choreographing himself. He remembered,

> I never did Jack Cole stuff for anybody unless it was asked for. Gene was the only one that asked for it, really. ...I wanted to get away from it. Even at that time, we had a TV set and you'd go watch TV and everybody was doing Jack Cole numbers—everywhere—all over the country. And I thought, well, I'm not going do that. So I tried to do [something different].... Now I did sneak in a step or two now and then, but I'd fix it so they would never know it was his.

Alex approached his work as an MGM contract assistant with enthusiasm and dedication. Although assistants rarely got film credit for their work, he was happy to be doing what he loved and glad to be able to provide for his family. The security of Alex's new job allowed him more financial freedom.[4] He gave up the dance studio in El Sereno and in 1948 he moved his family to a home on Fruitland Drive in Studio City. He remembered that when they moved into the new home, they had no furniture and the stove had not been put in yet. That first night, Mamacita came over and cooked dinner in the fireplace.[5]

After *Words and Music*, Alex assisted Charles Walters[6] on the Irving Berlin[7] musical *Easter Parade*.[8] The film starred Judy Garland, Ann Miller,[9] Peter Lawford, and Jules Munshin. Gene Kelly was slated for the male lead until he broke his ankle playing volleyball.[10] Fred Astaire, who

6. Words and Music *to* On the Town *(1947–1949)*

Backstage photograph of Alex staging "Thou Swell" with June Allyson and one of the Blackburn Twins for **Words and Music.**

had retired, was called in to replace him. Astaire and Alex worked for about five weeks preparing the dances for the film.[11]

Alex remembered one day when Astaire showed up early for rehearsal as he always did. Garland had not yet arrived. Astaire worked out steps with Alex, the hour grew later, and Astaire got more and more angry that Garland had not yet arrived. When she finally appeared, over three hours late, Astaire had been dancing heavily to work out his frustrations. He was covered in sweat. Garland strolled in and greeted Astaire with a big smile: "Hiya Freddie, what are we doing today?" Astaire, fuming, took the towel he had draped around his neck and wiped his face. "I'll show you," he said, and he launched into a complicated tap step. Garland said, "Oh, okay." She repeated the step almost perfectly on her first try.

In his book *Astaire: The Man, the Dancer*, Bob Thomas writes, "Fred was amazed at the facility with which Judy learned dance routines. Although not primarily a dancer, she could repeat steps after watching them twice. She was the best study Fred had known since Rita Hayworth."[12] In his autobiography, Astaire said that doing the numbers with Judy "remain with me as high spots of enjoyment in my career. Judy's uncanny knowledge of show business impressed me more than ever as I worked with her."[13]

After *Easter Parade*, Alex was hired to help on MGM's *The Kissing Bandit*, assisting Robert Alton.[14] The film starred Frank Sinatra and Kathryn Grayson. Cyd Charisse and Ricardo Montalban were featured, as was Ann Miller, who had danced with Alex twice before when he was dancing with Jack Cole. One of Alex's jobs was to teach Montalban the correct way to lift his leading ladies, Miller and Charisse, during a number called "The Dance of Fury." Alex was also hired as a dancer in the film, but his on-camera performances were cut.

Nineteen forty-nine was a big year for Alex at MGM. He did *The Barkleys of Broadway* with Fred Astaire and Ginger Rogers; *Take Me Out to the Ball Game* with Gene Kelly, Frank Sinatra, Betty Garret, Esther Williams, and the Blackburn Twins; *On the Town*, with Kelly and Sinatra; *Scene of the Crime* with Van Johnson; and *The Red Danube* with Janet Leigh.

Initially, *The Barkleys of Broadway* was to star Fred Astaire and Judy Garland. But when Garland became ill,[15] producer Arthur Freed hit upon

6. Words and Music to On the Town (1947–1949)

the idea of reuniting Astaire with Ginger Rogers. The two, a legendary dance duo in the past, had not worked together for over a decade. Alex was thrilled. "I was wild to meet this girl because I had seen them in the movies when I did vaudeville and I thought they were just so wonderful."

Robert Alton was the official choreographer on the film. Hermes Pan was also on board to help set Astaire's numbers. Alex was to assist Astaire. He remembered being in the rehearsal studio with the star, the first time he met Ginger Rogers:

> Fred and I, we had laid out some stuff. He does most of it and I learn it and I'm learning the girl's part. And all of a sudden a door opens and [Arthur] Freed comes in with Ginger and says, "Well, we got her. Here she is." And I looked at her and I couldn't believe it. I could see she was a little nervous because she hadn't even seen this guy in fifteen years. And I was standing there all smiles. And they talked a little bit and then [Astaire] said, "Come on. Go get your tap shoes. Let's get to work." In the meantime we were dancing and then he said, "You stand over there, Alex, and I'll stand here." Actually, we stood a little in front of her. And he started to go into this routine, whatever it was, I've forgotten. We're dancing. We're going....

Rogers put on her tap shoes. Alex remembered, "They were kind of dusty." Astaire started in with some fast, complicated tap steps. Then he and Alex both noticed that Rogers wasn't dancing.

> She wasn't doing anything. And so he steps back, and takes her hand, and I take her hand, and we go at it again. And now he starts to get mad. He's just mad as a hatter. He's all flushed. Finally he said, "What's the matter with you?"

Ginger Rogers didn't say anything, so Astaire finally said, "Oh, look, I guess you've been away from it a while. Alex, you take her in the other room and I don't want to see her until she's got the whole routine. I don't care if it takes you two months."

Alex led Rogers into another rehearsal studio and after calming her down, started teaching her the routine.

> I didn't go as fast as Fred did. I thought it was him that made her nervous and with me it'd be different, so I didn't take the real tempo. I took a slower tempo. And she couldn't get it. She couldn't get it. So I took her by the hand and started....

Alex worked on the routine with Rogers, and eventually she started to get the steps. As she grew more confident, Alex was able to stop mimicking Rogers' part for her to follow, and he switched over to Astaire's part beside her. After four days of rehearsal, Rogers had finally mastered the routine. Alex went back to the other rehearsal hall and informed Astaire, "She's ready now." Rogers put on her costume to show the dance, and then she and Alex performed together. Astaire beamed, and simply said, "Oh, that looks great." Later, when Alex recalled that first time they showed the dance to Astaire, he said under his breath, "And she danced just [great] ... was better than he did [it]."

When they actually shot the sequence for the film, Alex recalled, "I thought that she just looked so at ease. She wasn't looking down, and she was selling, and working the skirt, and doing all the things with Fred. I just can't say enough good things about her." After the film, Rogers gave Alex an autographed picture that she had inscribed, "Thanks so much for your wonderful help on Barkleys of Broadway."

Alex enjoyed working with Astaire and helped him with all the numbers in the film. "He was great with me. He used to actually say, 'You got something for me here? I'm stuck.' And I'd do it and most of the time he'd buy it. As I remember, all the time he bought it."

Take Me Out to the Ball Game and *On the Town* were both musically staged by Gene Kelly and Stanley Donen, although Alex recalled that Donen "never once, never once came into the rehearsal hall ... never once" for either movie.

Take Me Out to the Ball Game,[16] about a fictional baseball team called The Wolves, starred Kelly, Frank Sinatra, Esther Williams, and Betty Garrett.[17] "None of us knew how to play baseball. I never played baseball or football or anything. I was dancing!" He added, "They had me out in the backfield catching balls!"[18]

In addition to assisting on the creation of the numbers, Alex also dubbed the taps with Kelly after the movie was completed. Alex had already established a great working relationship with Kelly on *Words and Music*. Alex also recalled that the other star of the film, Frank Sinatra, and he "were great pals" as well.[19]

The team had three months of pre-production and Alex was put in charge of preparing Sinatra for the dancing he would have to do in the movie. When he met the singing idol for the first time, Alex was in the rehearsal hall with Gene Kelly working out the first number of the film. After introducing Sinatra to Alex, Kelly said, "Listen, Frank ... you've

6. Words and Music *to* On the Town *(1947–1949)*

been away from this for a long time. Now we've got the whole routine laid out and I've got a lot of pre-production to do, so you're going to come in here for the next two weeks and work on this thing. I want you in at 10 in the morning and you can break for lunch around one, and you don't leave until four. Is that clear? 'Cause that's what has to happen."

Sinatra nodded, "Sure, of course."

As he was leaving, Kelly looked back and said to Alex, "I want you to work the devil out of him."[20]

Alex got Sinatra up on the dance floor to begin teaching him the routine. However, Sinatra said, "Listen, Alex, could you do me a favor? I've gotta go. I have an appointment, and I gotta get outta here. Will you cover for me?" Alex said, "Sure."

As he was leaving, Sinatra added, "If anybody asks for me, just say I'm busy and I'm here. That's it. Say we're having a private rehearsal and nobody can come in. We can even lock the door."

As Sinatra was leaving, Alex called to him, "Where can I reach you?"

"You can't reach me, but I'll be on the lot."

Sinatra walked out and Alex was left in the dance studio with only the rehearsal pianist Eddie Becker. He waited for a while for Sinatra to return. When he didn't come back right away, Alex began working out a few dance steps on his own, with Becker accompanying him at the keys. A couple of hours passed and Sinatra was still not back. Then the rehearsal hall phone rang. Alex answered it and it was someone from the front office looking for Sinatra. Alex answered, "He'll be back shortly. Can I take a message?" Throughout the day, it was the same, the phone ringing with various people wanting to speak to Sinatra, who still had not returned to start learning his dances. Alex just kept covering for him.

Eventually producer Arthur Freed called. Alex remembered that he started to sweat as soon as he heard Freed's voice asking for Sinatra. Alex hesitated, then told Freed, "No, Arthur, he's gone for a little bit. He'll be right back. Should I have him call you?" Freed said, "No." He told Alex that he'd call back later that afternoon. Fortunately Freed never did, because Sinatra did not show up for the rest of the day. In fact, Sinatra didn't show his face at the rehearsal hall for the remainder of the week.

In the meantime, Alex found out that Sinatra had contacted Kelly and told him that the dancing at his rehearsals with Alex was so difficult that he needed more time to perfect the number. "Give me a break. I need another week to rehearse," Sinatra begged Kelly. Kelly relented and added a third week to the schedule for his co-star to study with Alex.

Alex kept showing up for work, but as the second week of rehearsals started, he still had not taught a single step to Sinatra. Halfway through the second week, Sinatra finally popped his head into the studio just to say hello. He started to leave again, but Alex stopped him. "Oh, Frank, you really gotta knock on it, because you only got about eight days. And, you know, he's gonna fire me! He's gonna be mad, and he's gonna blame me, not you!" Sinatra relented. He got his rehearsal clothes and returned to start learning the routine. As Alex remembered, Sinatra worked hard every day after that, until he got the whole thing down pat. The filming day arrived, and Kelly never knew what had happened.[21]

Take Me Out to the Ball Game was directed by Busby Berkeley. Conflicts developed on the set between Berkeley and Kelly, who was considered one of the most powerful men on the MGM lot.[22] In addition to being one of the stars, Kelly was also highly knowledgeable about the latest use of the camera and the newest techniques for shooting numbers. One day when they were to shoot the opening number, Berkeley called Alex in and asked him to dance in for Kelly as Berkeley set up the camera shots. Berkeley kept asking Alex to repeat the dance again and again, while the director was up on the boom setting up overhead shots, panning left and right, swooping in and out. The whole time, Alex was thinking, "Oh, Gene is not going to like this at all."

Finally the cast arrived for the actual filming, fully costumed and in makeup. The set was made to look like an old theater. Kelly and Sinatra slipped into the second row of seats as Kelly called to Berkeley to see the set-up, "Run it once for me."

Berkeley agreed, and Alex started the number. He had barely started, when he heard laughter. Alex recalled, "It was Frank and Gene, laughing and slapping their thighs." Kelly stood up, whistled shrilly and said, "Hold it, Buzz. That went out with high button shoes. Don't you know that? Get off the camera. I'm gonna do it." Alex remembered, "There was just silence and it was so embarrassing."[23]

Kelly also had disagreements with his leading lady Esther Williams. Williams had been called in to replace the studio's initial choice for the film, Judy Garland.[24] From the beginning, Kelly made life miserable for

6. Words and Music to On the Town (1947–1949)

Williams, partially because she was not a dancer, but mostly because she was so much taller than he was. Williams was 5'10" and Gene Kelly was only 5' 7". According to Williams' autobiography *The Million Dollar Mermaid*,

> There was no hiding the fact that I was half a head taller than he was. Looking at the two of us side by side in front of that rehearsal hall mirror, I thought back to my first meeting with Louis B. Mayer, when he talked about all the techniques the studio used to make short men look taller. "You can put Charles Boyer on a box and dig a hole for Loretta Young's horse, Mr. Mayer," I grumbled under my breath, "but for a dance number, the box won't work."[25]

The friction between Williams and Kelly and his cohort Donen[26] reached such a level that Berkeley was called in to mediate. He came up with an idea that would feature a swimming number for Williams, but Kelly nixed it. Instead he convinced Freed that they should include a Harry Warren-Johnny Mercer song called "Baby Doll" in the musical. Kelly had the costume department put Williams in a long crinoline so that she could dance without shoes, and appear shorter. Despite this, she was still taller than her leading man. Kelly then made her do the entire soft-shoe in a deep plié, confident that her bent knees would be hidden under the skirt. It was not an easy task. "The poor kid, I felt so sorry for her," Alex said later.

In the same number, Kelly inserted one of his favorite lifts. As Alex watched, he realized that because of Williams' height, and the bulk of the dress, when she was up in Kelly's arms, "it looked like he was dancing with a building." He told Kelly, "You've got to put her down and let me do it so you can watch." Alex lifted Williams, and Kelly realized that the lift made Williams look even taller. At that same moment, Freed entered the rehearsal hall. They showed the number to him with poor Esther Williams dancing in a squat, culminating with the lift. Freed made the decision then and there to cut the number from the film.[27]

Alex reluctantly told another story about *Take Me Out to the Ball Game*. Kelly and Sinatra were late for the start of filming for a scene set on the baseball field. Finally Berkeley shouted, "When the hell are those guys coming?"[28] He ordered the first assistant director to go get them. The first assistant was afraid of Kelly, so he approached Alex and begged him to go. He said to Alex, "Say we've been waiting for two hours." Alex went over to Sinatra's bungalow and knocked on the door. Sinatra answered the door totally nude, clutching a whisky bottle. Behind Sinatra, Alex saw a naked girl jump out of sight. Alex saw bottles strewn all over. Then he saw Kelly was there as well. Sinatra smiled and said, "Come on in, Alex, and have a drink." Alex said, "I can't. They're waiting for me [on the set] and they sent me to tell you you're late already, and that they're ready to shoot, and everybody's waiting." Sinatra responded, "Oh, we'll be there. We'll be here." Alex returned to the set and told everyone that they would be there shortly, but that they weren't quite ready yet. Forty-five minutes later, the two showed up, a little groggy, but ready for filming.

Alex's next assignment as an assistant was on the musical *On the Town*. In addition to working again with three of the stars from his previous picture, Gene Kelly, Frank Sinatra, and Betty Garrett, he also

Alex (left) in the rehearsal hall at MGM, assisting Gene Kelly and Carol Haney on the choreography for *On the Town*.

6. Words and Music *to* On the Town *(1947–1949)*

A shot from *On the Town's* "A Day in New York Ballet." Left to right: Lee Scott, Gene Kelly and Alex.

reunited with his friends Ann Miller and Vera-Ellen. The film had many dance sequences, so it was decided to hire female assistants. Alex suggested Carol Haney, his partner in Cole's company. Haney and another woman, Jeanne Coyne, joined Alex to set the dance sequences with Kelly.

On the Town marked the debut of Kelly as a director, sharing credit with his friend Stanley Donen. Rehearsals started on February 21, 1949, in Culver City. The cast worked 18-hour days in two adjacent rehearsal studios, sometimes even rehearsing on weekends.

Kelly and Donen had originally hoped to shoot the entire musical on location in New York City, but that proved too difficult and expensive.[29] Although some exterior shots were done in New York, the rest were shot on the soundstages and back lot at MGM.[30]

Alvin Yudkoff's biography of Gene Kelly states,

> Sinatra tortured them with his expected lackadaisical attitude towards rehearsals. To Gene, it didn't really matter with Sinatra's songs—which

were sublime, he thought — but he was determined to elevate the quality of the crooner's dancing. He practically imprisoned Sinatra to gain time to brush up the simple moves he required and was pleased when Sinatra applied himself, learning steps with good will and even mounting enthusiasm.[31]

All of the book scenes and other musical numbers were completed on the film by May 26, 1949, and rehearsals began in earnest for the dream ballet, "A Day in New York," that Kelly had planned to include in the movie. However, despite the fact that Sinatra's dancing had improved since *Take Me Out to the Ball Game*, Kelly knew that the challenges this number presented would be too much for both Sinatra and the other member of the sailor's trio, Jules Munshin. Kelly asked Alex if he would be one of the dancing sailors, doubling for Sinatra. Kelly also asked for suggestions from Alex for "another guy about your size that can do this stuff," to double for Munshin. Alex thought of his friend Lee Scott, who he knew was a great dancer. Carol Haney and Jeanne Coyne[32] also danced in the ballet sequence for Betty Garrett and Ann Miller. Shooting of the seven-minute-long "Day in New York" ballet was completed on July 2, 1949. The sequence has come to be regarded as one of the most outstanding examples of film musical dancing.

7

The Red Danube to *Two Weeks with Love* (1949–1950)

The Red Danube was the first film for which Alex was hired not as an assistant, but as the choreographer. Directed by George Sidney, it was also Alex's first non-musical. Janet Leigh had been hired to star in this story of a Russian spy whose cover was as a ballerina. Originally Sidney asked Alex to give Leigh only a few poses that could be used for close-up shots. Since Leigh had no training as a dancer, Sidney planned to cut away to a double for the majority of dance sections.

Sidney told Alex, "I'm going to put you in the Powell Bungalow because it's out of the way, and you won't be bothered and she won't be bothered." On the first day of rehearsal, Alex met Leigh. "She came in and she was only about seventeen. She was just a beautiful girl. That Janet, she was so beautiful."[1]

Alex started Leigh off with some simple warm-ups at the barre. He told her not to be afraid, explaining that she would have a dance double. After a couple of days, Leigh asked Alex if he could actually give her a few steps. He did. "She was just so ready for these things. And she started to look pretty good in these combinations. Then she surprised the devil out of me because she said, 'Alex, can I go up on toe?'" Knowing that pointe work required a lot of careful training, Alex told her, "No honey, you can't." But Leigh insisted: "I just want to try it." He reluctantly agreed. Because she didn't even know how to put on the pointe shoes, he had to show her how. Once she had them on, he suggested that she just stand at the barre and hold herself up as she slowly tried to go up on pointe.[2]

Leigh was determined and, after the first few painful attempts, she

Alex with Janet Leigh during the filming of *The Red Danube*.

was able to balance on pointe. She kept practicing. As she improved, she became more and more comfortable standing in the toe shoes. Alex decided to give her a simple step that she could do while still holding the barre. After a few days she was able to do the step without holding on, and Alex gave her more and more steps.

When Sidney came to see the progress, Alex told him that Leigh

7. The Red Danube to Two Weeks with Love *(1949–1950)*

was actually doing simple combinations on pointe. He suggested to the director that instead of cutting away to a dance double, he might get some great footage if he shot Leigh doing the first part of the dance herself. Sidney was thrilled, and informed Alex that the shooting schedule had just been pushed back, so they had two additional weeks to perfect the moves.

Because of Leigh's determination and Alex's patience, by the time the sequence was shot, Leigh was able to do much of the complicated routine on pointe. According to Alex, Sidney cut away to the dance double only for the very end piqué turns and final foutés.

Leigh recalled the rehearsals in her autobiography, *There Really Was a Hollywood*:

On the set of The *Red Danube*. Alex, by the camera, is giving directions to Janet Leigh. Leigh has a bandage on her left knee, a result of an injury sustained during rehearsals when her pointe shoe got caught in a crack in the floor.

The Man Who Made the Jailhouse Rock

Poor Alex Romero, a fine dancer and choreographer at MGM (and an angel), had the task of getting me on pointe. Do you have any idea how difficult it is to jam your feet into those toe shoes—those damn torture chambers—let alone stand on them? And the muscle strength needed to support one's body on one's toes? There was no way I could be expected to do the whole routine—it would have taken years—but I did have to execute a few steps for close-ups, and exude an aura of a prima ballerina. Oh, the pain! One day, I was practicing turns, and I turned but the toe shoe didn't. It stuck between two boards in the rehearsal hall floor and didn't budge—my knee hasn't been right since.[3]

Leigh and Alex formed a deep bond. After filming was completed, Leigh approached Alex and asked him to marry her. Alex smiled and told her, "I sure would like to, but I'm already married." Embarrassed, Leigh responded, "Oh, I'm so sorry!" Then she asked, "What can I do for your wife?" Alex told her that she didn't have to do anything, but Leigh arranged to have a huge bouquet of flowers sent to Faun. Alex later commented about how gracious he thought it was for Leigh to respond in that way. Even after many years in the business, working with countless celebrities, Alex said that of all the female stars he had worked with, Leigh was his favorite. The two became lifelong friends, and Leigh always asked Alex to choreograph numbers for her charity events.[4] In 2001, Leigh appeared on stage with Alex, introducing and narrating a short documentary film about him for the Jazz Dance LA "Tribute to Alex Romero."

After finishing *The Red Danube*, Alex worked on another non-musical feature, MGM's *Scene of the Crime*, a small detective film starring Van Johnson and Arlene Dahl. Alex choreographed the dances and the pseudo-strip numbers performed by Gloria DeHaven in a steamy nightclub setting.

Next Alex assisted choreographer Robert Alton on the film version of Irving Berlin's *Annie Get Your Gun*, directed by Busby Berkeley[5] and starring a 28-year-old Judy Garland. The male lead was newcomer Howard Keel[6] in his first major U.S. film. Alex was thrilled with the assignment because he had worked with Garland before and, as he put it, he and Judy "were great pals." He added, "I always loved working with her, but she drank all the time."

Garland's addiction to drugs and alcohol caused her more and more problems during this period in her life, and she often confided in Alex.

7. The Red Danube to Two Weeks with Love (1949–1950)

Alex remembered, "She'd say to me, 'Alex, would you please get me that Cola-Cola bottle over there,' and then she'd pour it out and put whiskey in it, and so she hid it all the time."

One time on the set, she said, "Alex, you'll never believe what happened to me this morning. They used to let me just drive right in. But now they got orders to search me for the goofballs [her word for her pills]. You know where I put them? I opened my Kotex box and put them way down in the bottom. They didn't find them." Garland showed Alex the box, reached in it, and pulled out some pills. Alex recalled, "She was so proud of that."

For *Annie Get Your Gun*, Alex was also cast as the white Indian Chief to perform in the "I'm an Indian Too" number. He was costumed in a huge, white-feathered headdress, white buckskins, and white war paint. Part of the choreography required him to run at full speed and jump on a trampoline held by some of the male dancers. The trick sent him soaring several feet in the air above Garland and the other performers. During one take, the men holding the trampoline tilted it and Alex flew off to one side and fell. Fortunately the crew had spread mats on the floor. Alex landed on the mats and wasn't seriously hurt.

Rehearsals and filming of the "I'm an Indian Too" number lasted for six days. During that time, Garland was physically weak and often confused. In his Garland biography, David Shipman writes, "She was required to sing and be funny in the midst of a large chorus of dancers dressed as Red Indians. She appears to be in a trance: Her singing is barely competent, and she completely lacks the *joie de vivre* the number demands. Rehearsing it with Alton, she could not stand up and had to be physically supported by his assistant, Alex Romero, who was fortunately appearing in the scene."[7]

Alex remembered that on the day they filmed the song, Garland arrived on the set an hour and a half late, and was particularly disoriented and unstable on her feet. She continued to drink heavily and became increasingly inebriated. When the cameras were rolling, Alex had to literally hold the star up and guide her around during the dance. When they finally finished shooting the number, Garland ended in her final pose, sitting unsteadily on Alex's knee. Producer Arthur Freed had slipped on to the set and was watching from behind the camera. As soon as the director[8] called, "Cut," Freed exploded. He shouted, "Judy, You're

The Man Who Made the Jailhouse Rock

Alex as the White Indian with Judy Garland in *Annie Get Your Gun*. Alex was also assistant choreographer on the film.

fired as of this minute. Get the hell out of here. I never want to see you on this stage again. Get out!"[9]

Garland was leaning into Alex's arms; as she clung to him, he felt her tremble, but she didn't say a word. Alex remembered that she held on to him tightly and tears started to well in her eyes.

Garland was replaced in *Annie Get Your Gun* by Betty Hutton.[10] MGM had already spent $100,000 on the Indian number alone, and wanted parts of it salvaged for the new version with Hutton. But after being shown the footage, Hutton vetoed the idea. She said she didn't want the Indian in white any more and demanded that the number have less dancing and more comedy. The original number that featured Alex as the white Indian was scrapped. Decades later, it was resurrected from the MGM vaults and inserted into *That's Entertainment III*.

After Hutton took over the role of Annie Oakley, she had problems with Howard Keel, although in Keel's autobiography he said that Hutton

7. The Red Danube *to* Two Weeks with Love *(1949–1950)*

was sweet and the difficulties were really with the rest of the cast and crew. Hutton wrote in her book, p. 232, "Keel proved to be my primary adversary during the shooting of the film. There was much bad blood between us."[11]

During the filming, Keel was pulled aside by fellow cast member Louis Calhern, who played Buffalo Bill.[12] Calhern told Keel that Hutton had been constantly upstaging him in their scenes together. Keel seemed to brush the warning aside. Being new to films, however, he turned to his new friend Alex and often looked to him for advice on how he was looking on camera. Alex explained, "I'm not [a director], but I've seen a lot of movies." Alex often squatted next the camera, mouthing movement directions to Keel when he was being upstaged. Alex said that on one occasion, "Hutton was screaming and I said to [Keel], 'Come down there. Move over. She's upstaging you.' And he did. But, she was looking at him...." It seems that Keel listened. Hutton demanded that one scene be re-shot 35 times because she was convinced Keel was now claiming camera and upstaging her.[13]

Alex's next film was *Pagan Love Song*, Robert Alton's first job as a director.[14] Alton asked Alex to assist him and told him, "Listen, Alex, I want you to do the numbers for me because I'm the director. I'll tell you

Alex setting a pose for Esther Williams in ***Pagan Love Song***.

I'm having a heck of a time with the script. I have no time to do the numbers."

The location sequences were shot in Kauai, which at that time was undeveloped and hard to reach. It rained constantly. Mail could only reach the cast once a month. The production was painfully slow as the weather prevented the crew and cast from filming.

In the big Tahitian dance production number, Alex utilized native dancers. In addition to using their traditional movements, he gave them what he called "jazzy steps." He remembered that they weren't too happy about that.

Alex also set numbers on Esther Williams, the star of the film.[15] Alex always tried out every bit of staging that he expected his performers to do to make sure it worked and was safe. He recalled, "I did the swimming number, but it was easy ... and you know I don't swim! We did it in a river." Because he had to swim against the current, and he didn't know how to swim, Alex held on to the long vines that hung over the river. In this way he was able to plot out the number. Underwater shots were created for Williams in a specially made pool in Hollywood.[16]

In addition to choreographing Williams, Alex worked with her co-star Howard Keel. Keel's left arm was disfigured, and he depended upon Alex to choreograph him in the swimming number with Williams so that it would not appear in the camera shots. In addition Keel broke his arm during Kauai filming and had to keep it disguised in certain scenes by draping a towel over it.

On the film, Alex also had the chance to work with a young dancer named Rita Moreno.[17] The two hit it off immediately. "We used to dance in between breaks and there were a lot of breaks because it rained like the devil...." In addition to staging the dances on *Pagan Love Song*, Alex also worked as an actor, playing the role of the coconut crab seller. At the end of May, after two months, shooting on Kauai wrapped and the cast and crew returned to Hollywood. To celebrate the completion of filming on the island, Williams hosted a huge cast party but, as Alex recalled, she asked everyone to "bring your own booze and bring your own steaks."

In 1950, Alex also acted as the choreographer for the Civil War western *The Outriders*, directed by Roy Rowland and starring Arlene Dahl and Joel McCrea. For the film he did a number in which the men in a

7. The Red Danube to Two Weeks with Love (1949–1950)

westward-bound caravan begin drinking and dancing. As the only woman in the group, Dahl dances with them all, eventually ending up with her love interest, McCrea.

Alex worked with Dahl again the same year when he assisted Hermes Pan on *Three Little Words*.[18] The musical also starred Fred Astaire, Red Skelton, Keenan Wynn, Vera-Ellen, and a young Debbie Reynolds performing "I Wanna Be Loved By You" with Carleton Carpenter.

The Toast of New Orleans starred Mario Lanza and Kathryn Grayson. Choreographer Eugene Loring hired Alex to dance in the "Tina Lina" number. It featured Alex's friend Rita Moreno, accompanied by James Mitchell.[19] Alex remembered the gossip on the set was about how Lanza had developed a mad crush on Grayson and had been caught trying to climb the fence at her Beverly Hills home to get into her bedroom. Grayson called the police before Lanza could get in.[20]

At the end of 1950, Alex was assistant choreographer to Busby Berkeley on *Two Weeks with Love*,[21] which starred Jane Powell and Ricardo Montalban. The film also featured 18-year-old Debbie Reynolds. In her autobiography *Debbie: My Life*, she mentions that Berkeley was brought in to shoot her number "Abba Dabba Honeymoon" which she did with Carleton Carpenter. The song was staged by choreographer Nick Castle. She writes,

> Buzz [Berkeley] would strap himself on his crane and go miles up into the air so you could barely see him. There are stories about how in the past he'd be drinking and fall off if they didn't tie him on. He'd fall asleep while they were doing the lighting. Carleton used to sing, "Somewhere there's Busby, how high the boom...." They'd have to wake him up when they were ready to shoot."[22]

8

An American in Paris to *The Band Wagon* (1950–1953)

On June 5, 1950, Alex began rehearsals for the musical *An American in Paris*. Gene Kelly, using the art director's and costume designer's drawings to inspire his dance ideas, asked Alex to work with him on plotting out the dances three months before filming. In addition to assisting Kelly on the choreography, Alex performed in the movie.

The film's largest number was the "American in Paris Ballet," a climactic 17-minute dance sequence. Alex danced in the section of the number that featured four "Americans in Paris," who wore straw boaters and different colored striped jackets. Alex was in the blue-stripped coat and tapped with Kelly in the Fourth of July section.

"American in Paris Ballet" was a physically grueling routine, and it was Kelly's intention that it be shot from beginning to end without cuts. Early in the morning of the first day of filming, however, the performers were three-quarters through the killer number when director Vincente Minnelli called, "Cut!" The surprised and exhausted dancers watched as the 75-foot-high camera crane slowly lowered to deposit Minnelli on the floor of the sound stage. He stepped off the crane and, whistling, slowly sauntered past Gene Kelly and the panting dancers to the back of the set. There he adjusted a flower, moving it about an inch. He started back to the crane. When he reached Kelly, the infuriated star pulled off his hat, threw it on the ground, and stomped on it, screaming, "Jesus Christ, Vince, if anyone could see that goddamned flower, we shouldn't even be dancing!"

Filming on the number had to be halted because Kelly had destroyed his one-of-a-kind hat, created specifically for the ballet. In order to

8. An American in Paris to The Band Wagon (1950–1953)

match shots, another had to be specially made in Paris. The production was shut down until it arrived.

Later, during the same number, the camera crane broke and crashed to the stage floor. Alex, who was right under it, jumped out the way and barely missed being hit. No one was hurt, but as the crane fell, it broke off part of the fountain in the center of the set and, again, filming was halted.

The "American in Paris Ballet" took a month to film and cost over half a million dollars.[1] Film historian Ted Sennett called it "both the *piece de résistance* of the film and its principal claim to fame. It is everything its defenders and detractors have claimed over the years: imaginative, audacious, spectacular, pretentious, and too ambitious for its own good."[2] *An American in Paris* went on to win the Best Picture Oscar.

In 1951, Alex worked on four MGM films, *Inside Straight, Texas Carnival, The Strip,* and *Show Boat*. He was hired as the choreographer on *Inside Straight*, a B picture starring Arlene Dahl and David Brian. On *Texas Carnival*, he was one of two specialty dancers in an Ann Miller number with Sasha Goudavich, the Russian dancer who had taught him the air tours on one of his first dancing jobs. The musical starred Esther Williams and Howard Keel.

During the filming of *Texas Carnival*, Williams and her radio-singer husband bought a restaurant called The Trails, located at 6501 South Sepulveda Boulevard, on the corner of Sepulveda and Centinela Avenue. They changed the name to Esther and Ben Gage's Trails. It had a large dance floor and a bandstand and became a hangout for workers at the Hughes and Douglas Aircraft plants, including Howard Hughes himself. Williams asked Alex to stage a floor show for the restaurant. Alex offered to choreograph it for free as a favor because he was so fond of Williams.

In *The Strip*, Alex danced with Sally Forrest and two other backup boys, Lee Scott and Bert May, in a technically challenging jazz tap number choreographed by Nick Castle.[3] The number required the male dancers to spin trays while dancing. The music for the dance, entitled "JT Jive," featured Louis Armstrong on the trumpet, Earl Hines on piano, and Jack Teagarden on trombone.

Alex was assistant choreographer to Robert Alton on *Show Boat*. Alton loved to play tricks on Alex, and during preparations for the Hammerstein-Kern musical he arranged for one of the film's stars, Ava Gard-

Alex (left) dancing with Ann Miller and Alexander "Sasha" Goudavich in *Texas Carnival*.

ner,[4] to be in on one of his jokes. Alton asked Alex to teach a waltz to the sex symbol during a special private rehearsal. When Gardner showed up, she was wearing a lace dress with no bra. The outfit was skin-tight and practically see-through. Alex avoided looking at Gardner as best he could, and tried to demonstrate the number. He suggested that before they danced together, Gardner should put on a rehearsal hoop skirt to give her a feel for the width of her actual costume. Playfully, she refused.

8. An American in Paris *to* The Band Wagon *(1950–1953)*

When they went in to dance position, Alex held his partner at arm's length, explaining again about the width of the skirt she would be wearing in the film. Gardner just nodded and pulled Alex tightly to her, smiling seductively.

The only other person there was the rehearsal pianist. Alex looked at him helplessly, blushing more and more with each movement. He was happily married to Faun, whom he adored, and one of the sexiest ladies in Hollywood was rubbing up against him. Alex said, "She pushed me, and pushed me, and pushed me. She was really going at me, and you could see through everything." When the rehearsal was finished, Gardner thanked him for the lesson and left the room. Soon Alex got a call on the studio phone from Robert Alton. Alex could hear laughing in the background as Alton kidded him about "enjoying his rehearsal with Ava." Later Alex found out it was all a friendly stunt to embarrass him. "He liked to tease me," Alex said. He was told that Ava Gardner scolded Alton, "That Alex guy was so nice. I shouldn't have done that."

In 1952, Alex choreographed *Across the Wide Missouri*, directed by William Wellman, and starring screen legend Clark Gable.[5] The cowboy picture was shot primarily in the High Sierras, and the location was difficult to reach. The altitude was so high that the actors and crew frequently became light-headed. Filming had to halt until they recovered. Although Faun was several months pregnant with their third child, Alex joined the production staff and moved to Colorado for filming.

Wellman had MGM build a base camp for the production in the mountains between Denver and the actual top of the Sierras. The camp was in the mountains, but not as high up as the actual filming location. Huge tents were constructed to house the cast and crew, with cots lined up dormitory-style. Dividers were hung to separate the men's side from the women's.

Barbeques were built at the site. Telephone poles with lights and speakers on them were used to illuminate the camp at night and make announcements. Wellman brought his stack of Nat King Cole records and broadcast the singer over the speakers to entertain the company. A large bullhorn was also used to communicate throughout the camp.

The two major numbers in the film were a comedy dance-fight and a Scottish sword dance.[6] In the comedy number, the cowboys disguised themselves as women to fool the Indians. The dance was to escalate into a huge fight. Alex recalled, "Clark Gable loved to rough house." The star watched Alex setting the fight stunts, something that Alex had done many times in the vaudeville act with his brother John. During one rehearsal, Gable pulled Alex aside and asked, "Hey, Alex, have you tried this one?" He showed Alex the trick of hitting a guy who at first doesn't react, then keels over when someone blows gently in his face. Alex knew the trick and gladly put it in the dance for Gable.

The sword dance featured Alan Napier. Because of the strenuous nature of the piece, Alex was concerned about the altitude and spoke to Wellman about it. Wellman solved the problem by taking Napier up to the location early and keeping him there so he could acclimate himself to the altitude before he had to perform the dance.

One day during filming, Alex was returning from the highest location site when he heard the bullhorn. "Alex Romero, come down please. Bill Wellman has something to say to you." As Alex approached the main camp, the director came out to meet him and led him away from the tents. He put his arm around Alex's shoulders and gently said, "We just got a call from your home, and your baby was stillborn." Alex was sent home on the next train to Los Angeles to care for Faun and his girls. As he recalled the incident, Alex choked up: "It was a boy and Faun always wanted a boy."

Around this time, as Faun was still recuperating, family conflicts began to escalate between Faun's sister Kate and Kate's two sons. Kate eventually threw her two high school–aged boys out of the house. Faun's other sister Denise took in the younger boy Bart, and Alex and Faun offered to take in the older Butch. For the next three years or so, Butch lived full-time with the family, becoming like a son to Alex and Faun.[7]

In 1952, Alex was asked to choreograph *The Bad and the Beautiful*, directed by Vincente Minnelli, and starring Lana Turner and Kirk Douglas.[8] On the Dean Martin-Jerry Lewis picture *Jumping Jacks,* the choreographer Bob Sidney became sick, so Alex stepped in and choreographed the tap number for the male dancers. On *Skirts Ahoy,* Alex assisted choreographer Nick Castle and worked with Esther Williams again. The film also featured Debbie Reynolds, Bobby Van, Joan Evans, and Vivian Blaine.

The Belle of New York was a musical directed by Charles Walters. Robert Alton was hired to choreograph and brought Alex along to

8. An American in Paris *to* The Band Wagon *(1950–1953)*

assist, but it was Fred Astaire who asked for Alex to help him on his numbers.[9]

One of Alex's fondest memories was when the two of them were working together on the "Dancin' Man" number. Astaire looked at Alex and said, "I'm kind of stuck a little bit. Do you have anything that would fit in here?" Alex was always making up his own steps in his free time during breaks. He showed Astaire something that he had made up earlier, about 16 bars of a routine. Astaire loved it: "Oh that's beautiful. Do it again." Alex repeated the piece of choreography. Astaire got more and more excited. Alex recalled, "He was like a kid."

At that moment, Arthur Freed came into the studio and Astaire called to him, "Arthur, I want you to see the wonderful stuff Alex just gave me." He asked Alex to demonstrate, and Alex did steps for Freed, who applauded. Alex recalled, "That really made me feel good."[10]

Another of Alex's favorite numbers in the film was the "Oops" number in which Astaire and Vera-Ellen danced on the streetcar. Alex remembered that while they were working on it, Astaire told him that he was worried that Vera-Ellen was anorexic. According to Alex, Astaire spoke to the producers about it and said to Vera-Ellen herself: "Honey, you have to eat. Your bones are showing." Alex remembered that when they were working out the lifts in the dance, she was sometimes so weak from the anorexia that she couldn't assist in propelling herself up in Astaire's arms. Alex remembered that Vera-Ellen was a very sweet woman, but was as intimated by Astaire as she had been with Gene Kelly.

In *The Belle of New York*, Alex had a hand in the staging of "Baby Doll," the same song that had been cut from *Take Me Out to the Ball Game*. He also assisted with Astaire's drum dance in the emporium. Alex recalled that it took an entire day to film. During the dance, Astaire was supposed to throw a drumstick on the floor and have it bounce back up into his hand. It wasn't until the 52nd take that the drumstick hit the right spot and bounced perfectly into Astaire's hand.

The Belle of New York was shot at the same time as *Singin' in the Rain*. The two productions were housed in MGM stages adjacent to each other. Although Alex was not officially involved in *Singin' in the Rain*, he was good friends with both Gene Kelly and Cyd Charisse. During the filming of Charisse's "Broadway" ballet scarf dance, Alex was asked to help work out how to use the 25-foot Chinese silk scarf in the dance.[11]

The Man Who Made the Jailhouse Rock

In 1953, a full year for Alex, he worked on six films at MGM: *Ride, Vaquero!*, *Lili*, *Small Town Girl*, *The Affairs of Dobie Gillis*, *Kiss Me Kate*, and *The Band Wagon*. Alex was hired as choreographer for *Ride Vaquero!*, a cowboy film with Howard Keel, Robert Taylor, Anthony Quinn, and his "close friend," Ava Gardner.

When director-choreographer Charles Walters became tied up with his directing duties on *Lili*, he had his assistant Alex choreograph the majority of the numbers, including Zsa Zsa Gabor's numbers and the climactic ballet with Mel Ferrer and Leslie Caron.

When the Metro front office called Alex about working on *Small Town Girl*, he was informed that he would immediately start assisting Busby Berkeley. Berkeley talked to Alex about creating a Flamenco tap number for Ann Miller. He told Alex to hold an audition and pick 18 to 20 men. Then Berkeley said, "You get the boys and I'll see you a little later because I have to go somewhere." Berkeley then left the stage. Alex continued, "I phoned in exactly whom I wanted. They needed big guys, because Ann Miller's very tall." The next morning, as the newly hired dancers were warming up, Berkeley showed up, saw the boys, approved them, turned to the pianist and said, "Play the music."

The pianist began to play a Spanish-sounding song. Berkeley stood by the piano for a while, thinking. Then he walked to the center of the stage. Alex moved in place behind him, ready to observe and learn the routine. Berkeley then walked back towards the piano, and Alex walked back as well. Berkeley stopped again to think. Alex stopped and waited. Berkeley repeated this several times with Alex continuing to shadow him. Finally Berkeley stopped, looked at his watch, and said, "Alex, I have to go see the art director. Would you start the number?" Then he left.

Alex recalled, "I was shocked out of my socks. I didn't have the faintest idea of what I was going to do. Usually if I'm going to assist and maybe think I'm going to [be asked to create steps], I start to think about the number. I just knew it was Spanish."

He asked Don Garza, the piano player, to play the music again.

> And I'm making up things and looking for patterns, and I finally got about eight or twelve bars, something like that. And I thought, I'd try them out on them. And I looked it over and made little changes, and I liked what I saw. And I keep looking at the door to see when he was going to come in.

8. An American in Paris *to* The Band Wagon *(1950–1953)*

A backstage shot of Alex with Leslie Caron (and others, unidentified) on the set of *Lili*.

And to make a long story short, [Berkeley] never came in at all. And people are calling and bringing in things like they do for the choreographer, changes or whatever they are, and I'd just put them on the piano. And I'd tell them, "He's expected right away."

Berkeley finally showed up at the end of the day, around five, and asked, "How's it going?" By then Alex had choreographed quite a bit. Berkeley said, "Show me what you've got." Alex ran the number for him, and Berkeley said, "Hey, that's great, I like it. I like it, Alex. Let's keep it." Then Berkeley announced to the dancers that rehearsal would be the same time tomorrow. The next day Berkeley didn't show up. He just phoned in at the end of the day and asked Alex how it was going. "And he did the same thing the next day and as it turns out, I did the whole number." Alex remembered that he never saw Berkeley at any rehearsals after that first day. In later years, Alex said, "I didn't expect, and knew I wasn't going to get, credit. But [doing this particular number] helped me a lot because a lot of people would come in, would see what was happening, and Ann [Miller] was telling people that I was her new choreographer. So from then on, it helped me a whole lot."[12]

Miller sent a note to Alex when he was being honored by Jazz Dance LA in 2001: "Of all people it's about time you should be honored. I so enjoyed working with you in *Small Town Girl* as that Spanish number we did was so outstanding and I am very proud of it today."[13]

In the fall of 1953, producer Arthur Lowe, Jr., pulled Alex aside and said, "I'd like you to work with me on something ... a movie, a 'B' picture. And I have Debbie [Reynolds] and Bob Fosse. It's low-budget and you're going to have to take a cut, but I want you to know that my father's read the script and thinks that this is going to be like the Andy Hardy family that went on for five years or so. And if so, you'll be getting more money...." The film was *The Affairs of Dobie Gillis*. It featured Debbie Reynolds,[14] Barbara Ruick, Bobby Van (in the part of Dobie), and a young Bob Fosse in his first movie role.

Alex went over the script with Lowe during pre-production meetings, and the producer was especially excited about a sequence that took place in an auditorium. Lowe wanted a barn dance but, as he told Alex, "I'd like an updated version of that. Like, put some swing dancing in ... and jazz and stuff like that." Swing was popular at the time and the idea of doing that type of number appealed to Alex as a choreographer. Then Loew added, "And we want you to be the caller...."[15]

Alex quickly agreed but later thought to himself, "You can't do a caller in swing dancing because there are no calls in swing dancing." After the meeting he went home and started to brainstorm. "I wrote this dumb song.... I think it's kind of corny now ... what I thought was an updated barn dance. I wrote the lyric for that. Now looking back, I just loved the things he was throwing at me. The number was at the time ... one of the best things I'd ever done."

In addition to the auditorium dance, there was a malt shop number

8. An American in Paris *to* The Band Wagon *(1950–1953)*

that featured what would later seem to be classic Fosse jazz moves. Alex approached Fosse before they started and told him, "Bobby, if you want to take over, if you want to do this, be my guest because I know you're a great dancer and you'd probably feel better doing it." Fosse replied, "No, no, no, Alex. I like the challenge of doing somebody else's work." Alex remembered, "That pleased me, and I went ahead and did it all."

For her book *Masters of Movement: Portraits of America's Great Choreographers,* Rose Eichenbaum interviewed Alex and watched the *Dobie Gillis* malt shop number with him. She writes:

> [Alex] slipped in *The Affairs of Dobie Gillis* [video], forwarding it to the Fosse solo. The energetic young dancer seemed to jump out of the screen. One minute he was on top of a piano, then he went up and down a staircase, then did a duet with a jukebox—all in a single number. I thought to myself, this looks like Fosse's style, but he's performing Alex's choreography?
>
> "Alex," I said, "are you in part responsible for Fosse's dance style?"
>
> "No, no. I would never take credit for influencing Bob Fosse. This was the dance style of the time. The only thing I might have done was give him the idea to use a hat."[16]

In addition to the standout performance of Fosse in this number, the dance also featured the other leads in the film, Reynolds, Van, and Ruick. Despite the stylistic differences in the four performers, the number holds together as a cohesive piece, combining jazz and tap, and building to a huge crescendo. It ends with Van pulling Reynolds up a flight of stairs while she sits in a chair.

Alex was next assigned to assist Hermes Pan[17] on *Kiss Me Kate.* Bobby Van and Bob Fosse were in the film, along with the superlative dancer Tommy Rall. The women were Carol Haney, Jeanne Coyne, and Ann Miller.[18] Alex knew Haney from his days with Jack Cole and Coyne from *On the Town.* He had worked with Miller on *Texas Carnival* and *Small Town Girl,* and had danced with her in films choreographed by Cole. The two stars of the film were Howard Keel and Kathryn Grayson.

Keel wrote in his autobiography, "Hermes Pan, the award-winning choreographer, was so busy with dance numbers, I asked him to lend me his assistant, Alex Romero, to work on my numbers."[19] Alex knew Keel well, having worked with him on *Pagan Love Song, Texas Carnival, Annie Get Your Gun, Show Boat,* and *Ride Vaquero!* In a 1987 interview, Keel recalled how Alex came to work with him on the film:

Hermes started with me and I said, "Hermes, you know, some of what you've got me doin' ... "I'm not a Fred Astaire or a Gene Kelly." I said, "I can't do that kinda thing." And his assistant, Alex Romero, was a very fine choreographer, and I said, "I think Alex knows me pretty well, would you mind?" And he said, "Go right ahead, I'm so busy I don't know what to do. You're absolutely right."[20]

Keel recalled that sometimes after shooting until 7:00 P.M., he'd "take a sandwich break, then work with Alex Romero until 10:00 P.M."[21] After setting Keel's numbers, Alex also helped him during filming. While shooting "Where Is the Life That Late I Led," Alex placed himself off camera to signal to Keel which direction to go.

Alex did not stay until the completion of *Kiss Me Kate*. After he finished his work with Keel, he was assigned to work on *The Band Wagon*,[22] directed by Vincente Minnelli.[23] Alex was hired to assist choreographer Michael Kidd, who was doing his first film choreography. Fred Astaire asked for Alex because Kidd did not tap. Alex was also the dancing stand-in for Astaire.[24]

Alex and his family lived quite far from MGM. Alex's old $25 Ford no longer was drivable, so he took the Pacific Electric Red Car Line to get to work. One day as he was heading to Metro to rehearse, he noticed a man at a shoeshine stand at the Pacific Electric Building Terminal in downtown Los Angeles, near Sixth and Main Streets. Alex watched as the man shined a businessman's shoes. The bootblack had an old jukebox next to his stand that played jazz music. He took two big brushes and hit the wooden part of them together as he worked, "making sounds you wouldn't believe." Then the man took a polishing rag and started "popping the rag to rhythm."

Alex was mesmerized by the display. He was wearing tennis shoes that day, so the next day on his way to work, he wore dress shoes, planning to get a shine from the man. He did, and as he was sitting in the chair, he asked him, "Where did you learn to do that?" The man said, "I just do it. I like music." Alex asked him if he also tap danced. The man said, "No. Sometimes I just move my feet around."

That day at rehearsal, Alex found Astaire playing the music and trying to decide what to do at a shoeshine stand in his number "Shine on Your Shoes." Astaire played around a bit and then told Alex, "You get up and see if you can find some things." Just as Alex was beginning

8. An American in Paris *to* The Band Wagon *(1950–1953)*

to experiment, Michael Kidd walked in to the rehearsal hall; Alex recalled, "[He was] so vivacious and all smiles." Kidd jumped on the shoeshine stand and turned around, and jumped off in what Alex called "Russian-type dance." Astaire got irritated and began pacing. Although he respected Kidd as a great choreographer, he knew that Kidd wasn't a tapper.

Astaire finally said, "Mike, do me a favor, please ... you go rehearse on something with Cyd [Charisse]. Alex has worked with me before and he'll help me here."

Later that day, while Astaire and Alex were figuring out steps, Alex couldn't stop thinking about the shoeshine he had gotten that morning. Finally, he just couldn't hold in his excitement any longer. He said, "Fred, I got something that might fit here ... an idea for you."

"What is it?"

"Well, I ran into this black kid...." Alex told him about Leroy Daniels, the bootblack he had met at the Pacific Electric Building. Alex said of Daniels' amazing rhythms, "I've never heard anything like it."

Astaire didn't hesitate. "Get him."

"Well, Fred ... he's not in the Guild. He doesn't have a card...."

"Just get him. Bring him in."

The next day on his way to work, Alex asked Daniels if he could come in to meet Astaire. Daniels immediately closed up his stand and went with Alex to MGM. When they got to the rehearsal hall, Alex introduced him to Astaire, then said, "Fred, why don't you have him do your shoes?" Astaire agreed, and as Daniels went into his routine, "Fred went out of his mind." The "Shine on Your Shoes" number became a classic and, after the film, Leroy Daniels gave up shining shoes and went into show business full-time.[25]

In addition to helping on the "Shine on Your Shoes" number, Alex assisted on the other staging in *The Band Wagon*. One of his favorites was the song "I Guess I'll Have to Change My Plan," with its simple, elegant movements featuring Astaire and Jack Buchanan. As an elderly man, Alex frequently sang this Schwartz-Dietz classic recreating the same choreography that he still remembered from working on the film 50 years earlier.

9

Seven Brides for Seven Brothers to *The Eddie Fisher Show* (1954–1957)

As the only staff assistant choreographer on the Metro-Goldwyn-Mayer lot, Alex Romero was frequently shifted from one project to another. "I didn't have any say about it. That was my job. I was real happy about it because, in essence, you learn different styles. My gosh, so many great choreographers."

In 1954, director Stanley Donen assigned Alex to work with choreographer Michael Kidd on *Seven Brides for Seven Brothers*. Although Alex had assisted Kidd on other projects, and the two got along well, Kidd was initially frustrated because he wanted to use his own assistant from New York.[1]

While they were prepping the numbers, Kidd asked Alex to go to the props department and bring back items that might be used in a barn-raising. Alex returned with lumber, hammers, axes, and anything else that he thought could work. The two men began experimenting with the props, eventually creating stunning acrobatic and balletic tricks that were used in the barn dance–fight. Kidd later said of Alex's prowess during this process, "Whatever you saw up there on the screen, Alex did it first."[2] Kidd also said, "Alex was endlessly creative and supportive."[3]

The movie featured some of the top male dancers in the business, including Tommy Rall, Jacques d'Amboise, Mark Platt, Matt Mattox, and Russ Tamblyn.[4] Alex remembered when Kidd was first working out the barn-raising tricks with the dancers:

> [Kidd] started out with that stuff [the acrobatics] first instead of the dancing.... Tommy [Rall] was very sullen ... looked mad all the time, a very

9. Seven Brides for ... to The Eddie Fisher Show (1954–1957)

quiet guy, never mentioned dancing or anything. [Kidd] was going to do a big trick, a big acrobatic thing with little balletic steps, but mostly acrobatic. He'd say what he wanted, like to Matt [Mattox] or one of the other guys. He'd mention the ballet terms and then for the tricks he'd say, "I want you to do this flip or that flip, or this or that." He'd say, "Try it." [Mattox] couldn't do it, so he'd say, "Try it." "I can't do that." He'd try someone else. "I can't do that." And he tried all the guys. I was standing very close to Tommy and he was looking like this [with his face in a scowl] ... real mad. And then [Kidd] said, "Tommy, could you do this?" And he'd say, "Sure." And whoosh, whoosh, whoosh, pow, pow ... and I thought "Wow, he's gonna give it to him. Isn't that great." But Kidd would look at one of the other guys and say, "Now you got to learn that." And to Tommy Rall, "You help them." He just wouldn't give him anything. He just didn't like Tommy. He seemed to hate him ... and Tommy wasn't too pleased with him. And this went on and on.

The filming of *Seven Brides for Seven Brothers* only took 34 days. Alex had the opportunity to work again with his close friend Howard Keel, and also with Jane Powell, whom he knew from *Two Weeks with Love* and *Small Town Girl*. Both stars later asked Alex to choreograph their nightclub acts.

Keel's nightclub act opened at the Last Frontier in Las Vegas shortly after *Seven Brides* completed shooting. After firing the writer he had hired to create his act, Keel turned to Alex. He recalled,

[Alex] created an act around my body of work at MGM. The MGM staff built a special stool and a complete dressing table that I could roll onstage. I'd sit there and in front of the audience, turn myself into Petruchio and sing "Where Is the Life That Late I Led?"[5]

Alex also wanted Keel to do a little tap dance in his act. At first, Keel resisted the notion, but Alex persisted, telling Keel, "Don't you say a word. When you hear me tapping, I'll stop and you do exactly what I did." Alex smiled when he recalled that Keel didn't really execute the steps very well, but he said that when Keel tapped in his act, "the people stood up and applauded."[6]

In 1955, Alex was assigned his first-big budget musical as solo choreographer, *Love Me or Leave Me* with Doris Day[7] and James Cagney. A newspaper publicity blurb from the period stated;

Alex Romero not only handles his first full choreographical assignment in staging the dances for MGM's CinemaScope musical drama *Love Me or Leave Me* based on the life of Ruth Etting, he also plays his first film role in the picture. ...Romero, in the past assistant to such choreographers as Hermes Pan, Busby Berkeley and Michael Kidd, duplicates his real-life role by portraying a dance director in *Love Me or Leave Me*, appearing in scenes revolving around the Hollywood phase of Miss Etting's career.[8]

Alex recalled, "That was probably the most exciting thing I've ever done. I don't know how I got the job. [Joe] Pasternak [the producer] just said, 'Alex, you're going to do *Love Me or Leave Me* as a choreographer.' That was my first big job, and you know, I never was afraid."

Rehearsals began on November 19, 1954, and ran until the 4th of December. When Day first came on the set and met Alex, she was with her husband Marty Melcher, whom Alex thought was the "greatest guy you'd ever want to know." The couple brought in a big tray of dried fruit and nuts. Melcher took the food into his wife's dressing room, and she invited Alex in to eat while she was being made up.

Alex and Day got along famously. Others had warned him that she was a problem to work with, but Alex didn't think so. "I've never had anybody more cooperative or sweet in my whole life. She was loved by everybody on the set."[9]

Alex started Day on the female comedy dance routines, including the opening song "Five Foot Two, Eyes of Blue (Has Anybody Seen My Gal?)."[10] Alex called these types of dances "the dumb numbers." When he was first teaching dance steps to the women, they laughed at how easily Alex was able to come up with fun, feminine moves. He later explained how his training with Jack Cole helped him learn how to choreograph for women. He said that Cole always asked his company dancers to learn both the male and female parts of a dance. He'd tell them, "I want you boys to dance like girls and I want you girls to dance like men." The purpose of this was so that they would be able to teach either sex when assigned on a movie. Alex said, "Thank God for Jack Cole."

During *Love Me or Leave Me*, Melcher came to the set every day and watched his wife and Alex work. After about a week of rehearsal, Melcher called Alex aside and told him, "Do you know what? After this movie, I'm going to get a Broadway show for Doris Day and you're going to be the choreographer."

One of Day's numbers was "Ten Cents a Dance." The staging Alex did was simple and restrained, with Day standing with her hands on her hips, legs in a wide stance. Alex wanted the fringed dance to provide the

9. Seven Brides for ... to The Eddie Fisher Show *(1954–1957)*

Alex and Doris Day review music on the set of *Love Me or Leave Me*.

only real movement. He explained that he knew he should not distract from the emotion of Day's performance or the power of the number with extraneous choreography. "Ten Cents a Dance" is now recognized as a film classic.

Several other numbers in the film were also choreographic standouts.[11] In "Shakin' the Blues Away," the male ensemble began with a Jack Cole–flavored modern jazz dance that transformed into a hat and cane production number featuring Day in a beaded aqua-blue gown. Pictures of Day in the number were later used in the film's publicity material.[12]

Cagney and Alex met during rehearsals to tap dance together. Alex recalled, "Every day he came in to dance." A 1955 article in the *Oakland Tribune* stated,

> James Cagney doesn't dance in MGM's CinemaScope picture *Love Me or Leave Me* ... but he matched Doris Day step by step during rehearsals for the film with choreographer Alex Romero. A firm believer in physical fitness, Cagney has long used dancing as a means to keep in shape. It is a practice he has followed ever since his hoofing days on Broadway. The star's first act on reporting to MGM for his first film at this studio was to contact Romero

and make arrangements to be called every time a dance rehearsal was scheduled.[13]

Cagney treated Alex with great respect: "He was the first guy to ever call me Mr. Romero." The star was curious about Alex's process while creating choreography. When Cagney asked him, "Do you make up the steps as you go along?" Alex responded, "Well, some of them, but mostly I come in early, and I dance and I get steps first ... get ahead of them a little bit. I don't have to do the whole number...." Cagney nodded and said, "Well, I like to tap dance every day."

In addition to dancing with Alex, Cagney attended all the other dance rehearsals.[14] "He watched them all. When we got to the big number, he'd leave the set [where he was working] to come on over." Cagney commented once to Alex, "If any of your chorus people here had been on Broadway, they would [have been] a dancing star. We didn't do that. We didn't do hard steps like that. You'd just get away with a soft shoe and you'd stop the show. And everybody here ... well, we never worked that hard.'"

During *Love Me or Leave Me*, Doris Day began to have marital troubles. Alex recalled that Melcher suddenly stopped showing up on the set and at the end of filming the movie there was an incident when Day ran out crying. Alex ran after her, calling "Doris, honey, Doris," seeking to console her, but Day didn't look back or stop. Although they were very close during the filming of *Love Me or Leave Me*, Alex was never able to reach her after the movie was completed.[15]

In 1955, Alex also choreographed the historical spectacle *The Prodigal* starring Lana Turner. "It was one of the hugest sets I've ever seen in my whole life. [Director] Richard Thorpe[16] took me in there and showed me this thing and he said, 'Alex, there's a lot of staging and I want you to do it all. We're going to have horses and whatnot.'"

For the ritual "sacrifice of the maiden" scene, Alex set a dance that was based on stylized hieroglyphic positions found in ancient friezes. He had 30 women in the number plus banner carriers and other extras. The dancers had to position their bodies so that they were turned sideways to the left. Alex asked Thorpe, "Is there any special place you want [the dancers] to enter from?" The director assured him, "No, wherever you want." So Alex decided to have the procession enter from the left.

> I wanted them to all come in doing this one step.... A little bit of it was Jack Cole-ish ... but it was Egyptian, you know, [sideways] like a frieze, turned

9. Seven Brides for ... to The Eddie Fisher Show (1954–1957)

this way. And it's kind of hard to walk that way. I gave them a little bit of movement ... they'd walk and move ... walk and move ... and it looked good to me. And when it was done, I said [to Thorpe], "I want you to look at this." And he looked and he said, "Oh, that's great. That's fine. That's very good."

Alex asked Thorpe again,

> I just wanted you to see the entrance.... I want to let you know that if you for some reason don't like this camera angle and want to do it to the right, let me know now, because it's going to take me at least a half-hour, because it's all on the left. It's pretty complicated for [the dancers] and we'll have to shut down for a half hour at least.

Thorpe responded, "No, that's fine."

On the day of filming, Thorpe was setting up the camera shots and, on the spur of the moment, changed his mind about the entrance. He apologized to Alex, and had to wait half an hour as the dancers reversed the routine. Alex said later that he regretted that most of the dance was cut from the final edit of the film.

Near the end of the year, Alex choreographed another huge musical feature, *I'll Cry Tomorrow*, starring Susan Hayward.[17] He remembered, "We did some wild dancing...."

It was Broadway director Daniel Mann's first film as director, and he said to Alex, "You're gonna have to help me." Alex asked if he could give the director a suggestion for the set. Mann agreed and Alex told him about his idea for a double-deck set. Alex said, "I can get a lot more action because I want to come down from this little nightclub where she's singing and then really cut loose and do some wide [shots]."

Mann was excited by the idea. Alex remembered, "He just let me take over. He didn't bother me ... didn't see the number until it was finished. And when he saw the run-through he said, 'God, it looks like a Broadway show.'"

One section of the number had dancers parading down the street after leaving the nightclub. Alex wanted one of the male dancers to come flying into the shot:

> So I built a trampoline and I did the trick. And I hit this trampoline, and it was Frank [Magrin] who caught me up like this [above his head]. I'd trust him with anything. I've done so many things that could have killed me and he saved my life. And then we did it and the guy came through and hit the bass drum. It's a great trick.

The Man Who Made the Jailhouse Rock

> I said [to the dancers], "I want one of you guys to do it." Frank couldn't do it. I needed him to catch, because I knew he could catch anybody. Nobody could do it. So I went to the director and said, "I've got this thing and I need a guy. I need a professional acrobat to do this thing."

The producers agreed and hired an acrobat to do the stunt. The man showed up and Alex explained the action he wanted, and when the cast began rehearsing the sequence the acrobat prepared to make the jump.

> Frank starts running down and this guy didn't jump. I said, "Are you okay?" And he said, "Yeah, but I can't do this. I can't hit the trampoline." I said, "Well, how are you hitting it?" "Well, like this." And he did one without going anywhere, and he was bending his knees. And you can't do it if you bend your knees. You only break [the momentum].... If you hit it stiff-legged, it throws you.

The acrobat told Alex that the stunt was impossible to do. Alex looked at the guy, signaled Frank Magrin, ran and hit the trampoline himself, and

A shot from the number "Sing You Sinners" in the movie *I'll Cry Tomorrow* starring Susan Hayward. In addition to choreographing the number, Alex created the concept for the set. This shot captures the moment just after an acrobat had hit a hidden off-stage trampoline and landed on the shoulders of two dancers to hit the drum.

9. Seven Brides for ... *to* The Eddie Fisher Show *(1954–1957)*

sailed through the air, landing above Magrin's head in the catch-hold. He said to the man, "You got it? Just stand here and watch how my feet hit that." Alex demonstrated again, but the acrobat could not get the trick.

Realizing he wasn't able to do the job he had been hired for, the man asked Alex, "Are you going to fire me?" Alex responded, "No, they're paying a lot of money for you...." He refused to have MGM pay the man for nothing. The acrobat eventually did some semblance of the stunt. Alex recalled, "It looks pretty darn good, but it isn't nearly the trick that we had."

After Alex's successes with *Love Me or Leave Me* and *I'll Cry Tomorrow*, he was approached by producer Jack Segasture about choreographing a new Broadway musical called *Pleasuredome*. It starred comedienne Kaye Ballard and comedian-songwriter Jimmie Komack, and featured Josephine Premice, who had danced for Katherine Dunham. After weeks of auditions and rehearsals, the production, a revue-type show publicized as "a Cook's tour of the Palaces of Mirth," opened in previews on December 1, 1955, at the Shubert Theatre in Washington DC. Unfortunately, Segasture had already run out of money. The show closed while still in previews and the never made it to New York. In 2012, Kaye Ballard recalled working on the project and said of Alex, "He was wonderful."[18]

Alex returned to Hollywood. In 1956, he was contracted to choreograph *Diane*, Lana Turner's last film under contract at MGM. The male lead was Roger Moore. Alex recalled:

> [Moore] was a big, tall, handsome, beautiful guy — great looking guy, but he moved like.... [Alex imitated Frankenstein]. He just can't walk hardly. The first day we got together and I had researched some stuff, and when you research, you got it, and then you make-up from there, and nobody ever knows it. And yet it looks typical.... And they had these great gowns and lots of bows and turns and this and that, and it was complicated.... And [Lana Turner] sees that it's impossible for [Roger Moore] right now. And she said, "Why don't I leave you two alone for a couple of days and you can work with him?" And I stayed with him for three or four days and I got him looking great and when Lana came back she said, "Oh, this looks great."

Alex recalled that he and Moore grew close during the process of making *Diane*: "We were kind of buddies during the rehearsal." After filming, Alex recalled, "He picked me up in his arms and said, 'God, Alex, you saved my life. I thank you so much.'"[19]

Immediately after finishing *Diane*, Alex began work on *The Fastest Gun Alive* with Glenn Ford and Jeanne Crain. The movie featured a spe-

The Man Who Made the Jailhouse Rock

cialty hoedown with Russ Tamblyn doing acrobatic tricks and hopping on a shovel as if it were a pogo stick. In an interview about the film, Tamblyn spoke of the experience:

> Alex had me swinging from rafters, doing acrobatics and dancing on top of a shovel. He was great with people who didn't know how to dance, like Elvis Presley in *Jailhouse Rock*. Elvis was really uncomfortable with choreography, but Alex got him to do all sorts of stuff. Alex would find out what you could do, and then he'd choreograph to your capability. I was a lot like Ray Bolger. Ray wasn't great at ballet, but if you got him to do some eccentric loose dancing, he was terrific.... Alex and I fastened a boot to the top of a shovel and I jumped around in this crazy routine.[20]

On all of his jobs, Alex prepared every stunt and step, making sure that he could do them before giving them to his dancers. His daughters Melinda and Judy remembered his preparing the shovel dance for *The Fastest Gun Alive*. Melinda said, "There are things I remember Dad working out at home with the shovel." Judy added, "It was hard on the wooden floor."

Alex recalled that one day while he was rehearsing the hoedown number with Tamblyn, Glenn Ford came into the rehearsal studio and saw the two working out some tap-like steps. Ford, who was then married to tap star Eleanor Powell, said to Alex, "Listen, if you're going to do tap, I'm leaving. That's all I hear at home. [Powell] taps in the bathroom and kitchen.... I absolutely hate it!"

In the summer of 1956, Alex was approached by producers Huntington Hartford and Ray Golden to choreograph a new stage musical revue called *Joyride*. The musical, with music by Max Gordon Showalter, featured such performers as Joel Grey, Dorothy Greener, Bernie West, and Conrad Janis. It was to open at the Huntington Hartford Theatre on Vine Street between Sunset and Hollywood Boulevards in Los Angeles, followed by a tour to Chicago. Alex began work on the project and finished the opening and closing numbers for the production before he had to drop out because of conflicts that developed when he was offered the chance to do another new Broadway show.[21]

In September of 1956, Alex took a break from Hollywood and traveled to New York to choreograph the musical *Happy Hunting*[22] with Ethel Merman and Fernando Lamas.[23] Twenty-five separate auditions were held in June at the Longacre Theatre at 220 West 48th Street in mid-

9. Seven Brides for ... to The Eddie Fisher Show *(1954–1957)*

town Manhattan, with 11,500 people showing up for 60 roles. Alex needed 12 dancers.[24] A newspaper article from the time stated,

> Alex Romero, our choreographer, worked a bit differently. Screening "terp" applicants, Alex asked them to change to practice clothes. Then he took groups of dancers (ten at a time) through steps evolved to test their skill. This quickly separates the pros from the beginners, but, like all good choreographers, Romero retained one or two novices who showed special promise.[25]

Alex went to New York to prep *Happy Hunting*[26] three weeks before the five-week rehearsal period started on September 13. He didn't like the music, and told the producer so. He remembered, "The music there I thought was terrible, especially the number they picked for the big production number. There were a couple of others, but the big production number was supposed to be a show-stopper." Alex was used to having input on numbers at MGM, and told the producer and writers, "I'll do

Alex's athletic choreography is on display in a number from the Broadway musical *Happy Hunting.*

the first chorus like you want, but then I want to go to rock and roll." The writers and musicians rolled their eyes. Alex said, "It's the coming thing." The producer said, "Look, we're going on the road for six weeks; [rock and roll] will be gone by then."

Despite this, Alex went on to create a show-stopping number in the first act. It occurred right before Ethel Merman's entrance. At the Philadelphia tryout,[27] the number received such extended applause that Merman threw a fit. She demanded that the dance number be edited so that her entrance would receive more applause. Because Merman was not only the box office draw, but also one of the producers, the number was trimmed. Despite these cuts, the number continued to garner one of the biggest responses of the evening.[28]

By 1957, Alex was working primarily as a choreographer in movies, and had stopped assisting at MGM. That year, however, Jack Cole was approached about doing a film called *Les Girls,* which was to star Gene Kelly (his last at MGM).[29] Cole had two conditions for accepting the job. First, he wanted "a fellow who used to work with him, Alex Romero, to assist him," and second, he demanded that "the male lead in the film, Gene Kelly, never, never come into the rehearsal hall."

Alex was approached about assisting Cole on *Les Girls* and was informed about Cole's conditions. He was honored that Cole had asked for him, but he was concerned about the second condition. "That had to be tough on Kelly because he's [a guy who] wants to do what he wants to do, you know ... he's a taskmaster."

During the first rehearsals to set the numbers, only Cole and Alex were in the hall. Alex was to learn both Kelly's and Mitzi Gaynor's parts. He would then be responsible for teaching the two stars, Kelly first. "I taught [Kelly] that and when he had it, [Cole] said, 'I don't want Mitzi to come in [and dance with Kelly] until she's got it ... and I want him to practice while Alex is working with Mitzi.' And they did it just like that. I knew that I'd be the fall guy if they didn't do every finger and every look ... and he's got beats you don't know with his head.... And they all mean something, and they look good on the screen."

After finishing the number with Kelly and Gaynor, Alex worked with Cole on another dance with one of the film's other leading ladies, Taina Elg. "Cole had this idea of doing this number with a rope ... a soft rope ... I thought it looked like [demonstrating the string game Cat's

9. Seven Brides for ... to The Eddie Fisher Show *(1954–1957)*

Cradle]. He'd do something and wrap it around her arm or leg and then turn and it would be a funny design because they're about twelve feet apart ... and he wouldn't settle until he had a great design he's making ... and that's what the number was mostly about... It was a hard number to learn because you had to untwist everything...."

One day while rehearsing the rope dance, Alex left the lot during a break to walk to the bank to deposit his paycheck. He and Cole had just worked on a complicated part of the routine, and Cole had said, "Alex, I like this one especially. Make sure you have that." Alex went on with the story:

> Now it's lunch time and it's payday and I have to go to the bank, and it's about three blocks away. And I'm going down the street walking to the bank, and when I get to the stoplight, I'm practicing, going ... [demonstrating a Cole jazz move] ... like that. And I don't know I'm doing it and I'm out in traffic. And the light goes on, and I cross the street and I'm evidently doing a little bit like that [showing some more moves], and there was a cop car that I didn't know was watching me.

Alex continued down the street, practicing the Cole routine, oblivious to everything around him. The police car pulled into a driveway and cut in front of Alex, stopping him up short. Alex started to go around the car, but the policemen got out and called to him: "Hey, hey, hey. Come over here. Come over here. Are you all right?"

"Yes, I'm fine."

"Are you sure you're all right? Have you been drinking?"

"No, I don't drink."

"Have you any identification?"

"I've just broken for lunch and I'm going to the bank and I have some identification here."

Alex pulled out his check and handed it to the two officers, who looked at it and whistled. One of them said, "What kind of money do you make?"

"Well, that's the salary. I didn't steal it. I'm working for it."

"Well, why were you acting so funny? You know, you could have caused an accident. Cars were putting on their brakes and looking at you. And that's very dangerous."

Alex explained he was working at MGM and was going through a routine. He recalled, "I thought they wouldn't buy it because who in the world would say he was practicing." He told the police, "I'm only assisting this man and I have to remember it for him. And I'm supposed to do it perfectly when I get back and it's very involved." One of the officers said, "I can see that." Alex continued on to the bank, but did no more practicing on the way.

Shortly after this incident, Cole contracted hepatitis and stopped his work on *Les Girls*. Alex also left the film, moving on to his next project, choreographing the historical drama *Raintree County*.

Raintree County was not a musical but featured a waltz with the two stars, Elizabeth Taylor and Montgomery Clift. Alex's daughters remembered that, during the filming of *Raintree County*, their father came home and talked about Taylor, describing what it was like "to be hypnotized by her beauty."

That same year, Alex choreographed Robert Wise's World War II drama *Until They Sail*. The film starred Jeanne Crain and featured Paul Newman. Six years later Alex ran into Newman again while setting choreography for the film *The Stripper* on Newman's wife, Joanne Woodward. He taught Newman to play jai-alai with rather disastrous results. *Until They Sail* also featured Joan Fontaine, Piper Laurie, and, in her first film, Sandra Dee.

While still working on *Until They Sail*, Alex was approached about being the dance director for NBC-TV's *The Eddie Fisher Show*.[30] Alex accepted the offer and worked as the series' staff choreographer for two years, staging numbers for such stars as Fisher's wife Debbie Reynolds, Bob Hope, George Burns, Jimmy Durante, Jerry Lewis, Eddie Cantor, Gordon MacRae, the Ames Brothers, Johnny Mathis, Peggy Lee, Ethel Merman, Kate Smith, Jane Powell, Red Buttons, George Gobel, Gisele MacKenzie, and a young dancer named Mary Tyler Moore, among others. The show was cancelled in March of 1959 because of the scandal created when Fisher divorced Debbie Reynolds to marry Debbie's best friend, Elizabeth Taylor.

In the fall of 1957, Alex was approached about doing a film starring a young rock and roll singer by the name of Elvis Presley. The film was *Jailhouse Rock*.

10
Jailhouse Rock (1957)

In 1957, Alex Romero was the youngest choreographer on the MGM lot. On May 6, producer Pandro Berman called him. "Alex, did you know that Elvis Presley's here at the studio? He just arrived today." Alex recalled, "I didn't know he was on the lot. Nobody did. He came on secretly and they put him in that Powell Bungalow. That's way out there away from everybody ... because he was only nineteen and he was a very shy boy."

Berman continued, "I checked everybody and none of the choreographers can do rock and roll and I understand you can do it."

"Yes, I do. I've been doing it for quite a while." Alex listened to the radio and records to keep up with the latest trends in music, and he was a fan of rock and roll. He liked the energy and rhythms. He had used rock and roll in the big production number in *Happy Hunting* the previous year and in other productions he had choreographed. "I knew there was a big market for rock and roll."

Berman said, "We want you to work with Elvis." He told Alex to go to the Powell Bungalow to meet the young singer right away.

> So I went to the Powell Bungalow and I'm standing outside of it because I hear all this [miming guitar playing]. They're singing and everybody plays guitar, not well, but they all play guitars. They sing and play.... And they're just a bunch of rough kids. And, he's got a couple of bodyguards in there, too, so he's got about eight of them. And I heard all that and I smiled to myself and I walked through the next door. I'm not through the main door yet that goes into the hall itself. And I stand there and listen and they're just having fun. It's cute.

Alex opened the two swinging doors and entered the room. Everyone turned to him.

> They were all over the floor. And Elvis was [there] too. And everybody does like this [turning to look]. Just staring at me, and very unfriendly

like.... And I think, "God, that just looks like *Blackboard Jungle* or something." So I walked to them and I said, "Hi guys."

Elvis Presley was sitting on a long table. Alex jumped up on it beside him, offering his hand. "Hi, Elvis, I'm Alex Romero and I got the assignment to do this movie, and I'm so happy about it because I like your work. I love what you do."

According to Alex, Elvis was hesitant at first. He recalled, "He's looking very unfriendly at this time. Oh, he didn't say anything. He was just looking at me. And I thought I better say something, so I said, 'I know what you're thinking. You're thinking that I'm gonna teach you a lot of fancy dancing, aren't you?'"

"Yeah, Hollywood dancin'."

"Elvis, I said I'm a fan of yours.... And that's what I do best [rock and roll]. I love this, and I've been doing it before you. My steps are going to be just like yours, so you'll pick 'em up."

Elvis looked at Alex and said, "Will you do one for me? Can you do something for me [now]?"

Alex nodded, got off the table, and went to the middle of the room. One of the other boys started strumming his guitar with a rock beat, and as Alex recalled, "I went into some stuff. And [Elvis] smiled. He smiled. And then I jumped back on [the table] and said, 'See, so you don't have to worry. I know how to stage you. I'll stage you so that you look like you.'" Elvis had a grin on his face, and as Alex remembered, "He was real happy."[1]

Alex's description of this meeting also appears in Peter Harry Brown's book *Down at the End of Lonely Street: The Life and Death of Elvis Presley*:

> Romero and Presley met for the first time in a rehearsal hall that had once been used by tap dance queen Eleanor Powell. "I don't want anybody to go and make a Hollywood boy out of me," warned Presley. Romero was amused. "I guess he thought that I was going to give him some slick dancing steps, like they had in the MGM musicals. No, I was gonna do Elvis. I chose steps that were foreign to him, but that were also like him, so he could pick them up." Initially, Elvis was terrified. "I could see it in his eyes," said Romero. "I think he was intimidated by MGM. After all, MGM is like playing the palace of motion picture studios. He felt he was out of his league."[2]

There have been other accounts of Alex's first meeting with Presley on *Jailhouse Rock*. In *Last Train to Memphis: The Rise of Elvis Presley*, author Peter Guralnick states:

10. Jailhouse Rock (1957)

> He met the choreographer too, Alex Romero, who was already planning the big dance sequence that was scheduled to be shot at the beginning of the following week. Romero had a dub of the song for the sequence "Jailhouse Rock," and showed Elvis some of the steps that he had devised for it along the lines of a typical Gene Kelly or Fred Astaire number.[3]

This version of the story has been widespread, and it frustrated Alex whenever he heard it. It was a real source of hurt and anger for him. He felt that the accounts of his showing Elvis elegant Astaire-like moves made him (Alex) look incompetent, calling into question his innate sense of what was required for a number. Alex had spent a good part of his life making celebrities look comfortable dancing on screen, and his work encompassed a wide variety of styles. That's how he approached his work with Elvis.

At MGM, Alex was recognized not only as a choreographer who moved easily from style to style as a project demanded, but also as an innovator who helped bring jazz and rock and roll dancing to the screen in the first place. Alex insisted, "They [other people who wrote accounts] said Elvis wanted to see some dancing and I got up there and did some Fred Astaire and Gene Kelly. Now, look, I got more sense than to try to sell him anything like that! If he's a rock and roll dancer and I can do rock and roll, why would I be doing Fred Astaire? It's all lies!"[4]

Alex recalled that Elvis and the other boys in the room were smiling as he left the Powell Bungalow to return to the main lot for a production meeting. When he entered the meeting room, he saw the full staff and crew.

> They were all lined up—the creative department ... the director, and the producer, and Colonel Parker, and all the way down [the sides of the table], the designer, the music director, and the set designer, and on like that ... and I happened to be sitting next to the set designer.

They all waded through the script, breaking down each scene in terms of what props needed to be made by the prop department. Other departments then got their chance to express their needs and ideas for the movie. It was a long and tedious process that took several hours. Alex recalled that, throughout the day, Elvis' manager always had his say.

> Colonel Parker is so funny. He's got the script in front of him and the title now is *The Jailhouse Kid*. He's smoking cigars. The only one smoking and they are this long [indicating a huge stogie] and he's a real cute guy and very smart. He says, "Wait a minute. Before we go anywhere with this

thing...." And he slams [the script] down, and he says, "See that? I don't want to use that title at all. You're gonna have to name the picture something else. You can name it anything else you want because they ain't comin' in to see the script. They're comin' in to see my boy. I don't care if you got a flop picture, he's gonna fill the theaters for you." He talks like that, see.[5]

Pandro Berman responded, "Don't worry, we'll come up with a name, but let's give this a chance." Parker also stated, "[Elvis] has to have a million dollars up front even before we see the script, just to come in. And the other thing: You have to have at least 10 songs in this thing — ten songs."

During the meeting all the music for the film was played. Alex remembered,

> When I hear the first one, I'm pretty excited. Boy, that's great. And now I've got all this time, and so I'm thinking what I can do with that. And things just started popping into my head. I could see the cyc, and I stole my own idea. I had the double deck thing [such as the set he had envisioned on *I'll Cry Tomorrow*] but here I had jail cells. And I wanted a sky-blue cyc in the back so that you could see through the bars ... they'd look like silhouettes. And then I thought, well, I need a spiral staircase to get the guys down from up there but I don't want Elvis to go with them.... Then I thought, "A pole, a steel pole, that's what I want here."

Pandro Berman said, "Well, Alex, tell me, what number there did you see that has the best production values?"

Alex answered, "Just the first one, 'Jailhouse Rock.' That's a showstopper and I've got some ideas for it."

Berman said, "No, no, Alex. I'm sorry, but that's going to be over the titles. We're not going to use that ... just for the titles."

Alex told the producer, "You don't know what you're missing. You're just missing a bet. I'll do anything that you want, but I wanna tell you, you're missing a bet." Berman and the others thought about it, and then Berman agreed, "Okay, you got it."

Alex turned to the set designer and said, "I want this, and I want that...." Alex explained his ideas for the set and recalled that the man just kept saying, "Good. Good. Yes. Yes." Alex smiled as he recalled, "And he's saying yes to everything I want. It just happened. It happened. And I was lucky and they bought it, and the number was good."

The "Jailhouse Rock" production number was to be shot the following week, so Alex's next job was to cast the 16 male dancers.

10. Jailhouse Rock *(1957)*

I had an audition and I picked the guys and of course I tried to pick guys that were rough-looking and there were a lot of them. When you pick the dancers, there isn't a big gang, although we picked 16 or 14 — I don't remember. The director said, "Alex, we're going to have to get some extra people here and fill it out because, you know, this is a big prison." I said, "That's okay." And I said, "Well, let's try to get some that can dance a little ... move, not dancers, 'cause you know, the camera's going to be primarily on the group, but if you're panning or whatever, you might see these people and I'll have them doing things." He said, "That's all right with me." And I started.

One dancer that Alex cast was a young man who was auditioning for him for the first time. Alex Ruiz was a powerful, athletic dancer who understood Romero's style immediately. After *Jailhouse Rock*, he went on to serve as Alex's assistant for the next 10 or 12 years.[6]

Alex also called in Sasha Goudavich. As Alex recalled, "We became good friends after that first movie on the hill [where Sasha taught Alex air tours]. I didn't have him in front. He couldn't do rock and roll too well, but he dances like mad. But he didn't look quite right. Anyway, I put him to the side, and I used him up high ... and I had him hanging by his legs upside down, and then from that he does a flip and lands down here and things like that...."

Goudavich had been in several movies by this point in his career and when it came time to film the number, he approached the first assistant director and said, "Listen, this is not ordinary dancing. We're jumping from up high and stuff like that, and we're going to have to have more money." The film was low-budget, so the production staff had to call the Guild that represented dancers. Alex thought, "Oh, the front office is going to be mad at me. I was only trying to make the thing exciting." A Guild representative came to the set and viewed the number, and decided that hazard pay was indeed warranted. To Alex's surprise, the front office approved the raise.

Another dancer in the film was Alex's close friend Frank Magrin, who had danced in *I'll Cry Tomorrow*.[7] A tough looking guy with a heart of gold, Magrin kidded Elvis during the filming. At one point Elvis said to Magrin, "I don't know what I'm doin' here. I can't dance." Magrin asked him, "Can you sing?" Elvis smiled and responded, "Oh, a Pat Boone fan, huh?"[8]

Alex worked with Elvis for four days to prepare him for filming. In

The Man Who Made the Jailhouse Rock

Elvis Presley in the "Jailhouse Rock" number choreographed by Alex. Dancer Frank Magrin is at left.

10. Jailhouse Rock (1957)

teaching Presley, Alex set the singer's movements to words instead of counts. "He's a rhythm guy, and I said, 'On this word, you're going to....' Words go better with him because he's following the song."

Alex often worked this way with the stars he was staging. He had learned to dance by making up steps to rhythms by finding the accents. Although he learned to count for staging performers who were trained in that method, for those like Elvis who didn't use counting, Alex always sang the rhythms while teaching a dance.

Presley also got some coaching from Russ Tamblyn.

> When Romero worked with Elvis Presley on *Jailhouse Rock*, he sent the nascent king of rock 'n' roll to Tamblyn who remembers, "Elvis showed me the leg thing that he was doing, and he asked me if I would help him with it, and I said yes, so I went back to his dressing room and worked with him for a while. At the time, I didn't think much of it until later on someone said, 'Wow! You worked with Elvis on his legs?'"[9]

Filming on the "Jailhouse Rock" number began on Monday, May 13, 1957, at MGM's Culver City Studios. Security was tight. Signs on the soundstage doors read, "Closed set." However, several movie stars, like Alex's friend Gene Kelly, came in to watch takes.[10] Richard Thorpe, whom Alex had worked with on *The Prodigal*, was the film's director. Known for his ability to keep things under budget, the efficient 61-year-old Thorpe was known for doing only one or two takes. As a result, Alex had prepped the dancers well. The number got a good response from the celebrities, according to Alex. He recalled, "Of course they were clapping for Elvis, I know, but it was partly that routine...."

Part of Alex's choreography required Elvis to slide down the fire pole, but in rehearsals, the singer told Alex he was afraid of heights. No matter how many times Alex demonstrated it for him, Elvis just couldn't manage the trick with the speed and daring that Alex wanted. Elvis eventually did try the trick, but on the second day of filming, he broke a porcelain cap off one of his teeth while sliding down the pole. Peter Guralnick relates the story in *Last Train to Memphis*:

> [Elvis] told the assistant director, Bob Relyea, that he thought he could feel something rattling around in his chest, and Reylea called a doctor to the set, but after examining him the doctor reassured Elvis and Relyea that it was just Elvis' imagination, no more than a scratch. "So now we get the entire crew and all the dancers down on their hands and knees looking for

the [cap], 'cause it's very, very small and must be on the floor someplace, and we decide it's all in his mind.[11]

The tooth actually went into Elvis' lung and he was rushed to Cedars of Lebanon Hospital. The surgeon had to separate Elvis' vocal chords to remove the tooth. Elvis's voice was hoarse for a few days, but his million dollar vocal chords were not damaged. He was released from the hospital and returned to film the number. Alex remembered that Elvis told him that the doctor suggested that Elvis eat a lot of bread after the surgery.

After shooting was completed, Elvis sought Alex out.[12] "He came up to me, and he put his hands right here on my shoulders and he says, 'You're a good ol' boy.' And went like that [patting him on the cheek] And that coming from Elvis, I took as a good compliment. And that's all he said about it, but then years later when he came back and I did three other movies, he said, "Alex, that's the best number I've ever done in anything, and I didn't tell you that before."

Alex shared that he was disappointed in parts of Presley's performance in the "Jailhouse Rock" number. He said, "Elvis wasn't as good as I thought he was going to be, and he made a lot of mistakes, and I couldn't rectify them because we got a one-take man [Thorpe, the director] down there, you know.... And so I left them in. Nobody sees them but me...."

The main part of the choreography that he wished had worked better was where Presley slid down the table.

> The stuff when they lift the table ... well, he was already sitting down when they lifted it and that's no big trick, see... These guys lift up the table, and I had great people and strong people and it just goes up and at the same time he should just lean into that [standing] and then he's on his side and he gets a good slide. Well, they got the thing up and then he laid down and he only slid about that much because when he lay down it wasn't high, it was here.... It [standing for the slide] was just more action and it would be more exciting, you see ... but the singing and the moves were great. It was all Elvis, but it was just a few places like that I was unhappy with, but nobody else complained....

There is a story that after the film was completed, Elvis himself recreated Alex's dance moves one night:

> If Elvis couldn't quite remember his dance steps for the camera, he remembered them one night when he was out with friends in Hollywood. They'd

10. Jailhouse Rock *(1957)*

Alex's choreography in *Jailhouse Rock* featuring Elvis Presley. Alex also created the concept for the set.

all just left a Doris Day movie because members of the audience recognized Elvis, and kept walking up and down the darkened aisles to get a look at him. Elvis and his friends climbed into his Cadillac and were headed back to his suite at the Knickerbocker Hotel when Elvis turned on the radio and chanced upon "Jailhouse Rock." "Hey, guys, hear that?" He loved to listen to himself on the radio. He turned up the sound and pulled the car over, cranking up the volume full blast. He climbed out of the car, and as his friends looked on, Elvis went through his "Jailhouse Rock" routine on a deserted Hollywood side street, in a light rain, as the headlights cast dancing shadows.[13]

Alex did not receive film credit for doing *Jailhouse Rock*. He finished his work on the movie and immediately flew to London to begin work as choreographer on the fantasy film *tom thumb* with Russ Tamblyn.

> I didn't get credited because the very next morning after we finished that number, I was going to England, and Elvis was going in the Army. And if I had been there, I would have seen.... I go to see the rushes, but I didn't see the complete number.... But if I was there, I would have said, "Hey, there's no credit up there...." But I was gone, and I was gone quite a while. Then [Pandro Berman] sent those notes to England. Well, he sent the whole *Variety*. I didn't get credit, but I thought that was pretty darn nice.

Berman had sent Alex a letter dated December 10, 1957, which also included an apology that he had had published in *Variety*. It read,

> Dear Alex,
> Due to an oversight, your name was ommitted [sic] from the screen credits of *Jailhouse Rock*. I am writing you this letter of apology because I feel that I have been guilty of a serious error.
> I am anxious to tell you of my feeling of the importance of your contribution to the film. I believe without question, that the most popular sequence in the picture is that musical number created by you which dramatized and illustrated the song "Jailhouse Rock," the section of the film which was commented on by members of the preview audience as their favorite.
> I hope you will forgive the error and that we will be working together again soon.
> Sincerely,
> Pandro S. Berman[14]

Ever since the release of the movie, stories have circulated that Elvis Presley himself choreographed his moves for the "Jailhouse Rock" number. In his book, *Elvis*, biographer Albert Goldman gave credit where credit was due.

10. Jailhouse Rock *(1957)*

This famous bit of footage was just an afterthought by the producers of the film. It wasn't part of the original scenario or budget, but when Alex Romero, the dance director, came up with the idea of choreographing the title song, another $25,000 was found for the sequence. Presley purists put this number down as too slick and chorus-boysy. Actually it was the one time in Elvis' entire career when somebody with a bit of skill and authority got the kid to move as if he knew where he was going. The jivey strutting style he adopts is perfectly in keeping with his natural body language; the only difference is that instead of faking all his moves with the force of a football lineman hurling himself down a row of staggered car tires, Elvis makes his moves with definition and style.[15]

The "Jailhouse Rock" number is seen by many as a groundbreaking sequence in the history of film dancing, a transitional number propelling the film musical into the modern era.

In their book *Elvis: Day by Day: The Definitive Record of His Life and Music*, Peter Guralnick and Ernst Jorgensen wrote:

> [*Jailhouse Rock*] is famous for the dance sequence in which Presley sings the title track while cavorting with other inmates through a block of jail cells. The sequence is widely acknowledged as the most memorable musical scene in Presley's 30 narrative movies, and it is credited by musical historians as the prototype for the modern music video.[16]

On March 4, 1985, *People* magazine stated, "The title song could stand today as a first-rate MTV video, so deftly was the Elvis strut transformed by choreographer Alex Romero into thrilling dance movement."[17] In 2010, *Time* magazine listed "Jailhouse Rock" as one of the top 10 movie dance scenes.[18]

Alex Romero was paid only $1,000 for choreographing "Jailhouse Rock," but it remained one his proudest achievements. As an older man, Alex recalled, "It was so easy to do."

11

tom thumb to "The Goulash" (1958–1962)

Immediately after finishing *Jailhouse Rock*, Alex Romero flew to Europe to begin work on *tom thumb*.

> *tom thumb* was supposed to be done at our studio, Metro, but they always look at the budget and in those days they didn't have cameras that ... today you can make a guy that big [showing a small space with his fingers]. They can make him do anything ... so many wonderful things with all this new technique they have, but then, they had to build everything [all the props] big. It came a couple of million dollars cheaper [to shoot in England] than here at home.

Alex made a short visit to Denmark to visit friends that he had met when he worked in vaudeville in the 1930s, then he flew to London to begin pre-production.[1]

> [Producer-director] George Pal gave me complete run of the show ... of that number ... so I told him what I wanted. Rusty [Tamblyn] had to start on the book, you know, so they were doing dialogue, and I was in this place all by myself and I would think of another prop, another thing to do, so I'd call [Pal] and he'd say, "Yeah, we'll have it made...." It was just great....

Huge props were created to give the illusion that Tamblyn was a tiny creature. Alex then took advantage of Tamblyn's amazing acrobatic talents.

> For instance, in one place [Tamblyn] was going to walk on a pencil. He wanted to get across this thing, and I had him put this pencil down and what he did, he kept shoving it, and danced out of it, and then pulled it up. And he did things on the pencil. And I said, "Well, if we solidify the pencil, can you do some tricks on it?" He did that thing with his knees [indicating

11. tom thumb *to "The Goulash" (1958–1962)*

Alex (right) with Russ Tamblyn on the set of *tom thumb*.

a back flip] and a lot of other things. And then he'd do a kip and pull up and jump, and ... well, you know how light he is on his feet.

The film featured live action and, at the suggestion of Alex, some animation as well. Alex recalled, "And then I thought to have him [Tamblyn] paint.... I took these big brushes, paint brushes, but he had to take them like this [as if holding a lance] and he was making some figures. And I asked [Pal], 'Could we jump those figures off the paper and do a dance with them?' And he said, 'Yes.' And we had so many things like that."

Alex was very proud that in the film he had given Tamblyn a backwards-walking movement similar to the moonwalk long before Michael Jackson created such a furor and popularized the step in the 1983 *Motown 25: Yesterday, Today and Forever* television special.

When Alex returned from London after the completion of *tom thumb*, he was asked by Charles Walters to assist on the musical *Gigi*. Vincente Minnelli originally had been hired as the director, but he became busy on other projects overseas. Walters, who had been hired as choreographer, took over the job of directing certain numbers. He asked Alex to stage some of the numbers for him, such as Leslie Caron's "The Night They Invented Champagne."

In 1959, Alex staged the dances in *A Private's Affair*, starring Gary Crosby, Sal Mineo,[2] and Barbara Eden. The director, Raoul Walsh, gave Alex free rein to do anything he wanted with the musical numbers. Again Alex used athletic movements to pump up the choreography. At one point he had the dancers pole vault to a tall platform and then pole vault off. They were terrified to try it, so Alex demonstrated how it could be done.

One of the female dancers was a young woman by the name of Betty Bunch. In a newspaper interview from 2011, she said that Alex "was my favorite choreographer in any medium. He was so kind and so masculine. When he wanted to move a girl to a different place, he put his arm gently around her or whispered to correct her."[3] Bunch described a number from the film:

> Alex devised a charming number, high-energy jazz, and had an Army Jeep drive onto the set, carrying Sal and Gary and one of the boy dancers on the back bumper. It screeched to a halt, the boys jumped off, joined us dancers, confetti was released overhead, and we did an armpit finish. After the first time through, Alex changed it slightly, having the three men grab a girl dancer and pull her into a sit-down on his knee. Alex had Gary pair with me, same armpit finish. Gary fumbled a little. Gary and I chatted easily. Then at "take one" at the end, Gary blew the action, didn't get off the Jeep bumper on the right count. The confetti was all over the set. The ADs had us break while the set was re-set, all the IATSE [union stagehands] grabbed brooms and helped the set director. The re-set took at least five minutes. "Places" from the top. Same thing happened again. Another re-set. Would you believe Gary blew 32 takes? He apologized charmingly every time. We were getting tired, the mistake always happening at the end. I asked Gary if there was anything I could help him with, he said no, he was just tired and

11. tom thumb to "The Goulash" (1958–1962)

would get it this time. As the stagehands cleaned up the confetti for take 33, Frankie, the boy dancer who rode on the bumper with Gary, casually said, "Gee, Gary, I hope you blow this one, too. We're only five minutes away from 'golden time.' That's double time for all of us." Gary said, "Oh, yeah?" The dear man did indeed blow take 33, gave us all a big grin, and we gave him a big cheer and sang, "For he's a jolly good fellow...."[4]

Alex Ruiz, Alex's assistant on the film, remembered his favorite number involved Crosby and Sal Mineo peeling potatoes and catching them. He said later, "Everything we ever worked on, I was amazed at what a great imagination [Romero] had. He came up with these great, great ideas. He was a thinker."[5]

Also in 1959, Alex choreographed *Say One for Me* at Twentieth Century–Fox. The film starred Bing Crosby, Debbie Reynolds, and Robert Wagner. A newspaper review of the film reads, "One of the major surprises of the film is Wagner's performance as a singer and dancer. He does both with high spirit, especially in two numbers with Miss Reynolds, 'The Girl

Rehearsing for *Say One for Me* are, from left to right, Alex, Debbie Reynolds, Robert Wagner, and Alex Ruiz.

Most Likely to Succeed' and 'Chico's Choo-Choo.' Alex Romero staged Miss Reynolds and Wagner's dance numbers with taste and style...."[6]

Alex worked for six months on *Say One for Me* while simultaneously choreographing *The Eddie Fisher Show*. He and Ruiz worked out a grueling schedule, shuttling back and forth between Fox and NBC so that Romero could create dances for both projects. Alex Romero would set the choreography, then rush to the other side of town while Ruiz would rehearse the dances that Romero had set. Both Alexes also frequently worked after hours. Ruiz remembered, "We'd go to stars' homes to rehearse with them. We worked day and night."[7]

Alex (right) and Eddie Fisher backstage on the set of *The Eddie Fisher Show*.

11. tom thumb to "The Goulash" (1958–1962)

During *Say One for Me,* Romero and Debbie Reynolds established a close working relationship as well as a deep friendship. In 1959, he was hired to choreograph Reynolds' first television special, "A Date with Debbie." Louella Parsons mentioned it in her gossip column on October 24, 1959: "Gower Champion will direct her first show and Debbie and Marge Champion will do the famous dance they did at the Thalians. Alex Romero is set for the choreography."[8]

Alex had staged a number for Reynolds earlier in the year for the SHARE Show benefit. SHARE (Self Help and Recovery Exchange) donated money to mentally challenged children. Their annual benefit, a popular cause among the Hollywood set, featured the top celebrities. For many years, Alex volunteered his services to choreograph the shows. In 1959, he worked up a number for Reynolds called "Tequila." It was performed at the Ambassador Hotel and proved to be the highlight of the evening. One member of the audience that night, director George Sidney, came backstage after the dance and offered Alex the film *Pepe.*

Reynolds was to appear in the film, and Sidney asked Alex to recreate the "Tequila" number for her as a dance with the film's star Cantinflas.[9] Later Alex expressed regrets about how the film version turned out. "What we had in the original dance was gone."[10]

Much of *Pepe* was shot on location in Mexico in 1960, and in addition to Reynolds' "Tequila," Alex created numbers for Dan Dailey, Shirley Jones, Maurice Chevalier, and Sammy Davis, Jr.[11] The film also featured cameos from such stars as Bing Crosby, Frank Sinatra, Kim Novak, Greer Garson, Zsa Zsa Gabor, Donna Reed, Dean Martin, Bobby Darin, Peter Lawford, Jack Lemmon, Jimmy Durante, Edward G. Robinson, Janet Leigh, and Tony Curtis. Because it was rainy and most of the locations were outdoors, filming moved at a snail's pace. Alex recalled,

> And so we're going out and it's raining and we can't shoot. And it's raining.... And we're on it for three months, and now the *real* rainy weather is going to start. And [director Sidney] said to me, "Alex, I want you to stay here and scout some locations and I'm going to go back. I've got something to shoot there. I've got a couple of things and I'll take some of the cast with me and you stay here with the artistic director and you go out every day and hunt for locations." ...And I had all the numbers down ... what we were going to shoot ... and he was gone forever — I spent practically another three months there.

Because of extended delays, one of the dances in the film, the rumble section, was assigned to Eugene Loring to choreograph back in Los Angeles.[12] Meanwhile, Sidney was having trouble casting two men for a dance with Shirley Jones. He asked Alex to search around Mexico to see if he could find any local talent that might work in the number.[13] "I started looking at variety shows and we'd go to nightclubs and see flamenco dancers and I just couldn't find the right looking pair. And finally I went to a variety house, which is like vaudeville ... and I saw these two Argentine boys and they did a Malambo, but the real Malambo. ...I liked 'em and so I hired them. They were just such fun and so good for her."[14]

After finishing *Pepe*, Alex flew to New York to stage the Macy's Thanksgiving Day Parade. Then he returned to Hollywood to begin work on MGM's *The Gazebo* with Glenn Ford and Debbie Reynolds. The movie was not a musical, but wanting to capitalize on Reynolds' singing and dancing abilities, it was decided to include a production number for her.

In an article "All in a Day's Work" is a description of the athletic number that Alex created for her:

[I]n the course of a dance number [Reynolds] sustained a number of bruises and other wounds. The studio had run off ten minutes of the film that afternoon, and one of the scenes I watched was the strenuous dance episode. With four boys, Debbie had pirouetted, done cartwheels, been thrown through the air from one to another, and ended up sliding backwards down the tilted top of a grand piano. "Pulled a muscle," she explained. "And some of the slides gave me floor burns."[15]

The article also featured an interview with Alex about working with Reynolds:

Says Alex Romero, dance coach and choreographer for the film, "She's an amazing dancer. Most people don't realize she started late and has only been dancing since she started in pictures. Since she also sings, there's the dividend of a sense of rhythm, and she has a great beat. When you design dance routines for a movie star who will be working with professionals, it's customary to assign them different steps from the supporting dancers. That's so the star won't suffer by comparison. This wasn't necessary for Debbie. In *Gazebo*, she works with four boys who are veterans, fitting right into the line-up and doing the same steps they do. She'll attempt anything. In fact, we don't treat her like a star at all. Her attitude is most un-starlike. When the second boy from the left stood out with spectacular leaps, she didn't demand his removal. She tried to be as good as he."[16]

11. tom thumb to "The Goulash" (1958–1962)

Alex Ruiz remembered one stunt they experimented with on the set of *The Gazebo*. Reynolds was to jump on a trampoline and land on top of a grand piano. Reynolds' dance-in during rehearsals, stuntwoman Patricia Saunders was asked to perform the bit and refused, saying, "You're crazy, I'll kill myself." Both Romero and Ruiz had already tried the stunt themselves and assured her that it was possible. She told them that it was different for her because she was wearing high heels.

Believing that the stunt Romero had envisioned was possible, Ruiz called wardrobe to have them send up a pair of extra large heels in his size so he could try it himself. Just then, Reynolds walked into the rehearsal room and, sensing the tension, asked what was going on. They explained the problem. Reynolds said, "That doesn't seem so hard." She went to the back of the hall, ran, hit the trampoline, and landed perfectly on top of the piano." As Ruiz said, "Bam! Stuck it perfectly!"[17] Saunders just lowered her head without saying a word and walked out, never coming back.

Alex adored working with Reynolds and admired her spunk and daring when it came to doing his choreography. He was disappointed, however, that there was one move in *The Gazebo* dance that she was not able to do.

> I had an idea to wire up a piano stool. She was working on a piano, doing some dancing on and off the piano, and I was looking at the stool and I thought, "I could do something with that," so I had the prop people wire it up real strong and it wouldn't turn and that way I could sit Debbie on it to do things ... lifts... I told them I wanted some casters on there that would go straight and then when I was by myself I'd run and then I'd jump and Debbie's pretty active and has always done things like that for me ... and I'd jump. I'd put the thing [on the floor] and I'd jump way out and land on my stomach and arch, and it would just go.... And then I thought if I did that, the guys would dance over there and grab her and then do some other things.... But she wouldn't do it. She was afraid of it. I don't know.... So I had one of the boys do it....

Alex's next project was *The George Raft Story*. For three months before filming, Alex gave daily dance lessons to the star of the film, Ray Danton. Danton was a slow and awkward learner. Trying to prepare him to portray Raft was a painstaking process[18] but a newspaper publicity piece made it sound simple.

> Because Raft was one of the world's greatest ballroom dancers, Danton had to learn how to dance. Previously he never had danced; in fact, had never enjoyed dancing. But for weeks before the start of the picture, he

was under the tutelage of choreographer Alex Romero and rehearsed eight hours daily. A fine, graceful athlete, Danton surprised all, even Raft, with his performance as a dancer. In the picture he does the Charleston, Tango and Bolero, dancing with Barrie Chase, who soared to fame overnight as the lovely dance partner of Fred Astaire in several television spectaculars.[19]

Barrie Chase did not like her co-star. As Alex put it, "She and Ray Danton hated each other from the word go ... wouldn't talk to each other.... She was just mad all the time." Chase also created problems on the set by not showing up for her calls on time. "She was late for everything. Oh, it cost them ... I don't know ... thousands of dollars ... never, never made anything on time ... the wardrobe, the hair ... nothing at all...." Despite the tension on the set, Alex was able to create several dances using Danton and Chase.[20]

During pre-production the studio had not decided if *The George Raft Story* would be shot in black and white or color. One morning Romero and Alex Ruiz were coming onto the lot when Danton ran up to them with his hands hidden behind his back. Excitedly he told them, "I have the best argument to shoot in color." He pulled out his left hand. In it was a black and white self-portrait. Danton asked them, "What's that? What do you see?" Before they could respond, he said, "A good-looking, handsome guy!" Both Alex and his assistant looked at each other, well accustomed to these demonstrations of Danton's huge ego. They nodded simultaneously and said, "Sure, Ray." Then Danton pulled out his right hand and in it was the same photo in color. He held out the picture and said triumphantly, "That's glamour, baby!"

In 1961, Alex did *The Four Horsemen of the Apocalypse* with Glenn Ford. A newspaper article about the movie mentioned a tango that Alex choreographed for Ford and his co-star Ingrid Thulin:

> [O]n a Hollywood sound stage under the direction of Vincente Minnelli, not even 300 pairs of feet could interfere with the whirls, dips and glides of [Ford and Thulin], who tangoed to the beat of "Boulevard of Broken Dreams." On the sidelines, dance director Alex Romero watched Ford and Miss Thulin with expert eyes and as the two were about to go into their dance gave them detailed instructions on just what makes a Tango untangle a movie. "When you see a Tango danced as it should be, you've seen the last word in sophisticated dances," Romero states. "However, there was a time when it was known as a bawdy dance of the waterfront."[21]

11. tom thumb *to "The Goulash" (1958–1962)*

Alex (right) working with Ray Danton on the set of *The George Raft Story*.

Alex also did a big number for the film called the Malambo. He remembered, "Minnelli had called me up and told me a little bit about [the film] and said, 'Do you know the Malambo?' I said, 'Yes,' but I didn't know the Malambo!"

Minnelli explained to Alex that one of the actors, Lee J. Cobb,[22] had to learn the dance, and would be doing most of it on film. Ford was to do some of it as well, supported by an ensemble of male dancers. Minnelli also told Alex that he needed to choreograph "a very wild gypsy number...."[23]

Alex knew he had to learn about the Malambo, "and I thought, 'What am I going to do?'" Not sure how to research the dance, he decided to at least learn the rhythm of it. At a local record store he listened to a recording that the store clerk said was a Malambo.

> And what it is, they dance to the sound of horses ... pahrump, pahrump, pahrump [demonstrating the rhythm]. That's the basic thing. And I get home and start doing my own thing and I'm going pahrump, pahrump, pahrump-pa-pa pum, and I faked the whole thing. I went [to the studio] and I took my guys, and Lee Cobb hasn't shown yet. I told him I just wanted to practice and get it together with some of the boys. And there was an Argentine kid there and he did the Malambo! And I thought I'd be found out and he'd open his mouth and tell Vincente, "That ain't no Malambo." And I'm going pahrump, pahrump, pahrump-pa-pa pum, and I then look over at this kid and he's smiling and he says, "That's great, Alex. That's it! That's it!" [I was] lucky as can be!

Although he had worked with Minnelli on several films, Alex remembered that he was particularly difficult to work with on *Four Horsemen of the Apocalypse*. "He screamed at everyone all the time." Minnelli requested that several macaws be put in the trees to decorate the set for the Malambo number. The birds were large and colorful, and cost the studio about $3,000–$5,000 each. Before stepping behind the camera to begin shooting, Minnelli meticulously directed the prop men to position the birds exactly where he wanted among the branches. As the music started, the birds were startled and naturally moved along the branches of the trees. In a few moments, Minnelli screamed, "Cut!" He pointed at one of the birds and shouted, "Will you tell that bird not to move? Tell him! Tell him!" The prop men re-positioned the bird.

Shooting began again, and again the various macaws shifted. Minnelli went ballistic. "Tie them up. Tie them to the branches," he shouted. The prop men secured the macaws talons to the branches with wire and shooting recommenced.

The Malambo dance had loud music, pounding feet, and Minnelli had added some smoke for extra effect. When the birds couldn't move, they started screeching and flapping their wings frantically. The birds eventually ended up hanging upside down. Filming stopped.

Minnelli conceded that the birds had to be untied, so the prop men

11. tom thumb to "The Goulash" (1958–1962)

untied them. What they did not realize was that the soundstage doors had been opened to cool off the studio in between takes. The over-excited macaws saw their opportunity and all of them flew out the open doors to freedom. Alex remembered, "And off they go to Argentina or someplace."

At the end of 1961, Alex worked with two Hollywood legends, Joan Crawford and Bette Davis, on *What Ever Happened to Baby Jane*. Alex said, "Well, that was just complete fun." The two stars did not get along at all. "They were fighting like cats and dogs, I mean, screaming and throwing things, so it was very awkward."

Alex's job was to stage the Baby Jane character's vaudeville performances as a little girl, and to work with Bette Davis, setting her scene in front of the mirror when she screeched out the song "I'm Writing a Letter to Daddy." Alex remembered, "When [Davis] went crazy [in the film], that was fun to do.... And she said, 'I want to move. I don't want to look like a dancer, but I want to move.' I said, 'I know exactly what you're talking about. I like the idea. It's going to be very dramatic and weird.'"

In 1962 he helped Alice Faye with her numbers in *State Fair*. Alex was not officially on the film, which was choreographed by Nick Castle, but he knew Faye and Castle well and stepped in to coach and stage the star's numbers.

In 1962 Alex also worked on the MGM film *The Wonderful World of the Brothers Grimm*, a musical fantasy that featured extensive choreography. The movie, shot in Cinerama three-panel-wide vision, presented extra challenges for Alex as he had to fill the screen, especially in the long shots.

As he did on most of his films, Alex was involved in several aspects of the production. In January 1962, *Dance Magazine* featured an article about his work on the film. The article begins with a description of how Alex had attended the orchestra recording session to set tempi. The story includes several photographs. The caption on one of them reads, "Staging movement is only part of a Hollywood dance director's job. Here, Alex Romero supervises a shoe fitting for Yvette Mimieux ... to be sure she will both look right and be comfortable for her dancing role in *The Brothers Grimm*." Another caption reads, "Romero exhorts a designer to devise a better coordination between costume and makeup." A third caption reads, "The choreographer participates in hair-dressing sessions to be sure his star will have good line of movement."[24]

119

The Man Who Made the Jailhouse Rock

Alex works with Yvette Mimieux on *The Wonderful World of the Brothers Grimm*.

When Alex was starting in films as a young man, he had tried to learn as much as he could about the business. He learned new steps from other dancers who took the time to share them, and he carefully studied how dance directors set up shots and moved their dancers around for maximum effect. He also became fascinated with the technical aspects of filmmaking. Later he said, "When I was first in Hollywood doing extra work I was so interested in the camera, I wanted to learn everything about it. I would always sneak up because they wouldn't let people go near the camera. And I'd stay in the dock somewhere and listen and watch what they were doing and what lens they were changing...." Alex's curiosity paid off as he became integrally involved in all aspects of creating dance numbers on film—from camera angles and lighting effects,

11. tom thumb to "The Goulash" (1958–1962)

to costume and set design, as Alex had done in creating set ideas for *I'll Cry Tomorrow* and *Jailhouse Rock*. Alex's contribution to the total look of any film on which he worked was extensive.

In addition to being involved in production aspects of the film, Alex often had to act as dance teacher because many times his actors were not trained dancers. This was the case with Yvette Mimieux on *Brothers Grimm*.[25] Alex's assistant Alex Ruiz commented about how Alex had a particular talent for making non-dancers look comfortable dancing on screen. He said, "Alex was a miracle worker."[26]

Mimieux was featured in the "Dancing Princess" section of the film and partnered with one of Alex's favorite performers, Russ Tamblyn. Tamblyn's gymnastic abilities made him a perfect match for Alex, who loved to include acrobatic tricks in his work. For this number, Alex had Tamblyn swinging on the arched hoops over a gypsy wagon as if he were on the parallel bars. After a wild gypsy dance with members of the dancing ensemble, Tamblyn and Mimieux glided into a romantic pas de deux.

Tamblyn remembered another number that was planned, but didn't make it into the film:

> [It] was kind of like a dream sequence. I was dancing with Yvette Mimieux and it went into a dream sequence, and Alex and I wanted to do this dance on a cloud. We wanted to have it going over the castle, and it was a great idea — dancing in the clouds. And we got the Cinerama people to all approve it. And we were going to start rehearsing and we were thinking about it, and how we were going to fall into clouds, and dance around, and then at the last minute the studio nixed it and said, "We just can't afford it." 'Cause you'd have to go up and shoot helicopter shots...[27]

The *Dance Magazine* article about the making of the film concluded with the following: "Immediately upon completion of *The Brothers Grimm*, Alex starts a new picture. In his free time he will be staging a big charity show and working privately with stars on night club acts and special material. It all seems so effortless."[28]

Alex was always busy. He staged charity events for SHARE, and beginning in 1958 served as the regular choreographer for the Thalian Shows. The Thalians, a charitable organization of show business people, raised millions to help children with mental health issues. The group was responsible for building the Thalians Community Mental Health Center at Cedars Sinai Hospital to provide psychiatric care. Alex's relationship with the Thalians lasted for many years. He worked with numerous celebrities, creating specialty dances for them as well as staging volunteers in elaborate production numbers for Thalians' benefits.[29]

Alex also staged nightclub acts for Bobby Short at the Hacienda, Howard Keel and Kathryn Grayson at the Stardust, Van Johnson at the Sands, Sammy Lewis at the Riviera, German singing star Manuela at the Casino de Paris, as well as Jane Powell, Huntz Hall, Marilyn Monroe imitator Paula Lane, and the warm-up for Debbie Reynolds' act.[30] In 1962, he choreographed the 14th Annual Screenwriters Guild Awards at the Hollywood Palladium. He also choreographed and appeared in the TV special "Arthur Godfrey in Hollywood" and staged the *CBS Repertoire Workshop* television production of "Who Tied the Can to Modern Man?" The same year, Alex was asked to create a social dance that debuted on the TV show *Surfside 6*. The dance was called "The Goulash." A newspaper account explained how the new dance came to be:

> Teamed with beautiful Diane McBain of Warner Bros.' *Surfside 6* series, Roger Carroll, an actor–disc jockey heard on Los Angeles' station KMPC, demonstrates the West Coast's answer to the Twist — a new dance called The Goulash. It will be seen on "A Private Eye for Beauty" segment, showing on May 21 on ABC. Actually the whole thing started as a gag, Carroll confesses. Back at his turntables after judging a Twist contest at the Hollywood Palladium, Carroll was about to spin the *Hungarian Rhapsody* when, in commenting on his earlier activities of the evening, he impulsively stated that a new dance had been invented and any listener could have a diagram of the steps by writing in. He called the dance The Goulash. More than 6,000 letters clogged the station's mail boxes the next day. Necessity then became the mother of invention. Dance instructor Alex Romero was pressed into service to create a dance. Sy Zeitner [Si Zentner] rushed in the breach to record a Goulash tune and faster than you can toss your yo-yo the craze took off into outer space. Lionel Hampton incorporated the Goulash into his act at Las Vegas' Thunderbird Hotel. The Twist crowd at Frank Sennes' Crazy Horse began to alternate its gyrations between the Twist and the Goulash.
>
> When actors on the set of *Surfside 6* discovered that a nervous but nervy bit player making his debut in the "A Private Eye for Beauty" segment was disc jockey Roger Carroll, who originated the Goulash, he was swamped with demands for lessons. Requests of diagrams of the Goulash steps still come into the radio station at the rate of 1,000 a day.
>
> Have you tried the Goulash?[31]

12

The Stripper to *Hustle* (1963–1975)

In 1963, Alex did a movie with Joanne Woodward called *The Stripper* at Twentieth Century–Fox Studios. Franklin Schaffner, the director, sent him to meet Woodward for the first time, and Alex remembered, "She was so nice ... so young and beautiful." Woodward told him, "Well, Alex, I just want to get acquainted with you, and see what you have in mind.... What do you think we ought to do?" Alex responded, "Well, [the director] told me not to go too wild with you, but it's got to look like a strip number.... We can do many things wardrobe-wise...."

While he was talking with Woodward, Alex thought of an idea. "What if we get a whole bunch of balloons and put helium in them, and tie them to a string, and tie them to your body in some way? ... Put them on or pin them on ... and they're all different heights ... and then you come out, and do some dancing, and you've got a pair of scissors on, and you go to the man in the front row, and you hand him the scissors, and he cuts it and the [balloon] goes up...."

Woodward loved the idea and so did the director, but after filming, Alex was disappointed to find that the balloon number was heavily edited when the film was released. "They cut the hell out of it. It's not as long as it was."

During rehearsals, while Alex made up steps for the routine, Woodward sat in the room knitting a sweater. The sweater was made of soft alpaca wool with an intricate design, and one day, she asked Alex if she could hold it up to his back to measure it. She told him that she was making the sweater for her husband, Paul Newman, and she thought Alex might be about the same size. At the end of the movie, Woodward handed Alex a box and inside was the sweater. Alex was touched that Woodward "had been knitting it for months for me."[1]

One day Woodward was called away to rehearse some dialogue. Alex and his assistant Alex Ruiz were playing jai-alai against the walls of the rehearsal studio while they waited for her to return.[2] The drummer and piano player were "participating" by accenting the hits with music. After a while, a handsome young man came in the rehearsal hall. It was Paul Newman. He asked for his wife, and Alex told him that Joanne was on the set doing dialogue. Newman asked Alex what he and Ruiz were doing. Alex explained that they were playing jai-alai. Intrigued, Newman asked, "Hey, do you suppose I could do that?" Alex put the glove on him and warned him, "I got to tell you one thing that everybody does. Everybody, when they first use this, you throw it like that, you see ... [demonstrating how to do it wrong], but that sestas is curved like that. And you throw it and the first one always goes to the back of the house. I just want you to know that." Newman assured Alex, "Aw, I won't do that." Newman tried it, and did exactly what Alex had warned him not to do. Alex showed him again how to correctly toss the ball, and after some coaching, Newman started to get the hang of it.

Then Alex said, "Okay, now try a little harder." Alex remembered what happened next. Newman tossed the ball so hard he lost control of it and it flew up and hit the sprinkler nozzle on the ceiling of the rehearsal studio. The nozzle bent and water shot out. The room started to fill with water, and the men ran around looking for the shut-off. In the midst of the chaos they heard sirens. Newman shouted, "Listen, I wasn't here. I don't belong here. I should be at Warner Brothers. I wasn't here ... and don't mention my name." Then he ran out.

As the sirens grew closer, Alex thought to himself, "What the hell. I'm going to get fired. What am I going to do?" Right before the firemen rushed in, he hit upon an idea. He picked up one of Joanne Woodward's high-heeled rehearsal shoes, put his foot in one, and kicked it up to the ceiling. It went all the way up, near the broken valve, then fell back at his feet. He thought his explanation might work, so he ran over to a nail he saw on the studio wall and put a big scratch on the heel.

The Beverly Hills Fire Department and the studio fire department, as well as the Fox production heads, rushed into the hall. The fire chief asked him, "How did this happen, Mr. Romero?" Alex put on his most

12. The Stripper *to* Hustle (1963–1975)

innocent face and answered, "Well, she's doing this strip number. She can kick, but I just wanted to see if it's easy for her, otherwise I'd do something else. And I went like that [kicking his foot] and would you believe it, it flew up and hit that thing and bent it." The fire chief looked at the big scratch on the heel and said, "Yeah, that did it."

Rehearsals were halted for the day and crews had to mop up the water. Alex remembered, "It took them forever." The cleanup was particularly messy because the floor beneath the studio had been converted into a temporary wardrobe storage and the entire space was flooded.

During rehearsals for *The Stripper*, Woodward took Alex over to another soundstage on the Fox lot to meet her friend, Marilyn Monroe. Monroe was filming the swimming pool scene in *Something's Gotta Give*, and it was a closed set. Alex recalled, "They let us in simply because [Woodward] is who she is...." He had always wanted to meet Monroe, and as they entered the soundstage, she was swimming in the pool. Alex described seeing her for the first time.

> They were setting up camera, doing another shot or something, and she was not too far from the edge, and she was floating, and in the nude, and she just looked gorgeous. And she happened to turn around, and she saw Joanne, and she raised her hand up and said, "Hi, Joanne." She kinda came out of the water, and there she was in all her splendor, and she was just gorgeous, and finally [she] came over to the edge, and pushed herself up a little bit to talk. And she was not affected by being nude there in front of me ... and all the crew was there too. And she was so sweet, and so nice, and asked what we were doing. And [Woodward] introduced me as her choreographer. And [Monroe] had done a lot of work with Jack Cole, and she said, "Oh." But, she didn't ask about him, but I wish I'd talked about him and let her know I'd been with him for a long time. Anyway, she was just so nice. I can't say enough nice things about her.[3]

In the early 1960s, Alex began to divide his time more and more between movies and television. In the fall of '63, he choreographed a CBS special, *Opening Night*, which ran on September 23. The production was a preview of the 1963–1964 season on the network, and featured performances by Lucille Ball, Jack Benny, Garry Moore, Andy Griffith, Danny Thomas, Phil Silvers and Don Wilson.

In January of 1964, Russ Tamblyn was asked to do *The Perry Como Special* for *The Kraft Music Hall* on NBC. The producers told him that that they had hired a choreographer for him. Tamblyn said he would not do the special without Alex as his choreographer. Later that year, Alex choreographed a *Lucille Ball Comedy Hour Special* for Desilu Studios entitled "Mr. and Mrs." Guest star Bob Hope joined Lucy's regular, Gale Gordon. The special aired on CBS on April 19.

The same year, Alex returned to films to stage the dances in *Seven Faces of Dr. Lao* at MGM. The film was directed by George Pal, who had used Alex as choreographer on *tom thumb* and *Brothers Grimm*. It starred Tony Randall, John Ericson and Barbara Eden. One of the number's Alex staged was Pan's dance for Ericson and Eden.

In 1966, Alex returned to television to work with his friend Gene Kelly on a Hanna-Barbera special called *Jack and the Beanstalk*. The movie combined live action with animation. Kelly played a character named Jeremy Keen, a man-of-all-trades who meets up with a young Jack played by Bobby Riha. The two climb the beanstalk together and have various adventures. Kelly did a dance with a group of animated mice and a romantic pas de deux with an animated Princess Serena. Alex assisted Kelly on all the choreography and also did stunts on the film.

An article about the movie in *Dance Magazine* (February 1967) said, "Working closely with Kelly was Alex Romero, himself a highly regarded member of Hollywood's choreographic fraternity. He danced-in for Gene, performed as a woggle-bird and cued the camera while Kelly was being filmed in his dances."[4] *Jack and the Beanstalk* won an Emmy for Outstanding Children's Special after it aired in 1967.

In 1967, Alex also choreographed and acted in the television series *Please Don't Eat the Daisies*. The episode, "None So Righteous," featured the Righteous Brothers. That same year, some producers asked Alex if he was interested in being the staff choreographer for a new comedy show called *Laugh-In*. When Alex told Faun about the offer, she advised him to turn it down since she had never heard of the two leads, Rowan and Martin. In later years, whenever they disagreed with Faun's take on things, Alex's two daughters reminded her of her advice not to take the show.

Around this same time, Alex's brother John, a realtor, convinced Alex to go into real estate. Despite the fact that Alex was working regularly as a choreographer, he wanted to stop his brother pestering him. He studied and passed the exam. In between his choreography jobs, he sold a couple of houses, but he hated the process. When Elvis Presley

12. The Stripper to Hustle (1963–1975)

called him to do another film, he informed John that he was quitting real estate for good and sticking to show business.

Alex ended up doing three Elvis films in a row: *Clambake, Double Trouble,* and *Speedway.*[5]

Clambake[6] was Elvis' 25th film. The film co-starred Shelley Fabares and featured a special cameo appearance by the dolphin Flipper. Alex remembered that when he reunited with Elvis, he noticed that he'd gained weight. Concerned studio executives ordered the star to shed the extra pounds, and the film's director, Arthur Nadel, had wardrobe redesign costumes to hide Elvis' bulk. Elvis began taking diet pills. One night the drugs made him dizzy, and he fell and hit his head on the bathtub. Elvis had a mild concussion. Filming, which was supposed to begin on March 10, 1967, was delayed two weeks.

While *Clambake* was being filmed, Elvis was dating his future wife Priscilla Beaulieu. Alex revealed that Elvis often took other young ladies into his trailer for sexual rendezvous while on the set. Although he tried to stay out of the personal business of the people he worked with, Alex found this particularly distressing. He knew Elvis' marriage was impending, and he thought Priscilla was such a "sweet girl."[7]

Alex remembered the choreographic challenges that came up during *Clambake,* although he said the film was "a whole lot of fun — extra fun."

> We did a lot of hard numbers. It was all dirt. It was supposed to be the beach, but it was dirt and we were doing a lot of hard dancing, and dust kept flying up and making everybody's eyes water.... And finally they'd have to water that down and it'd be too muddy and it was just a hard thing to do. [For another number] I had some dancers on the rooftop dancing. And [Elvis] got up there somehow, and did a little bit and then came down. I got him down by catching him in a blanket, and it was just a lot of fun and he enjoyed that.

Alex's assistant on the movie, Lance LeGault,[8] said, "Elvis liked Alex because he never made him do dance for the sake of dance. It was movement. And, it was apropos of the character and the situation, which was comfortable for Elvis."[9] LeGault also worked as the dance-in for Elvis on the film. Alex set all the choreography on LeGault first, then showed it to the director to block out the camera moves, before Alex taught the dance to Elvis. LeGault remembered, "I'm not a dancer. If I could get it, well, [Elvis] could get it."[10]

The Man Who Made the Jailhouse Rock

On the set of ***Clambake***. Alex is on the merry-go-round demonstrating to Elvis' double, Lance LeGault, how to hold the female dancer.

Alex worked on *Double Trouble*[11] in the summer of 1966.[12] "That had to do with the disco kind of stuff—the easiest kind of stuff I ever had to do.... All of it was ad lib." Alex hired 140 dancers for the film. The female lead was an English actress by the name of Annette Day. Alex remembered that Presley was fond of the lady. "She was very young and very sweet and Elvis liked her a lot and gave her a Cadillac before she left and was going to pay for the freight to have it shipped over so it would be there when she got home. Elvis did that for a lot of people. He was very generous. I didn't get any gifts. He probably thought I was rich. But he was very nice to me."

For *Double Trouble*, Alex choreographed a flamenco-type number for Elvis. After Alex had finished preparing it, Elvis and the director, Norman Taurog, asked for a preview of it. Upon seeing it, Elvis turned to Alex and asked, "Who's going to do that?" Alex smiled at him and answered, "You are."

12. The Stripper to Hustle (1963–1975)

When asked about *Speedway*,[13] Alex remembered, "That was with Nancy Sinatra.[14] She was great, so nice. She gave me a gold money clip and on the back she wrote, 'Love, Boots,' because she did that number. I staged 'These Boots Are Made for Walkin.' That was her first hit."

Alex's assistant on the film was again Lance LeGault. He remembered how Alex put Nancy Sinatra through the paces when rehearsing her number.

> Alex worked her ass off, I mean hard. See Alex, he's physical. He's strong. He comes from another school, another world — the Jack Cole school. So, if you wanna work with him you better come with two changes of clothes and a lot of oatmeal. Yeah, 'cause he'll work your ass off. Some people handle it and some people don't. Nancy handled it. She never complained one time.[15]

Unfortunately, most of the "These Boots Are Made for Walkin'" number was cut from the final edit of the film, according to Alex.

In 1968, Alex was approached by producer-director George Pal about choreographing a new fantasy film called *The Young Rip*. The script, written by George Wells, contained such characters from Washington Irving stories as Rip Van Winkle and Ichabod Crane. An article in *Dance Magazine Annual 1968* contained a brief blurb touting the

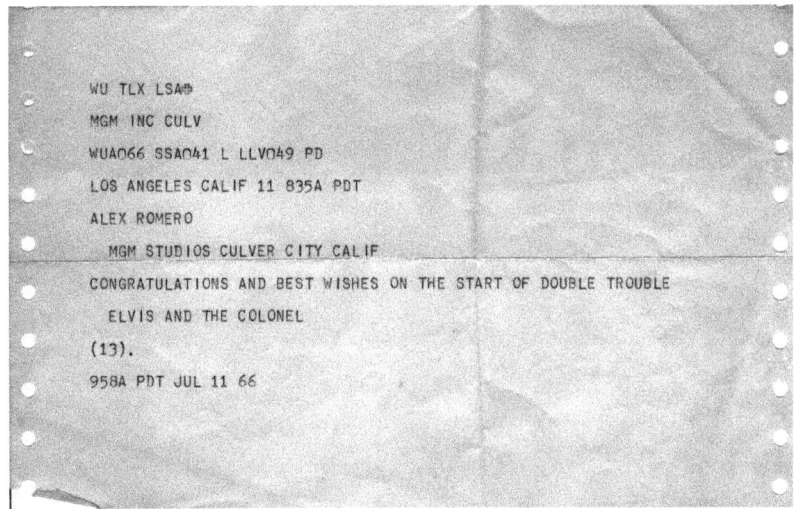

Telegram from Elvis Presley and Colonel Parker sent to Alex at the beginning of *Double Trouble*.

The Man Who Made the Jailhouse Rock

upcoming project. Pal was quoted as saying, "We'll have the kind of imaginative choreography Alex Romero did for me in *tom thumb*, in *Seven Faces of Dr. Lao*, and *The Wonderful World of the Brothers Grimm*."[16] Alex talked about working on his preparations for the film,

> In creating fantasy dance for motion pictures, you must first set out to do the impossible. Forget realism and restrictions. Let choreography and cinematography merge. Instead of choreographing routine steps and then expecting the camera to give them a touch of fantasy by filming them out of focus or in slow motion, I like to think from the beginning in terms of camera potentials.[17]

Although Alex worked several weeks in creating concepts and dances for the fantasy film, Pal eventually decided to scrap the project.

In 1969, Alex choreographed *For Singles Only* with John Saxon, Mary Ann Mobley, Lana Wood, and comedian Marty Ingels in a B-movie about a landlord, played by Milton Berle, who only rents the apartments in his complex to singles. Alex recalled, "It was just a fun

Alex in 1968, working out choreography for *The Young Rip*. The George Pal fantasy film about Rip Van Winkle was eventually shelved.

12. The Stripper to Hustle (1963–1975)

movie to do. I did a lot of dancing, but it was around a pool always. They'd dance a little bit and then dive...."

In the fall of 1969, Alex was approached by director Robert Aldrich about choreographing a screen test for an upcoming picture called *The Greatest Mother of 'Em All*. The film was about a horrible stage mother who pushes her 15-year-old daughter into stardom via stripping. A newspaper article described the process: "She was supposed to be stripping in a sleazy San Fernando Valley club. Choreographer Alex Romero had worked out a sleazy San Fernando Valley club routine, and she was going through it grimly — throwing her clothes, piece by piece, into the wings and chewing gum and making love to a pink drape."[18]

Aldrich spent six days and almost $80,000 on the screen test for a young performer by the name of Alexandra Hay. The screen test was used as a promotional short, but the film was never made.

In 1971, Alex choreographed *The Grissom Gang* for director-producer Aldrich. Aldrich had built his own studio as an independent producer and asked Alex to come on board to stage a tap dance for Connie Stevens. Alex had worked with Stevens before: He'd created a tap number for her in the Academy Awards show.[19]

In 1973, Alex choreographed a film entitled *Some Call It Loving*, a version of the *Sleeping Beauty* story in which a young woman, who has been asleep for eight years, is bought by a young man from a carnival. In 1974 Aldrich brought Alex on board for his film *The Longest Yard*, starring Burt Reynolds. Alex choreographed prison inmates performing a cheerleading routine.

In 1974, Alex took some time off from Hollywood when he was approached by Gene Kelly about appearing in a stage production of *Take Me Along*. Alex agreed to tour with the musical and perform with Kelly on the road.[20] The *Dallas Times Herald* included the following in its review of the show: "Kelly's entrance where he is joined by Alex Romero and Roy Palmer is an engaging mixture of tap, soft-shoe and Kelly's traditional athleticism...."[21]

Take Me Along played in Dallas, and while there, Kelly was approached by theatrical producer John Kenley. The show and its principals were bought for Kenley's circuit. The show moved to Warren, Ohio, where it rehearsed for a week to put in new ensemble members, and after playing a week there, went for a one-week engagement in Dayton and a one-week engagement in Columbus. Brian Byers, who performed in the ensemble, remembered that at each performance the cast would pack themselves in the wings of the theater to watch Kelly and the other Hollywood veterans. When asked about Alex in the show, Byers said, "Alex was just such a gent. He was such a cool guy. He was a charming, soft-spoken guy."[22]

After returning from the tour of *Take Me Along*, Alex joined producer Robert Aldrich to work on another Burt Reynolds film, *Hustle*, at Paramount. Aldrich said, "Alex, I want a girl to do a strip number, and she's gotta really go kinda wild, and yet we have to hide it a little bit." Alex went home and brainstormed about how to accomplish this. He came up with the idea of getting a big hoop, about eight feet wide, that had silks hanging from it. The idea was that the crew would turn the hoop, and the more it turned, the more the silks would open to reveal the girl.

13

Endings (1976–2007)

In 1976, Alex returned to MGM in the same capacity as when he started there in 1948: He was to assist Gene Kelly. Alex was brought in to help stage a dance-off between Kelly and Fred Astaire *in That's Entertainment, Part II*. Saul Chaplin,[1] the producer, knew that at age 76, Astaire preferred not to dance on film any more, but he had approached Kelly about trying to persuade Astaire to do the documentary and get Astaire to dance. Kelly convinced Astaire to do the film and Astaire thought that he would only be introducing the old filmclips.

Alex remembered that Astaire came into the rehearsal hall the first day and, along with Kelly, began learning his speeches. After a couple of days, however, Kelly approached Astaire and said, "Fred, you know what, I've been thinking. The audiences are going to be really disappointed if they don't see us move a little bit, do a little dancing, just simple dancing.... Don't you think we ought to do it?"

Astaire responded, "Well, all right."

Kelly started experimenting with a few steps. Then he asked Alex to join him and work up some more complex steps. Astaire sat and watched. Eventually he hit the seat of the chair next to him with a loud "thwack!" "Gene, You told me we were just going to talk, and now you got me dancing, and that's pretty complicated stuff...."

Kelly said, "Oh come on ... Alex has got it and he'll show it to you."

Alex could tell that Astaire was mad. He had worked with him before. He remembered, "He doesn't like to learn other people's stuff."

Kelly began working on his part. Alex worked with Astaire. Astaire continually grumbled to Alex, "Can you believe this guy [Kelly]? Can you believe this guy? Just going to talk and walk and now this!"

As rehearsals progressed, Kelly added more and more dancing until

The Man Who Made the Jailhouse Rock

the rather complex number was complete. Astaire grumbled throughout the entire process, but did the dance. It would be his last on film.

In 1976, Alex also choreographed *F. Scott Fitzgerald in Hollywood*, an ABC Movie of the Week. He worked with Tuesday Weld, who played the part of Zelda. Beginning in 1977, Alex was the regular choreographer on the television series *Fantasy Island*, staging numbers for 18 episodes throughout the run of the series until 1984.

In 1977, Alex was Gene Kelly's stunt double on the film *Viva Knievel!* Alex had never ridden a motorcycle before, but accepted the challenge with the same fervor he approached every thing he did. A program bio written for one of the Thalian performances stated, "[Alex is] fresh off of the set of *Viva Knievel!* starring Evel Knievel. Alex performed motorcycle challenges with the daredevil king."[2] Alex was 64 years old at the time.

A performance shot taken from Gene Kelly's television special, *An American in Pasadena*. From left to right: Alex, Kelly, and Danny Daniels.

13. Endings (1976–2007)

In 1978, Kelly called his friend Alex again, asking him to dance with him on his television special *An American in Pasadena*. The show featured many of Alex's friends from earlier years at MGM, including Lucille Ball, Frank Sinatra, Cyd Charisse, Betty Garrett, and Kathryn Grayson. Alex performed a precision soft-shoe with Kelly and tap master Danny Daniels. The dance was done to the music of "Poor Butterfly."[3]

In August, Alex traveled with Kelly and Daniels to perform at the Resorts International Hotel and Casino in Atlantic City to reprise their *American in Pasadena* dance. A review in *Variety* stated, "Kelly does what he likes to do best — dance. He breaks up the routine with a rundown on his films and the women leads.... Hoofers Danny Daniels and Alex Romero do a 'challenge dance.' It gets a standing ovation...."[4]

Love at First Bite (1979) gave Alex an opportunity to take advantage of the disco craze. He created a comedy number for the film's star George Hamilton, who played a disco-dancing Dracula. Alex told Hamilton he planned to put some lifts in the dance, but Hamilton said he wasn't sure whether or not he could handle them. Alex reassured him that he would work out the lifts so that Hamilton could do them. Alex waited until the star was out of the rehearsal room to try out the lifts with Hamilton's co-star Susan Saint James.[5] Saint James was fearless according to Alex, and he was able to work out a back flip over the arm that went right into a death drop. They showed it to Hamilton when he returned and sold him on the idea.

Alex next did a made-for-television movie starring Catherine Hicks, *Marilyn: The Untold Story,* about the life of Marilyn Monroe. For the film, Alex recreated Jack Cole's original choreography for "Diamonds Are a Girl's Best Friend," as well as other numbers.[6]

While working on the roller disco film *Xanadu* as dance consultant to Gene Kelly, Alex was asked to contract dancers to do the sound dubbing for the soundtrack. Because the picture involved roller-skating, the studio asked the dancers to wear skates so the sounds would be more authentic. Lysa Baugher Klein, one of the dancers, said, "You know how insane that is. The floor [where they were to dub the taps] is this big ... as big as this table, and there were ten of us, for crying out loud! ...What we did was, we used our hands."[7] She explained that because it was impossible to actually skate in the sound studio, the dubbers put the skates on their hands and hit them rhythmically on the floor in some imitation of the choreography. Alex himself dubbed all of Kelly's taps on the film.

In 1981, Alex danced in the flophouse number in the MGM musical *Pennies from Heaven*. The movie was choreographed by Danny Daniels, who had performed with Alex in the Gene Kelly special *An American in Pasadena*.

In 1982, Alex began work as a regular choreographer for two television series, *T.J. Hooker* and *Remington Steele*. He also choreographed an animated movie called *Heidi's Song*, produced by Hanna-Barbera and released by Paramount. It featured the voices of Lorne Greene, Margery Gray, and Sammy Davis, Jr. Alex had worked for Hanna-Barbera before and understood the complex challenges involved in creating appropriate movement for cartoon characters. For the polka song "Arm Full of Sunshine," for example, he used a variety of traditional dance steps and positions. The animators then used a metronome to sync their drawings of Alex's choreography to the music so that the characters moved in rhythm.

The same year, Alex was hired to find dancers to dub the taps for the movie musical *Annie*. Alex was originally told that his group would work for four or five weeks on the film as Foley artists, reproducing the tap choreography and other dance sounds. The dancers arrived, learned the steps and started to lay down the tracks. However, Alex and his dancers learned that the studio was going to try to save money by using multi-tracks. Even for the big dance numbers in the film, the small group of Alex's dubbers were recorded only once; the sound engineers overlaid their taps several times to make it seem as if several people were dancing. The job lasted only a day and a half rather than a month. Alex himself dubbed some of the taps.

In 1982, Alex choreographed another George Hamilton film, *Zorro, the Gay Blade*. Hamilton told Alex that he wanted to do a flamenco dance. Alex told him, "George, this is really going to take time, because it's different than tap dancing or anything...." Hamilton insisted, and so Alex agreed. Hamilton worked hard to master the moves.

> Then we got to the dance, and now we're in Mexico ... and the director comes up to me and says, "Alex, you've worked this guy so hard, he's wasting away, and so let's do the number last ... [at] the end of the movie when he's rested." And I said, "Yes, but you've got to let me [keep rehearsing

13. Endings (1976–2007)

him], even if I have to go at night over to his house, and do this a couple of times so he won't forget it." The director agreed, and we kept the thing alive.

The budget for *Zorro, the Gay Blade* was $11,000,000, small for a feature film. Alex recalled that the director, Peter Medak, was "a wonderful director, but he was slow, as slow as Minnelli." When filming extended, the film's producers told the cast and crew that they had to return home from Mexico because the budget had ballooned to 12 million. Medak ignored the order and kept filming. "It went on and on and then it got up to 14 million until eventually the producers themselves flew to Mexico, stormed on the set, and demanded that filming stop." Concerned that he wouldn't be able to do the flamenco dance, Hamilton took Alex with him to the producers and begged them to let him do the number. He told them, "You don't understand. It isn't going to cost you anything. We have this thing. We saved it for last, and I have it perfectly. We could probably do it in an hour and a half or two." The producers adamantly refused. The producers said, "No. No. We're leaving." The flamenco number never made it into the film. Alex said, "And it was seventeen times better than anything that they did in that [film.]"

As Alex approached his seventieth birthday, he continued to stay busy in the business that he loved. In March of 1983, at Warner Brothers, he staged the dances for Rachel Ward and Bryan Brown for *The Thornbirds* mini-series Show Two. On November 14 of that year, he served on the "Elements of Choreography" panel for "The Dance Makers," sharing his knowledge of the craft and his process of creating dances for the screen with young choreographers. The program was presented by the Los Angeles Area Dance Alliance in association with the Professional Dancers Society at the Pilot Theatre.

In 1984, he worked again with his friend Robert Wagner on the television show *Hart to Hart*, choreographing a production number for an episode called "Whisper in the Wings." The hat-and-cane tap dance featured Wagner and his co-star Stefanie Powers, along with guest star Karen Akers and an ensemble of dancing men and women. Alex also choreographed two other episodes of *Hart to Hart*.

In 1984, Alex was brought in to choreograph new material for *That's Dancing*, the retrospective documentary about screen dancing. The film also featured some of Alex's earlier work, including clips from *Love Me or Leave Me* and *tom thumb*. Alex also did the Warner Brothers movie *City Heat* (1984) with Clint Eastwood and Burt Reynolds, an action-comedy set in the 1930s.[8]

In his eighties, Alex continued to dance every day in his home studio. Although work was less available, he did keep his hand in the business. Between 1987 and 1990, he choreographed an episode for *The Tracy Ullman Show*. On December 4, 1990, he was honored by the Southern California Motion Picture Council with their Lifetime Dance Achievement Award.

In his later years Alex became active in the Professional Dancers Society, a charitable organization made up of dancers and choreographers raising money to set up a retirement home for professional dancers. Alex served on the associate board and worked on many special events, helping to plan them and coordinate talent. He was active in creating the P.D.S. performing arts company and staging the young performers for the Society's benefits. In 1993, he was given the Gypsy Robe,[9] a tradition that began among Broadway dancers and was adopted by P.D.S. to honor the members of its own Hollywood community.

On April 27, 1997, Alex's beloved wife Faun passed away, a month before their 62nd anniversary. Alex grieved deeply. He had never been sick in his life and had never been in the hospital, yet shortly after Faun's passing, he began to experience serious tachycardia. The episodes worsened and Alex's daughters insisted he go to a cardiologist. Alex wore a monitor for two weeks. The doctor discovered abnormal rhythms, and a pacemaker was installed.

Faun's ashes had been interred on April 29, 1997, at the San Fernando Mission Cemetery and Mausoleum in Mission Hills, California. Alex was not happy with the location. He told his daughters that he thought Faun would rather be with Butch, the nephew she cared for in the early 1950s and who was like a son to her. Butch had passed away in 1988 from polycystic kidney disease. Alex's daughters agreed with their father's decision to disinter Faun's ashes, and did so on June 16, 1999. The family scattered Faun and Butch's ashes in the ocean at Dana Point.

Alex continued to grieve, but he also continued to dance. In the fall of that year, 84-year-old Alex performed in the opening number of the Jerry Lewis MDA Telethon. The production number featured over

13. Endings (1976–2007)

40 dancers from the 1940s, '50s, '60s, and '70s and was staged by choreographer Anita Mann.[10] Mann had been Alex's assistant on the film *Speedway*.

On October 13, 2001, Jazz Dance LA presented "Tribute to Alex Romero," honoring Alex with the Foundation's Lifetime Achievement Award. Held at the Harriet and Charles Luckman Fine Arts Complex at California State University, Los Angeles, the gala was introduced by Oscar-winner George Chakiris. Chakiris began by saying, "This year, for the first time, the Jazz Dance LA Lifetime Achievement Award will go to a choreographer — one whose name may not be known to the general public, but whose work has been seen and enjoyed by movie audiences worldwide for over half a century." Chakiris then introduced Janet Leigh, who said in her speech:

> Tonight Jazz Dance LA is honoring a man who played a tremendous role in the development of movie musicals, as both dancer and choreographer, Mr. Alex Romero. Many dancers here tonight, especially the young ones, may not know about Mr. Romero and we are here to fix that. Alex worked at MGM when I did — when it was the colossus of movie studios and the Hollywood musical was [in] its golden era. As a staff contract artist, Alex never received compensation or credit in proportion to his creative contributions to the movies. But those contributions were recorded on film and, as you'll see, they include moments in dance that have thrilled and inspired moviegoers all over the world. I am here because [in] one of my earliest films at MGM, *The Red Danube*, I was cast as a Russian ballerina. This film happened to be Alex's first as a credited dance director. It was so typical. I was a Russian ballerina ... who had never danced! Alex had two months to get me in shape, to build the muscles and the strength needed to hold me up. The director [and] I didn't want the usual [close-up shot] on my waist and then cut to a long shot and using the double.... Well our magician did it. He got me on pointe. He had the patience of Job and the determination of a Mount Everest climber. I never worked so damn hard or hurt so damn much in my entire life. Thank the Lord that I could move fairly well and had a sense of rhythm.... You know, actually, I think I've always been a frustrated gypsy.... And, the camera was able to show me full length, on pointe, and even doing several combinations. Don't misunderstand, a real dancer did the whole intricate number in the long shot, but we had our triumph! And we formed not only muscles, but a friendship which I treasure that has lasted a lifetime — 53 years.

Leigh then introduced Danny Daniels, whom Alex had danced with in the Kelly special *An American in Pasadena*. Daniels said,

The Man Who Made the Jailhouse Rock

When Alex Romero came to Hollywood to work in 1939, you had to be able to hoof — you *had* to be able to hoof. But in the late '40s the heat of Dixie and swing in jazz was challenged by a shift toward the cool and a new kind of jazz dance in which the feet [that] were silent started to push tap off the screen. This change took about ten years. Alex Romero, who was [sic] a tap dancer to this day, didn't just ride out this change, he was an integral part of it. For in addition to his hoofing, which he learned in vaudeville, Alex was a student of the legendary Jack Cole. Cole developed a style and technique in nightclubs that was seminal to the new jazz that gradually took over the movies. This technique remains the cornerstone of jazz dance today from isolations to knee slides. Look at funk and even hip-hop and you'll find elements of Jack Cole. But Cole was unhappy in Hollywood and after four years at Columbia Studios took his dancers back on the road. It was Alex Romero who brought Cole's style front and center into the movies at MGM where they signed and kept him for a long time because he could do anything.

Daniels then introduced a film tribute to Alex with clips of his performances and the films he had choreographed. Directed by Richard Kuller and edited by Gregory Gast, the mini-documentary was narrated by Janet Leigh. After the film, Leigh escorted Alex onto stage to receive the award. A spry 88, Alex proceeded to do a tap dance that he had worked up for the event. Leigh, Russ Tamblyn, and other friends from the movies, along with a new generation of young dancers, cheered him on. The event ended with a recreation of Alex's original choreography of "Jailhouse Rock" performed by 16 male dancers.

Several colleagues sent letters of congratulations to Alex. Leslie Caron, who had worked with him on *An American in Paris, Lili,* and *Gigi,* wrote, "I remember Alex Romero as the most hard-working dancer — endlessly enthusiastic, endlessly patient — great support — You could rely on Alex...."

Shirley Jones, who was choreographed by Alex in *Pepe,* wrote,

> I'm lucky. I've got three million friends. A million I "love." A couple of hundred thousand I "respect" and "admire." Maybe a few hundred I'm "smitten" with; and probably 16 or 17 I "revere," maybe even "worship." But I do believe that I could count on the fingers of one hand the creative souls from which I "learned" ... but I mean really & truly LEARNED — and Alex would be one of those. And it would seem that that legacy might stand as the proudest of any man's.

In his note, director George Sidney wrote, "'Little Alex,' as we called him, was a wonderful creator and talent." Howard Keel maintained a

13. Endings (1976–2007)

long and lasting friendship with Alex. When he and his wife Judy were unable to attend the event, Keel wrote, "Dear Alex — Please know how much I respect, admire, and love you and all you did for the movies."

At age 90, Alex moved into the Motion Picture Home in Calabasas, California. As active and gregarious as always, he quickly fit in, making friends with the other residents, many of whom he knew from his years in the industry. He still danced every day. For the next three years, he loved his surroundings, but he began to experience minor memory confusions that troubled his doctors. Despite the protests of his family, the social worker assigned to Alex's case insisted that he be relocated to a room in the facility's Alzheimer's wing on February, 13, 2007.

It was a lonely time for Alex when he discovered that he had no one to talk with in the new wing except the nurses. Visits from family and friends could not prevent depression from quickly taking hold of him.

At the end of August, several friends gathered to celebrate his 93rd birthday at a restaurant near the Motion Picture Home. Betty Garrett and Russ Tamblyn were there. But after Alex returned to his room at the facility, he quickly settled into depression again and announced that he would no longer eat. He contracted pneumonia, but recovered and continued his hunger fast, only eating a little when urged by friends or family. His condition worsened rapidly, and on September 8, 2007, he passed away. His daughter and a few close friends were by his side as he passed.[11]

Shortly before he died, Alex reminisced about his life as a dancer and choreographer. He said, "If you love something, you're going to do it well, and you don't ever forget it." He smiled and added, "I'm glad I did this for a living. I had so much fun."

Filmography

THE HEAT'S ON (1943) Columbia
Produced and directed by Gregory Ratoff; *Choreographed by* David Lichine
Mae West, Victor Moore, William Gaxton, Lester Allen, Alan Dinehart, Lloyd Bridges
Alex Romero: *dancer*

ALI BABA AND THE FORTY THIEVES (1944) Universal
Produced by Paul Malvern; *Directed by* Arthur Lubin; *Choreographed by* Paul Oscard
Maria Montez, Jon Hall, Turhan Bey, Andy Devine, Kurt Katch, Frank Puglia, Fortunio Bonanova, Moroni Olsen
Alex Romero: dancer

FOUR JILLS IN A JEEP (1944) Twentieth Century–Fox
Produced by William A. Seiter; *Directed by* Irving Starr; *Choreographed by* Don Loper
Kay Francis, Carole Landis, Martha Raye, Mitzi Mayfair, Jimmy Dorsey, John Harvey, Phil Silvers, Dick Haymes, Alice Faye, Betty Grable
Alex Romero: dancer

THE MERRY MONAHANS (1944) Universal
Produced by Michael Fessier and Ernest Pagano; *Directed by* Charles Lamont; *Choreographed by* Carlos Romero and Louis DaPron
Donald O'Connor, Peggy Ryan, Jack Oakie, Anne Blyth, Rosemary DeCamp, John Miljan, Gavin Muir
Alex Romero: dance-in for Donald O'Connor (not in film)

FOLLOW THE BOYS aka **THREE CHEERS FOR THE BOYS** (1944) Universal
Produced by Charles K. Feldman; *Directed by* A. Edward Sutherland; *Choreographed by* George Hale and George Balanchine
George Raft, Vera Zorina, Jeanette McDonald, Marlene Dietrich, Orson Welles, Dinah Shore, W.C. Fields, The Andrews Sisters, Donald O'Connor, Peggy Ryan, Sophie Tucker
Alex Romero: *dancer*

EADIE WAS A LADY (1945) Columbia
Produced by Michael Kraike; *Directed by* Arthur Dreifuss; *Choreographed by* Jack Cole

Filmography

Ann Miller, Joe Besser, William Wright, Jeff Donnell, Jimmy Little, Marion Martin, Kathleen Howard, Tom Dugan
Alex Romero: *dancer*

TONIGHT AND EVERY NIGHT (1945) Columbia

Produced by Victor Saville; *Directed by* Victor Saville; *Choreographed by* Jack Cole and Val Raset
Rita Hayworth, Lee Bowman, Janet Blair, Marc Platt, Marc Platt, Leslie Brooks, Professor Lamberti, Dusty Anderson
Alex Romero: *dancer*

ZIEGFELD FOLLIES (1946) MGM

Produced by Arthur Freed; *Directed by* Vincente Minnelli; *Choreographed by* Robert Alton, Roy Del Ruth, Eugene Loring, Charles Walters
William Powell, Judy Garland, Lucille Ball, Fred Astaire, Lucille Bremer, Fanny Brice, Kathryn Grayson, Lena Horne, Gene Kelly
Alex Romero: *dancer*

MEET ME ON BROADWAY (1946) Columbia

Produced by Burt Kelly; *Directed by* Leigh Jason; *Choreographed by* Jack Cole
Marjorie Reynolds, Frederick Brady, Jinx Falkenburg, Spring Byington, Allen Jenkins, Gene Lockhart, Loren Tindall, Eddie Acuff
Alex Romero: *dancer*

TARS AND SPARS (1946) Columbia

Produced by Milton H. Bren; *Directed by* Alfred E. Green; *Choreographed by* Jack Cole
Janet Blair, Alfred Drake, Marc Platt, Sid Caesar, Jeff Donnell, Noel Neill, Anita Alvarez, Tom Dugan
Alex Romero: *dancer*

THE JOLSON STORY (1946) Columbia

Produced by Sidney Skolsky and Sidney Buchman; *Directed by* Alfred E. Green; *Choreographed by* Jack Cole
Larry Parks, Evelyn Keyes, William Demarest, Bob Goodwin, Ludwig Donath, Scotty Beckett, Tamara Shayne
Alex Romero: *dancer*

THE THRILL OF BRAZIL (1946) Columbia

Produced by Sydney Biddell and Allen Rivkin; *Directed by* S. Sylvan Simon; *Choreographed by* Jack Cole
Evely Keyes, Keenan Wynn, Ann Miller, Allyn Joslyn, Tito Guizar, Felix Brassart, Sid Tomack
Alex Romero: *dancer*

TWO BLONDS AND A REDHEAD (1947) Columbia

Produced by Sam Katzman; *Directed by* Arthur Dreifuss; *Choreographed by* Audrene Brier

Filmography

Jean Porter, Jimmy Lloyd, June Preisser, Judy Clark, Rick Vallin, Charles Smith, Regina Wallace
Alex Romero: *dancer*

DOWN TO EARTH (1947) Columbia
Produced by Don Hartman; *Directed by* Alexander Hall; *Choreographed by* Jack Cole
Rita Hayworth, Larry Parks, Marc Platt, Roland Culver, James Gleason, Edward Everett Horton, Adele Jergens, George Macready, William Frawley
Alex Romero: *dancer*

EASTER PARADE (1948) MGM
Produced by Arthur Freed; *Directed and choreographed by* Charles Walters
Fred Astaire, Judy Garland, Ann Miller, Peter Lawford, Jules Munshin, Clinton Sundberg, Lola Albright
Alex Romero: *assistant choreographer*

THE KISSING BANDIT (1948) MGM
Produced by Joe Pasternak; *Directed by* Laslo Benedek; *Choreographed by* Stanley Donen
Frank Sinatra, Kathryn Grayson, J. Carrol Naish, Mildred Natwick, Mikhail Rasumny, Ricardo Montalban, Ann Miller, Cyd Charisse
Alex Romero: *assistant choreographer*

WORDS AND MUSIC (1948) MGM
Produced by Arthur Freed; *Directed by* Norman Taurog; *Choreographed by* Robert Alton and Alex Romero (assistant)
Gene Kelly, June Allyson, Perry Como, Judy Garland, Lena Horne, Mickey Rooney, Ann Sothern, Tom Drake, Cyd Charisse, Betty Garrett, Janet Leigh, Mel Torme, Vera-Ellen, the Blackburn Twins
Alex Romero: *assistant choreographer* to Robert Alton; *assistant choreographer* to Gene Kelly on "Slaughter on Tenth Avenue"; *choreographer* of "Thou Swell" and "The Lady Is a Tramp."

TAKE ME OUT TO THE BALL GAME (EVERYBODY'S CHEERING) (1949) MGM
Produced by Arthur Freed; *Directed by* Busby Berkeley, *Musical numbers staged by* Stanley Donen and Gene Kelly
Frank Sinatra, Esther Williams, Gene Kelly, Betty Garrett, Edward Arnold, Jules Munshin, Richard Lane, Tom Dugan, Douglas Fowley, Eddie Parkes, James Burke, The Blackburn Twins
Alex Romero: *assistant choreographer*

ON THE TOWN (1949) MGM
Produced by Arthur Freed; *Directed and choreographed by* Stanley Donen and Gene Kelly
Gene Kelly, Frank Sinatra, Betty Garrett, Ann Miller, Jules Munshin, Vera-Ellen, Florence Bates, George Meader
Alex Romero: *assistant choreographer, Sailor* (dancing for Frank Sinatra in the "Day in New York" ballet)

Filmography

THE RED DANUBE (1949) MGM
Produced by Carey Wilson; *Directed by* George Sidney
Janet Leigh, Walter Pidgeon, Ethel Barrymore, Peter Lawford, Angela Lansbury, Louis Calhern, Francis L. Sullivan
Alex Romero: *choreographer*

THE BARKLEYS OF BROADWAY (1949) MGM
Produced by Arthur Freed; *Directed by* Charles Walters; *Choreographed by* Robert Alton
Fred Astaire, Ginger Rogers, Oscar Levant, Billie Burke, Gale Robbins, Jacques Francoise, George Zucco
Alex Romero: *assistant choreographer*

SCENE OF THE CRIME (1949) MGM
Produced by Harry Rapf; *Directed by* Roy Rowland
Van Johnson, Arlene Dahl, Gloria DeHaven, Tom Drake, Leon Ames, John McIntire, Norman Lloyd
Alex Romero: *choreographer*

ANNIE GET YOUR GUN (1950) MGM
Produced by Arthur Freed; *Directed by* George Sidney; *Choreographed by* Robert Alton
Judy Garland, Betty Hutton, Howard Keel, Louis Calhern, J. Carrol Naish, Edward Arnold, Keenan Wynn
Alex Romero: *assistant choreographer, white Indian dancer*

PAGAN LOVE SONG (1950) MGM
Produced by Arthur Freed; *Directed and choreographed by* Robert Alton
Esther Williams, Howard Keel, Rita Moreno, Minna Gombell
Alex Romero: *assistant choreographer, actor (coconut crab man)*

THE OUTRIDERS (1950) MGM
Produced by Richard Goldstone; *Directed by* Roy Rowland
Joel McCrea, Arlene Dahl, Barry Sullivan, Claude Jarman, Jr., James Whitmore, Ramon Novarro, Jeff Corey
Alex Romero: *choreographer*

THREE LITTLE WORDS (1950) MGM
Produced by Jack Cummings; *Directed by* Richard Thorpe; *Choreographed by* Hermes Pan and Fred Astaire
Fred Astaire, Vera-Ellen, Red Skelton, Keenan Wynn, Arlene Dahl, Debbie Reynolds, Carleton Carpenter, Gale Robbins, Gloria DeHaven
Alex Romero: *assistant choreographer*

TWO WEEKS WITH LOVE (1950) MGM
Produced by Jack Cummings; *Directed by* Roy Rowland; *Choreographed by* Busby Berkeley
Jane Powell, Ricardo Montalban, Debbie Reynolds, Louis Calhern, Ann Harding, Phyllis Kirk, Carleton Carpenter

Filmography

Alex Romero: *assistant choreographer*

THE TOAST OF NEW ORLEANS (1950) MGM
Produced by Joe Pasternak; *Directed by* Norman Taurog; *Choreographed by* Eugene Loring
Kathryn Grayson, Mario Lanza, David Niven, Rita Moreno, James Mitchell, J. Carrol Naish, Richard Hageman
Alex Romero: *dancer*

AN AMERICAN IN PARIS (1951) MGM
Produced by Arthur Freed; *Directed by* Vincente Minnelli; *Choreographed by* Gene Kelly
Gene Kelly, Leslie Caron, Oscar Levant, George Guetary, Nina Foch, Martha Bamattre, Anna Q. Nilsson
Alex Romero: *assistant choreographer, dancing G.I.*

INSIDE STRAIGHT (1951) MGM
Produced by Richard Goldstone; *Directed by* Gerald Mayer
David Brian, Arlene Dahl, Barry Sullivan, Mercedes McCambridge, Paula Raymond, Claude Jarman, Jr., Lon Chaney, Jr.
Alex Romero: *choreographer*

SHOW BOAT (1951) MGM
Produced by Arthur Freed; *Directed by* George Sidney; *Choreographed by* Robert Alton
Ava Gardner, Howard Keel, Kathryn Grayson, Joe E. Brown, Marge Champion, Gower Champion, Robert Sterling, Agnes Moorehead
Alex Romero: *assistant choreographer*

TEXAS CARNIVAL (1951) MGM
Produced by Jack Cummings; *Directed by* Charles Walters; *Choreographed by* Hermes Pan
Esther Williams, Red Skelton, Howard Keel, Ann Miller, Paula Raymond, Keenan Wynn, Tom Tully, Alex Goudavich
Alex Romero: *specialty dancer*

THE STRIP (1951) MGM
Produced by Joe Pasternak; *Directed by* Laszlo Kardos; *Choreographed by* Nick Castle
Mickey Rooney, Sally Forrest, Louis Armstrong, William Demarest, James Craig, Kay Brown, Tommy Rettig
Alex Romero: *dancer*

ACROSS THE WIDE MISSOURI (1952) MGM
Produced by Robert Sisk; *Directed by* William Wellman
Clark Gable, Ricardo Montalban, John Hodiak, Adolphe Menjou, J. Carrol Naish, Jack Holt, Alan Napier
Alex Romero: *choreographer*

THE BAD AND THE BEAUTIFUL (1952) MGM
Produced by John Houseman; *Directed by* Vincente Minnelli

Filmography

Lana Turner, Kirk Douglas, Walter Pidgeon, Dick Powell, Barry Sullivan, Gloria Grahame, Gilbert Roland, Leo G. Carroll
Alex Romero: *choreographer*

THE BELLE OF NEW YORK (1952) MGM
Produced by Arthur Freed; *Directed by* Charles Walters; *Choreographed by* Robert Alton
Fred Astaire, Vera-Ellen, Marjorie Main, Keenan Wynn, Alice Pearce, Clinton Sundberg, Gale Robbins
Alex Romero: *assistant choreographer*

JUMPING JACKS (1952) Paramount
Produced by Hal B. Wallis; *Directed by* Norman Taurog; *Choreographed by* Robert Sidney
Dean Martin, Jerry Lewis, Mona Freeman, Don DeFore, Robert Strauss, Richard Erdman, Ray Teal
Alex Romero: *assistant choreographer, choreographed tap number*

SINGIN' IN THE RAIN (1952) MGM
Produced by Arthur Freed; *Directed and choreographed* by Gene Kelly and Stanley Donen
Gene Kelly, Donald O'Connor, Debbie Reynolds, Jean Hagen, Millard Mitchell, Rita Moreno, Douglas Fowley, Cyd Charisse, Madge Blake, King Donovan, Kathleen Freeman, Bobby Watson, Tommy Farrell
Alex Romero: *choreographic consultant on* Cyd Charisse's "Broadway" ballet scarf number

SKIRTS AHOY (1952) MGM
Produced by Joe Pasternak; *Directed by* Sidney Lanfield; *Choreographed by* Nick Castle
Esther Williams, Joan Evans, Vivian Blaine, Barry Sullivan, Keefe Brasselle
Alex Romero: *assistant choreographer*

THE AFFAIRS OF DOBIE GILLIS (1953) MGM
Produced by Arthur Loew; *Directed by* Don Weis
Debbie Reynolds, Bobby Van, Barbara Ruick, Bob Fosse, Hanley Stafford, Lurene Tuttle, Hans Conried
Alex Romero: *choreographer, actor (swing dance caller)*

KISS ME KATE (1953) MGM
Produced by Jack Cummings; *Directed by* George Sidney; *Choreographed by* Hermes Pan
Kathryn Grayson, Howard Keel, Ann Miller, Bobby Van, Tommy Rall, Bob Fosse, James Whitmore, Kurt Kasznar, Bob Fosse
Alex Romero: *assistant choreographer*

LILI (1953) MGM
Produced by Edwin H. Knopf; *Directed and choreographed by* Charles Walters

Filmography

Leslie Caron, Mel Ferrer, Zsa Zsa Gabor, Jean-Pierre Aumont, Kurt Kasznar, Amanda Blake, Alex Gerry
Alex Romero: *assistant choreographer (choreographed several numbers)*

RIDE VAQUERO! (1953) MGM
Produced by Stephan Ames; *Directed by* John Farrow
Robert Taylor, Ava Gardner, Howard Keel, Anthony Quinn, Kurt Kasznar, Ted de Corsia, Charlita, Jack Elam
Alex Romero: *choreographer*

SMALL TOWN GIRL (1953) MGM
Produced by Joe Pasternak; *Directed by* Leslie Kardos; *Choreographed by* Busby Berkeley
Jane Powell, Farley Granger, Ann Miller, Bobby Van, Billie Burke, S.Z. Sakall, Robert Keith, Fay Wray
Alex Romero: *assistant choreographer, choreographer of Ann Miller's Spanish tap number*

THE BAND WAGON (1953) MGM
Produced by Arthur Freed; *Directed by* Vincente Minnelli; *Choreographed by* Michael Kidd
Fred Astaire, Cyd Charisse, Oscar Levant, Nanette Fabray, Jack Buchanan, James Mitchell, Robert Gist
Alex Romero: *assistant choreographer, dance stand-in for Fred Astaire*

SEVEN BRIDES FOR SEVEN BROTHERS (1954) MGM
Produced by Jack Cummings; *Directed by* Stanley Donen; *Choreographed by* Michael Kidd
Howard Keel, Jane Powell, Tommy Rall, Russ Tamblyn, Marc Platt, Matt Mattox, Jeff Richards, Jacques d'Amboise
Alex Romero: *assistant choreographer*

LOVE ME OR LEAVE ME (1955) MGM
Produced by Joe Pasternak; *Directed by* Charles Vidor
Doris Day, James Cagney, Cameron Mitchell, Robert Keith, Tom Tully, Harry Bellaver, Richard Gaines
Alex Romero: *choreographer, actor (dance director)*

THE PRODIGAL (1955) MGM
Produced by Charles Schnee; *Directed by* Richard Thorpe
Lana Turner, Edmund Purdom, Louis Calhern, Audrey Dalton, James Mitchell, Neville Brand, Walter Hampden
Alex Romero: *choreographer*

I'LL CRY TOMORROW (1955) MGM
Produced by Lawrence Weingarten; *Directed by* Daniel Mann
Susan Hayward, Richard Conte, Eddie Albert, Jo Van Fleet, Ray Danton, Don Taylor, Margo, Virginia Gregg

Filmography

Alex Romero: *choreographer*

DIANE (1955) MGM

Produced by Edwin H. Knopf; *Directed by* David Miller

Lana Turner, Roger Moore, Pedro Armendariz, Marisa Pavan, Sir Cedric Hardwicke, Torin Thatcher, Taina Elg

Alex Romero: *choreographer*

THE FASTEST GUN ALIVE (1956) MGM

Produced by Clarence Greene; *Directed by* Russell Rouse

Glenn Ford, Jeanne Crain, Russ Tamblyn, Broderick Crawford, Allyn Joslyn, Leif Erickson, John Dehner, Noah Beery, Jr.

Alex Romero: *choreographer*

RAINTREE COUNTY (1957) MGM

Produced by David Lewis; *Directed by* Edward Dmytryk

Elizabeth Taylor, Montgomery Clift, Eva Marie Saint, Nigel Patrick, Lee Marvin, Rod Taylor, Agnes Moorehead

Alex Romero: *choreographer*

UNTIL THEY SAIL (1957) MGM

Produced by Charles Schnee; *Directed by* Robert Wise

Jean Simmons, Joan Fontaine, Paul Newman, Piper Laurie, Sandra Dee, Alan Napier, Charles Drake

Alex Romero: *choreographer*

LES GIRLS (1957) MGM

Produced by Sol E. Siegel; *Directed by* George Cukor; *Choreographed by* Jack Cole

Gene Kelly, Mitzi Gaynor, Kay Kendall, Taina Elg, Jacques Bergerac, Leslie Phillips, Henry Daniell, Patrick Macnee, Stephen Vercoe

Alex Romero: *assistant choreographer*

JAILHOUSE ROCK (1957) MGM

Produced by Pandro Berman; *Directed by* Richard Thorpe

Elvis Presley, Judy Tyler, Mickey Shaughnessy, Vaughn Taylor, Jennifer Holden, Dean Jones, Anne Neyland

Alex Romero: *choreographer*

GIGI (1958) MGM

Produced by Arthur Freed; *Directed by* Vincente Minnelli; *Choreographed by* Charles Walters

Leslie Caron, Maurice Chevalier, Louis Jourdan, Hermione Gingold, Eva Gabor, Jacques Bergerac, Isabel Jeans

Alex Romero: *assistant choreographer, choreographed "The Night They Invented Champagne"*

tom thumb (1958) MGM

Produced and directed by George Pal

Filmography

Russ Tamblyn, June Thorburn, Peter Sellers, Terry-Thomas, Alan Young, Bernard Miles, Jessie Matthews

Alex Romero: *choreographer*

A PRIVATE'S AFFAIR (1959) 20th Century-Fox

Produced by David Weisbart; *Directed by* Raoul Walsh

Sal Mineo, Christine Carere, Barry Coe, Barbara Eden, Gary Crosby, Terry Moore, Jim Backus

Alex Romero: *choreographer*

SAY ONE FOR ME (1959) 20th Century-Fox

Produced and directed by Frank Tashlin

Bing Crosby, Debbie Reynolds, Robert Wagner, Ray Walston, Les Tremayne, Connie Gilchrist, Frank McHugh

Alex Romero: *choreographer*

PEPE (1960) Columbia

Produced and directed by George Sidney

Cantinflas, Dan Dailey, Shirley Jones, Carlos Montalban, Vicki Trickett, Matt Mattox, Hank Henry

Alex Romero and Eugene Loring: *choreographers*

THE GAZEBO (1959) MGM

Produced by Lawrence Weingarten; *Directed by* George Marshall

Glenn Ford, Debbie Reynolds, Carl Reiner, John McGiver, Mabel Albertson, Doro Merande, Bert Freed

Alex Romero: *choreographer*

THE GEORGE RAFT STORY (1961) Allied Artists

Produced by Ben Schwalb; *Directed by* Joseph M. Newman

Ray Danton, Jayne Mansfield, Julie London, Barrie Chase, Barbara Nichols, Frank Gorshin, Margo Moore

Alex Romero: *choreographer*

THE FOUR HORSEMEN OF THE APOCALYPSE (1962) MGM

Produced by Julian Blaustein, Olallo Rubio, Jr.; *Directed by* Vincente Minnelli

Glenn Ford, Ingrid Thulin, Charles Boyer, Lee J. Cobb, Paul Lukas, Yvette Mimieux, Paul Henreid

Alex Romero: *choreographer*

WHAT EVER HAPPENED TO BABY JANE (1962) Warner Brothers

Produced and directed by Robert Aldrich

Bette Davis, Joan Crawford, Victor Buono, Wesley Addy, Anne Barton, Marjorie Bennett

Alex Romero: *choreographer*

THE WONDERFUL WORLD OF THE BROTHERS GRIMM (1962) MGM

Produced by George Pal; *Directed by* Henry Levin and George Pal

Filmography

Laurence Harvey, Karlheinz Bohm, Claire Bloom, Walter Slezak, Barbara Eden, Yvette Mimieux, Russ Tamblyn
Alex Romero: *choreographer*

STATE FAIR (1962) 20th Century–Fox
Produced by Charles Brackett; *Directed by* Jose Ferrer; *Choreographed by* Nick Castle
Alice Faye, Pat Boone, Bobby Darin, Ann-Margret, Pamela Tiffin, Tom Ewell, Wally Cox
Alex Romero: *helped Alice Faye on kitchen number*

THE STRIPPER (1963) 20th Century–Fox
Produced by Jerry Wald; *Directed by* Franklin Schaffner
Joanne Woodward, Richard Beymer, Claire Trevor, Carol Lynley, Robert Webber, Louis Nye, Gypsy Rose Lee
Alex Romero: *choreographer*

THE SEVEN FACES OF DR. LAO (1964) MGM
Produced and directed by George Pal
Tony Randall, Barbara Eden, Arthur O'Connell, John Ericson, Noah Beery, Jr., Lee Patrick, John Derek
Alex Romero: *choreographer*

CLAMBAKE (1967) United Artists
Produced by Arthur Gardner, Arnold Laven, Jules V. Levy and Tom Rolf; *Directed by* Arthur Nadel
Elvis Presley, Shelley Fabares, Will Hutchins, Bill Bixby, Gary Merrill, James Gregory, Suzie Kaye
Alex Romero: *choreographer*

DOUBLE TROUBLE (1967) MGM
Produced by Judd Bernard and Irwin Winkler; *Directed by* Norman Taurog
Elvis Presley, Annette Day, John Williams, Yvonne Romain, The Wiere Brothers, Chips Rafferty, Norman Rossington
Alex Romero: *choreographer*

SPEEDWAY (1968) MGM
Produced by Douglas Laurence; *Directed by* Norman Taurog
Elvis Presley, Nancy Sinatra, Bill Bixby, Gale Gordon, William Schallert, Victoria Paige Meyerink, Ross Hagen
Alex Romero: *choreographer*

FOR SINGLES ONLY (1968) Columbia
Produced by Sam Katzman; *Directed by* Arthur Dreifuss
John Saxon, Mary Ann Mobley, Lana Wood, Peter Mark Richman, Ann Elder, Chris Noel, Marty Ingels
Alex Romero: *choreographer*

THE GRISSOM GANG (1971) Cinerama
Produced and directed by Robert Aldrich

Filmography

Kim Darby, Scott Wilson, Tony Musante, Robert Lansing, Connie Stevens, Irene Dailey, Wesley Addy
Alex Romero: *choreographer*

SOME CALL IT LOVING (1973) Cine Globe
Produced and directed by James P. Harris
Zalman King, Carol White, Tisa Farrow, Richard Pryor, Veronica Anderson, Logan Ramsey, Brandy Herred
Alex Romero: *choreographer*

THE LONGEST YARD (1974) Paramount
Produced by Albert S. Ruddy; *Directed by* Robert Aldrich
Burt Reynolds, Eddie Albert, Ed Lauter, Michael Conrad, James Hampton, Harry Caesar, John Steadman
Alex Romero: *choreographer*

HUSTLE (1975) Paramount
Produced and directed by Robert Aldrich
Burt Reynolds, Catherine Deneuve, Ben Johnson, Paul Winfield, Eileen Brennan, Eddie Albert, Ernest Borgnine
Alex Romero: *Choreographer*

THAT'S ENTERTAINMENT II (1976) MGM
Produced by Saul Chaplin and Daniel Melnick; *Directed by* Gene Kelly
Fred Astaire, Gene Kelly
Alex Romero: *assistant choreographer*

VIVA KNIEVEL! (1977) Warner Brothers
Produced by Stanley Hough; *Directed by* Gordon Douglas
Evel Knievel, Gene Kelly, Red Button, Lauren Hutton, Leslie Nielsen, Frank Gifford, Cameron Mitchell, Eric Olsen, Sheila Allen, Marjoe Gortner
Alex Romero: *stunt double for Gene Kelly*

THE FRISCO KID (1979) Warner Brothers
Produced by Howard W. Koch, Jr., Mace Neufeld; *Directed by* Robert Aldrich
Gene Wilder, Harrison Ford, Raymond Bieri, Val Bisoglio, George DiCenzo, Leo Fuchs, Penny Peyser
Alex Romero: *choreographer, actor "Wise Old Man"*

LOVE AT FIRST BITE (1979) American International Pictures
Produced by Joel Freeman and Melvin Simon; *Directed by* George Hamilton and Robert Kaufman
George Hamilton, Susan Saint James, Richard Benjamin, Dick Shawn, Arte Johnson, Sherman Hemsley, Isabel Sanford
Alex Romero: *choreographer*

XANADU (1980) Universal
Produced by Lawrence Gordon; *Directed by* Robert Greenwald; *Choreographed by* Jerry Trent

Filmography

Michael Beck, Olivia Newton-John, Gene Kelly, Sandra Katie Hanley, Fred McKarren, Ron Woods, Carol Browne, Wilfrid Hyde-White
Alex Romero: *dance effects supervisor, dance consultant to Gene Kelly, dubbed Gene Kelly's taps*

A SMALL CIRCLE OF FRIENDS (1980) MGM
Produced by Tim Zinnemann; *Directed by* Rob Cohen
Brad Davis, Karen Allen, Jameson Parker, Shelley Long, John Friedrich, Gary Springer, Craig Richardson Nelson
Alex Romero: *choreographer*

PENNIES FROM HEAVEN (1981) MGM
Produced by Richard McCallum, Nora Kaye and Herbert Ross; *Directed by* Herbert Ross; *Choreographed by* Danny Daniels
Steve Martin, Bernadette Peters, Jessica Harper, Vernel Bagneris, John McMartin, John Karlen, Jay Garner
Alex Romero: *dancer*

ANNIE (1982) Columbia
Produced by Joe Layton, Carol Sobieski and Ray Stark; *Directed by* John Huston; *Choreographed by* Arlene Phillips
Aileen Quinn, Albert Finney, Carol Burnett, Ann Reinking, Tim Curry, Bernadette Peters, Geoffrey Holder
Alex Romero: *dubbed taps*

ZORRO, THE GAY BLADE (1982) 20th Century–Fox
Produced by George Hamilton and C.O. Erickson; *Directed by* Peter Medak
George Hamilton, Lauren Hutton, Brenda Vacarro, Ron Leibman, Donovan Scott, James Booth, Helen Burns
Alex Romero: *choreographer*

CITY HEAT (1984) Warner Brothers
Produced by Fritz Manes; *Directed by* Richard Benjamin
Clint Eastwood, Burt Reynolds, Jane Alexander, Madeline Kahn, Rip Torn, Irene Cara, Richard Roundtree
Alex Romero: *choreographer*

THAT'S DANCING (1985) MGM
Produced by Jack Haley, Jr., David Niven, Jr., Gene Kelly and Bud Friedgen, *Written and Directed by* Jack Haley Jr.
Mikhail Baryshnikov, Ray Bolger, Sammy Davis, Jr., Gene Kelly, Liza Minnelli, Tommy Abbott, June Allyson, Ann-Margret, Fred Astaire, Lucille Ball
Alex Romero: *choreographer of new material*

Television Shows

THE EDDY FISHER SHOW (1957–1959) NBC
Produced by Gregory Ratoff
Eddie Fisher, George Gobel, Gisele MacKenzie, Mary Tyler Moore, Debbie Reynolds

A DATE WITH DEBBIE (1960) ABC
Produced and directed by Bill Colleran
Debbie Reynolds, Cannonball Adderley, Walter Brennan, Carleton Carpenter, Carl Reiner, Nelson Riddle, Charles Ruggles

ARTHUR GODFREY IN HOLLYWOOD (1962) CBS
Produced and directed by Perry Lafferty
Arthur Godfrey, Pat Buttram, June Foray, Jerry Hausner

WHO TIED THE CAN TO MODERN MAN (1962) CBS
Musical direction by Billy Liebert
Diana Hall, Dick Hoyt, Arte Johnson, Suzie Kaye, Jim Luize, Marilyn Mason, Bill Mullikan

SURFSIDE 6 (1962) ABC
Season two, episode 35: "A Private Eye for Beauty"
Produced by William T. Orr
Troy Donahue, Van Williams, Diane McBain, John Dehner, Scotty Morrow, Dawn Wells

OPENING NIGHT (1963) CBS
Preview of 1963–1964 Season
Choreographed by Alex Romero
Lucille Ball, Jack Benny, Garry Moore, Andy Griffith, Danny Thomas, Phil Silvers, Don Wilson.

MR. AND MRS. (LUCILLE BALL COMEDY HOUR SPECIAL) (1964)
Produced by Edward H. Feldman and Jess Oppenheimer; *Directed by* Jack Donohue
Lucille Ball, Bob Hope, Gale Gordon, John Banner, John Dehner, Rudy Dolan, Stanley Farrar

KRAFT MUSIC HALL — THE PERRY COMO SHOW (1964) NBC
Season six, episode two—from the State Fair Music Hall in Dallas, Texas

Television Shows

Produced by Marlo Lewis; *Directed by* Dwight Hemion, *Russ Tamblyn's number choreographed by* Alex Romero
Jimmy Durante, Dorothy Provine, Russ Tamblyn, The Texas Boys Choir

JACK AND THE BEANSTALK (1967) NBC
Produced by Joseph Barbera, William Hanna, Gene Kelly, Bill Perez and Arthur Pierson; *Directed by* Gene Kelly; *Choreographed by* Gene Kelly; *Assistant choreography by* Alex Romero (also appeared as Woggle Bird)
Gene Kelly, Bobby Riha, Ted Cassidy, Marian McKnight

PLEASE DON'T EAT THE DAISIES (1967) NBC
Season two, episode 20: "None So Righteous"
Produced by Robert Stambler and Paul West; *Directed by* Bruce Bilson (also appeared on screen as actor)
Pat Crowley, Mark Miller, Kim Tyler, Brian Nash, Jeff Fithian, Joe Fithian, Bobby Hatfield, Bill Medley

FANTASY ISLAND (1977–1984) ABC
Eighteen episodes choreographed by Alex Romero
Ricardo Montalban, Herve Villechaize

F. SCOTT FITZGERALD IN HOLLYWOOD
movie of the week (1977) ABC
Produced by Robert Berger; *Directed by* Anthony Page
Jason Miller, Tuesday Weld, Julia Foster

AN AMERICAN IN PASADENA (1978) CBS
Produced by Buz Kohan; *Directed by* Marty Pasetta; *Choreographed by* Gene Kelly; *Assistant Choreography by* Alex Romero
Gene Kelly, Lucille Ball, Cyd Charisse, Gloria DeHaven, Betty Garrett, Kathryn Grayson, Bridget Kelly, Janet Leigh, Liza Minnelli, Alex Romero (tap dancer), Frank Sinatra, Cindy Williams

MARILYN, THE UNTOLD STORY (1980)
Produced by Lawrence Schiller; *Directed by* Jack Arnold, John Flynn and Lawrence Schiller
Catherine Hicks, Richard Basehart, Frank Converse, John Ireland, Viveca Lindfors, Jason Miller, Sheree North

HEIDI'S SONG (1982) Paramount
Produced by Joseph Barbera, William Hanna and Iwao Takamoto; *Directed by* Robert Taylor
Voices: Lorne Greene, Sammy Davis, Jr., Margery Gray, Michael Bell, Peter Cullen, Roger DeWitt, Richard Erdman

T.J. HOOKER (1982–1986) ABC (4 seasons), CBS (1 season)
Assorted episodes choreographed by Alex Romero
William Shatner, Heather Locklear, Adrian Zmed

Television Shows

REMINGTON STEELE (1982–1987) NBC
Assorted episodes choreographed by Alex Romero
Stephanie Zimbalist, Pierce Brosnan, Doris Roberts

THE THORNBIRDS (1983) ABC
Show Two
Produced by Irving Paul Lazar, Edward Lewis, Stan Margulies and David L. Wolper; *Directed by* Daryl Duke
Richard Chamberlain, Rachel Ward, Christopher Plummer, Bryan Brown, Brett Cullen, Stephanie Faracy, Barry Corbin

HART TO HART (1979–1984) ABC
Two episodes choreographed by Alex Romero
Produced by Aaron Spelling and Leonard Goldberg
Robert Wagner, Stefanie Powers, Lionel Stander

THE TRACY ULLMAN SHOW (1987–1990) Fox
Produced by Jerry Belsen, James L. Brooks, Ken Estin, Heide Perlman and Sam Simon; *Directed by* Ted Bessell, Art Wolff and Paul Flaherty; *One episode choreographed by* Alex Romero
Tracy Ullman, Dan Castellaneta, Julie Kavner, Sam McMurray, Joseph Malone

The Theater

FANCHON AND MARCO (1930–1933) Family Vaudeville act touring several cites in the U.S.
Dancer

THE CALIFORNIANS aka THE TWO CALIFORNIANS (1933–1939) Vaudeville act with brother John touring in Europe
Dancer-straight man

JACK COLE'S ACT (1947–1948) Assorted cities in the U.S.
Dancer

PLEASUREDOME (1955) closed out of town in Washington, DC, during previews
Choreographer

JOYRIDE (1956) Huntington Hartford Theater, Los Angeles
Original choreographer (replaced by Nick Castle)

HAPPY HUNTING (1956) Majestic Theatre, Broadway, New York
Original Choreographer with additional staging by Bob Herget

THE THALIANS BENEFIT SHOWS (1958–1975)
Choreographer

SHARE BENEFIT SHOWS (1950s and 1960s)
Choreographer

THE ACADEMY AWARDS (1950s and 1960s)
Choreographer or assistant choreographer on five shows (unable to confirm)

MACY'S THANKSGIVING DAY PARADE (1960)
Choreographer

14TH ANNUAL SCREENWRITERS GUILD AWARDS (1962)
Choreographer

LAS VEGAS ACTS (late 1940s through the 1960s)
Choreographer—Bobby Short at the Hacienda, Howard Keel and Kathryn Grayson at the Stardust, Sammy Lewis at the Riviera, Manuela at the Casino de Paris, and

The Theater

Debbie Reynolds (warm-up), Jane Powell, Huntz Hall, and Paula Lane.
Created the dance "The Goulash" used by Lionel Hampton at the Thunderbird.
Assistant choreographer to Bob Alton for Andy Williams at El Rancho (1947)
Assistant choreographer to Nick Castle for Van Johnson at the Sands (1953) (eventually took over as choreographer)

TAKE ME ALONG (1974) (summer stock season with Gene Kelly) Dallas and assorted cities in Ohio
Featured dancer, played a drunk

GENE KELLY ACT (1978)
Resorts International Hotel and Casino in Atlantic City
Specialty dancer

PROFESSIONAL DANCERS SOCIETY SHOWS (1970s and 1980s)
Choreographer

Chapter Notes

Chapter 1

1. "General don Miguel Quiroga Cantu was born in Monterrey, Mexico, on September 29, 1871. He attended the *Colegio Seminario Conciliar de Monterrey* (Seminary of Monterrey) where he excelled in his studies and demonstrated a great aptitude in sports. After graduating, he became a successful businessman. He owned several pieces of real estate in Monterrey including the Independence Theatre, the American Hotel, and a bank that was dedicated to the promotion of agriculture, arranging loans for the Mexican proletariat to buy real estate. During various interviews, Alex said his father also owned the opera house and the post office in Monterrey. A prominent member of Monterrey society, Quiroga was a member of the prestigious International Club within the city. Also active in San Antonio, Texas, he was a partner with his friend, druggist Francisco A. Chapa, in the Garza Mercantile Company, and one of the proprietors of a newspaper called *El Imparcial de Texas*. Considered the most influential Spanish-language newspaper in the state of Texas, it catered to Mexican intellectual exiles. His other business holdings in the U.S. included the Librería de Quiroga, a publishing house that specialized in printing light reading and romance novels for housewives. He had a home at 817 San Pedro Avenue in San Antonio, Texas, as well as Casa de Quiroga, a huge mansion in Monterrey. Alex once said that his parents were "rich as heck," one of the wealthiest families in Mexico.

While he was a first reservist in the North Mexican Republic army, Miguel Quiroga developed a close friendship with General Bernardo Reyes, acting as his campaign manager when Reyes was running for the presidency. He also supported Reyes in his attempt to overthrow President Madero. In October of 1911, General Reyes set up headquarters in Quiroga's San Antonio mansion to plan his attack on Mexico through the town of Laredo.

According to *The San Antonio Light*, San Antonio, TX, December 5, 1911, p.1:

[M]uch excitement had been aroused by the rumor that Gen. Bernardo Reyes and his two secretaries, David Reyes Retana and Miguel Quiroga, had left the city last night, presumably for the border. In particular did Maderista secret service agents grow busy, it being the determination, as stated, to prevent him from crossing into Mexico.

Two days later, the same paper included the following mention:

A broken-down automobile identified by officials there as Miguel Quiroga's, the one in which General Reyes always rode while he was in San Antonio and in which he was last seen here, forms the nucleus around which the bits of evidence have been gathered. Dispatches from Mexico state that General Reyes and party are headed for Gaicana (?), Nuevo Leon, his former stronghold. The car at Karnes City, bearing the initials "M.Q.," is reported to have reached there at 9:30 Monday night with two passengers—a large middle-aged man and a young man of slight build.

When Reyes was imprisoned in 1911 for his coup, Quiroga fled into exile in Canada where he stayed until Pascual Orozco was made general and called for the removal of Madero. Quiroga returned to Mexico and was given the title of Private Secretary to Orozco. In February 1913, Quiroga was in Mexico City as part of the *Decena Tragica* ("Ten Days of Tragedy") in which the military coup against Madero erupted into horrible violence in the capital city. When Victoriano Huerta turned against Madero and eventually established his interim gov-

Notes—Chapter 1

ernment, Quiroga was ordered to organize a force of 1000 irregulars in Monterrey, Nuevo Leon, and on April 9, 1913, was commissioned as brigadier general. His men were known as the *Brigada Quiroga*, and had many successful campaigns against the rebel bandit forces that threatened the northern areas of Mexico.

El Imparcial de Texas, Book IV, October 30, 1913, p. 4, the newspaper of which Quiroga was part owner, presented the following tribute after the general's death:

[T]he man, the hero called to glory, necessary for the salvation of the Country and of society, and the proof of civilization, rose up and Death claimed him — the powerful General don Miguel Quiroga. General Quiroga was a loving father and a caring husband at home — a man respected by society and admired for all of his cultural gifts— a sober worker, moved by an extraordinary love, inspiring his Country, his family and society — a man who never stopped to think about the dangers threatening society but only thought of the future, knowing that his nation was waiting for him. He was serenely resolved and with extreme valor, he guided the troops under his command, encountering the infamous traitors without fear. With firm character and singular bravery, he stoically confronted the rebels, despite the lack of numbers in his force, showing them that the true beauty of fighting for one's country lay in preventing it from being stained with blood by the impious mercenaries who tormented it without reason. The fight had been started with fierce rudeness and the sides were not equally balanced. Machine guns, cannons and bayonets were used in the struggle between both sides. But not even the roar of the cannons nor the sound of rifle shots could deter the sacred fighting spirit of General Quiroga, who did not stop encouraging his valiant soldiers fighting at the front of the battle, until he was mortally wounded by an enemy bullet.

(The above is a translation done by Maria Santana from the original Spanish.)

2. Soledad Chapa Quiroga was born around 1871. She was also called Choli or Chole. Her children and grandchildren called her Mamacita. The family knows that she had at least one brother, Pedro. Soledad was 5'5." She died in the 1950s in Los Angeles.

3. Once when relating his history, Alex Romero stated that in addition to all the public rooms such as ballrooms, receiving rooms, sitting rooms, and such, the palace, known as Casa de Quiroga, was so large that it had a private bedroom for each of the 23 children. In addition, each child had a personal nanny or governess, each of whom also had a private room. Because of the large number of children, many of the boys would have outgrown the need for a governess by the time the younger sons needed one. In any case, the palace was certainly one of the biggest homes in Monterrey at the time. Alex also told me that his father and mother had several vacation homes in other Mexican cities, and often traveled to the seashore and hosted parties there.

According to *The San Antonio Light*, San Antonio, TX, November 10, 1913, p.2,

General Miguel Quiroga, whose residence was one of the finest in northern Mexico, was burned to death when Constitutionalists destroyed the house by fire.

This is the only mention I could find of Miguel Quiroga burning to death.

4. Alex mentioned that his mother told him that his father was actually being groomed to become president himself at some time in the future.

5. Alex and the members of his family always insisted that General Quiroga was shot during an ambush as he was preparing to ride out to meet the forces of Carranza. *El Imparcial de Texas*, Book IV, October 30, 1913, p. 8, stated the following:

On the 23rd of this month, from 10 in the morning until one in the afternoon of the same day, the brave troops of General don Miguel Quiroga, with their chief leading them, fought against the two cannons and various machine guns of the Carrancistas, without ceasing, defending against the attack of the rebels. General Quiroga, who fought with ardor against the rebels, was killed moments before the arrival of Generals Ocaranza, Pena and Amaya.

(Translated from the original in Spanish by Maria Santana.)

In *La Prensa*, October 30, 1913, p. 1, there was the following account of the battle:

Thursday the 23rd of the present month, a large group of revolutionary soldiers, composed of about 6000 men, transporting a regular number of cannons and machine guns, and under the orders of Jesus Carranza and Pablo Gonzalez, began a vigorous attack on the city of Monterrey, fighting against the federal garrison of about 3000 men that fought in the city's defense. The

Notes — Chapter 1

rebels quickly achieved general success in penetrating certain areas of the city, only to be ejected later by the federal forces, who after three days of bloody battles, completely deterred the assailants, so that they were obligated to flee, convinced of the uselessness of trying to capture Monterrey, and at the same time subjecting them to sharpshooters' fire, causing at every moment, great ruin among the undisciplined rebel forces.

The federal forces also extracted a heavy price during the escape of the assailants, sending a powerful column of men to persecute them and to follow closely in pursuit, finishing the defeat that they had suffered in Monterrey.

On Saturday night, a message was received by the Mexican Consulate, recounting the death of Brigadier don Miguel Quiroga, a well-known person in this city, and who was one of the principal members of the Reyista Revolution, occupying the distinguished post of secretary to the late General don Bernardo Reyes.

Brigadier Quiroga took an active part in the defense of Monterrey, heading the troops that he had also organized and which carried his name, staying in the most dangerous sites of the battle during the final attack until bad luck touched him, and he paid with his life — a life of valor and activity which was so obviously displayed during this fight in defense of the actual government, and one that he had served loyally since the fall of the Madero Administration. (Translated from the original in Spanish by Maria Santana.)

Both of these accounts conflict with the family story and suggest that Quiroga was killed in battle after fighting for at least three hours. Alex's brother Carlos was there at the time of the attack and consistently said that his father was killed by a single bullet while preparing to ride out to meet the rebel forces. I did find a note I had made during one interview with Alex when he told me that his father had stuffed a handkerchief in the bullet hole and lived for three days before dying. This was the only time I remember Alex mentioning that.

6. Alex told me that his father's body was hidden in a cistern to prevent it from being beheaded by rebel troops, but never told me what happened to it. In a newspaper account of the battle of Monterrey, in *La Prensa*, October 30, 1913, p. 1, it states, "[Quiroga's] body was buried last Saturday without the corresponding military honors." That would suggest that Alex's father was buried on October 25, two days after the battle.

7. Alex said that some of his older brothers were sent to military academies in the United States and Europe to prepare them to follow in their father's footsteps and become officers in the Mexican army. The family has pictures of unidentified male siblings of Alex's posing stiffly in cadet uniforms. The oldest brother Miguel attended the Western Military Academy in Alton, Illinois. Founded by Edward Wyman in 1879, it was initially known as the Wyman Institute. The cadets followed a rigorous schedule that included military classes and training, and sports. They were required to march to and from classes and other activities and were not allowed to speak any language except English, even if they were from a foreign country. The school closed in 1971.

8. In *Masters of Movement* by Rose Eichenbaum, p. 165, Alex states, "My mother birthed twenty-three sons and one daughter." This is consistent with what he always told me — that he was one of 24 children. Alex's older brother Carlos stated in two interviews that there were 22 brothers and 2 sisters. Carlos' wife Malvina told Alex's daughter Melinda that some of the births were miscarriages and therefore there were never really that many living children born. Sydney, John's wife, told Alex that there had been three sets of twins born to the Quirogas. In a letter I received from John Romero Jr., he stated that his grandmother "had 22 children, including three sets of twins, but many died by miscarriage, at birth or early in life. Apparently only nine children (eight brothers, one sister) grew into adulthood." Those nine would be Miguel (the son), Alfonso, Humberto, Carlos, John, Oscar, Judith, Mario, and Alex. Alex stated in an interview with Rose Eichenbaum for her book *Masters of Movement*, p. 165, that 13 of his brothers were killed in the Battle of Monterrey. If 13 were killed in Monterrey, and 8 boys, including Alex, survived, that adds up to 21 sons. With Judith, that would make 22 children total as John Romero, Jr. stated in his letter to me. If Carlos or Alex were correct about the total, one or two children are unaccounted for.

9. Alex was christened Alejandro Bernardo Quiroga. He was given his middle name in honor of General Bernardo Reyes, who had

Notes — Chapter 1

been a close family friend and was Alex's godfather. One of Reyes' sons was also named Alejandro. Alex's birth certificate, written in Spanish, stated that he was born in the city of San Antonio on August 19, 1913, but his mother told him that since he was born at two o'clock in the morning, his birthday was actually on the 20th of the month, and that is the day he always celebrated as his birthday. He was baptized on January 20, 1914, in the Cathedral of San Fernando in San Antonio. Alex never questioned his birth date but there is a mystery. If Soledad Quiroga was three months pregnant at the time of his father's death and his father was killed near the end of October 1913, how is it possible for Alex to have been born prior to October in August of the same year? If Alex was born in August of 1914, that would mean Soledad Quiroga was pregnant for 13 months. Either scenario is impossible. There is perhaps no way to completely unravel this mystery, although Alex himself remembers hearing his mother telling him that "things would be easier if Alex was born in America." There is a strong possibility that Alex's birth date is correct — August 19 or 20, 1913 — but that he was actually born in Mexico, before his father was killed, and not in San Antonio afterwards. Alex would have been about two months old when his mother fled Monterrey. There is a strong likelihood that Alex's birth was registered in San Antonio to make U.S. citizenship easier. In an July 4, 2004, interview with Alex's daughters Melinda and Judy, they revealed that Judy's husband, Richard George, had found in his research into the family history a document that listed Alex's birth year as 1912, not 1913 as on his official birth certificate. (I was not able to find that document.)

There is little doubt that Miguel Quiroga was actually Alex's father, if family resemblance is proof. Alex not only looked like his father, but also closely resembled his brothers who survived the attack. When I was discussing with Alex's daughters the mysteries surrounding his birth, his daughter Judy said jokingly, "Maybe he was Hitler's illegitimate son!"

10. Alex's older brother Carlos, who later became a successful choreographer in his own right, did an interview in a local paper (date and paper unknown, probably some time in the 1930s) and gave a slightly different account of the events of the family's escape:

Then in the year of 1913 came the revolution and with it the name of Villa, the Bandit. My father, who was brigadier general in the Mexican army as well as a merchant of solid financial standing, was naturally hated and despised by Villa — so much so that he was assassinated by one of Villa's men. The fatal shot was fired from the second story window directly across from our house, as my father, sitting erect and proud on his horse, was leading his men off to battle. Following various threats to destroy all property owned by my family and after one terrifying night spent in the dark silence of our own theater in Monterrey, which Villa had promised to blow to bits, my mother decided to leave Mexico forever. So with my brothers and sisters, we made our way to the border and proceeded on to San Antonio, Texas.

Another undated article states:

Carlos saw his father, Brigadier General Quiroga, fall from his horse, victim of an assassin's bullet in 1913, while the son was still a small boy. He saw Huerta's soldiers with shots of victory pilfer and take possession of their great white home which housed a family of 22 boys and two girls under parental control. Proud, handsome Señora Quiroga hid her vast brood among friends in Mexico City, two girls in one place, three boys in another, and abided her time to escape her enemies. Her jewelry, fine filigreed silver, delicately spun threads of gold, fire opals of elegant texture, diamonds that were in their possession since the time of [sic] Andres de Concha arrived to paint the high altar of Santa Domingo church in Yanhuitlan, Oaxaca — one by one the senora disposed of them in order that her 24 children might be educated.

Carlos was 11 years old at the time of the attack of Monterrey and therefore would have remembered the events himself. His account of his mother's departure from Mexico up to San Antonio also explains why there were a few valuables passed down through the family, such as crystal, china, and some furniture. In addition, General Quiroga had strong ties to the elite in San Antonio, where he owned a home and other property. Soledad Quiroga's family was also from the area and would in all likelihood have helped the refugees when they arrived in the city. Alex's daughter Melinda remembered hearing that her family had a richly furnished home in San Antonio and that they survived by selling off the possessions in the house one by one in order to live. Carlos Jr. had a full silver service that belonged to the family that he had inherited

Notes — Chapter 2

and there were also pieces of fine crystal that survived and were handed down.

11. Alex's mother told him she remembered one time when the train that she and Norma were riding on stopped and the revolutionaries engaged in a fight while the women hid under the train cars.

12. *Los Angeles Times*, September 18, 2007, Sec. B, p.9, col. 1. Alex Romero's obituary. Quote by dance historian and author Larry Billman.

Chapter 2

1. Alex mentioned in one interview that his mother had only been able to take a few of her jewels with her when she escaped during the attack of Monterrey; after she sold them to support her children, she was forced to work herself. One wonders why, if Alex's father had extensive holdings in San Antonio, and his mother had relatives there, Soledad and her children were living in a mud hut. The mystery is compounded by the fact that pieces of silver and crystal, and even some furniture that had been owned by their father, were passed down to Carlos and John. When Carlos was older and would visit his niece Judy and her husband Dick, he'd bring little mementoes from the Quiroga family past, such as crystal knife rests, and a mantilla of Mamacita's that was made of black lace, covered with roses and encrusted with sequins. Judy remembered thinking, "How strange that he's got all of this." The older daughter Melinda explained, "According to stories I have heard, Mamacita was a very selfish woman. She may have just hung on to these things out of pride." Carlos and his wife Malvina sold most of the Quiroga silver and crystal when they ran into financial trouble later in life, so very few artifacts are currently owned by Miguel Quiroga's descendants.

2. Alex's daughter Melinda told me that her father's memories of playing with the chicken bones were from when the family lived in Los Angeles, not in San Antonio in a mud hut as Alex suggested. When Soledad and her children first came to Los Angeles, they struggled financially. Alex's daughter Judy said, "[Mamacita] was living in LA in squalor." Alex mentioned being poor several times during many interviews. In Rose Eichenbaum's book *Masters of Movement*, p. 165, he said that after the family moved to Los Angeles, they lived "in a poor Mexican neighborhood... We were so poor I didn't own a pair of shoes until I was twelve years old."

3. In one interview Alex said the mud hut was 12 feet by 12 feet, but in a second, that it was 16 by 16. In the second interview he added that the hut belonged to relatives of the maid Norma. According to Alex, Norma lived apart from the family in a separate hut until she married and her husband took her to his own home in San Antonio. Alex remembered that she cried and cried the day she had to move away from the family and that she "hung around me all the time."

4. The story about Carlos deciding to form an act was told to me several times by Alex. After Alex's death, I received an article from Carlos' daughter-in-law Alix Bainbridge; written by drama editor Virginia Wright and called *cine matters* (date unknown), it states: Wealthy Mexican families in San Antonio lent aid to the Romeros, and it was at one of their functions that Carlos Romero was first asked to dance. He had never danced before, but a partner was needed for one of the young ladies, and he was selected. She taught him to use the castanets, and their Spanish number was such a success, that the boy decided there might be something in this dancing business after all.

5. *The Mission Play* was a 4 and one-half hour spectacle that told the story of the founding of California. It was first produced in 1912, and was presented at the San Gabriel Mission. The beautiful San Gabriel Mission Playhouse, dedicated in 1927, was built to house the production and is still in use today.

6. Ginette Vallon also performed with Carlos on the Fanchon and Marco Circuit and partnered him in Chaplin's film *A Woman of Paris*. The two were known for their Latin tangos and Apache dances.

7. I do not know if this family legend is true or not, but I did find that Soledad Quiroga crossed the border from Mexico into the United States at Laredo in March of 1921. This is perhaps when she was returning from this trip to Mexico.

8. According to Alex, Norma lived with his family in San Antonio until she married and her husband made her move out of the house. He also said that when his family moved to Los Angeles, Norma made a trip there to help his mother for a while. When Norma returned to San Antonio, Alex said he cried for three days. He was very fond of Norma, who treated him like a son. He remembered playing catch with her as a little boy.

Notes—Chapter 2

9. Humberto also eventually came to Los Angeles although I was unable to confirm that he lived with the family in the house that Carlos rented. Alfonso returned to Mexico, only visiting Los Angeles from time to time.

It is next to impossible to find a complete list of Miguel Quiroga's children, particularly in light of the fact that birth records were destroyed in the Revolution in Mexico. Alex's family had a few family records and photographs, but the various children in the pictures were not all identified. In addition to Carlos, John, Oscar, and Mario, Alex did remember two other older brothers, Alfonso and Humberto. I also found written references to an older son, Miguel, who was named after his father. The children that I can confirm are:

a. Miguel Quiroga

Alton Evening Telegraph, Alton, IL, September 24, 1906, p. 1, stated:

The party from Mexico consisting of Miguel Quiroga and son, Miguel, Alberta Ostos, Jr., Jose Quiroga and Alejandro Reyes, arrived at 10 o'clock and went to the military academy.

Both General Quiroga and his superior Bernardo Reyes sent their sons to the Western Military Academy in Illinois. As part of their training, the boys were required to learn English at once, and were penalized for speaking any Spanish, even socially with each other. Jose Quiroga, also mentioned in the clipping above, was the general's brother. He was a lawyer and defended his brother in court when Miguel was charged with violating the neutrality laws. He was also the owner of the San Antonio newspapers *El Nacional* and *La Epoca*. He died at age 37 on April 8, 1925. General Quiroga also had three sisters that I was able to find: Concepcion Vida de Chapa, Isabel Perez, and Maria de Salinas.

Later in life Miguel Quiroga, the son, was mentioned in the *Laredo Times*, Laredo, TX, March 25, 1917, p. 8:

Miguel Quiroga, son of General Miguel Quiroga and one of the most prominent young business men of Monterey [sic], has arrived in Laredo to act as the local representative of the Marconi Wireless Stock Co.

This item indicates that Miguel did survive the Revolution.

b. Alfonso Quiroga

Alex spoke fondly of Alfonso and somewhat idolized him, calling him the brightest of the brothers. Family lore does include a story of Alfonso hiding out during part of the Revolution in the United States and visiting the family in California. He told them that he could never live permanently in the U.S. since he had to sneak his gun into the country, and he could never live in a place where he was not allowed to carry his gun. (After Alex's death, some family members maintained that this was said by Humberto, not Alfonso. Alex told me it was Alfonso.) Alfonso was a bullfighter in Mexico and there are several old family photos of him performing in the ring. He was also involved in the aviation business, flying a biplane. According to Alex, he was a very wealthy man. Alex suggested that he was actually one of the founders of Compañía Mexicana de Aviación, Mexico's oldest airline. As a little boy Alex used to dream of being a pilot when he grew up. Alfonso heard of this and, on one visit to Los Angeles, he paid five dollars for someone to take Alex up in a biplane. Alex remembered the plane had two cockpits and he was put in the front. He was so small he couldn't see when he sat down, so he did the whole flight standing up. Upon landing, Alfonso ran out to meet him and asked if Alex had liked the flight. When he said yes, Alfonso paid another five dollars to have Alex go up a second time. I saw an article from the family archives taken from the *San Jose Mercury Herald* dated October 4, 1928, that had a picture of Carlos and Judith posing with the city's postmaster. It said that Judith was sending the first airmail letter to be delivered to Mexico City from San Jose. The letter was to her brother Alfonso. Alfonso died of tuberculosis in Mexico, date unknown. There was a writer by the name of Alfonso Quiroga who wrote the first Mexican mystery, *Vila y milagros de Pancho Reyes, detective Mexicano*, but I do not know if it is the same Alfonso Quiroga.

c. Humberto (also Hombert or Humbert) Quiroga

I found some immigration documents that list Humberto as living at a Los Angeles address, although Alex never mentioned him as living with the family for any length of time. Alex did say that Humberto owned a gas station and car

Notes — Chapter 2

wash in the US. Humberto bought a Jitney Ford flat bed and put about six benches on it and started a taxi service. He called it Jitney Services. Humberto died some time in the late 1920s, probably around 1928, of a drug overdose. I found an old photograph of a young Mexican girl by the name of Olga, inscribed to Alex and dated 1930, and recorded as "your niece." Alex said that Olga was the illegitimate daughter of Humberto and the maid Norma.

d. Jeronimo (Jerome) Quiroga aka Carlos Quiroga, Carlos Romero

Carlos was born on August 10, 1902, in Monterrey, Mexico, and died in September 1969 at the Norumbega Sanitorium in Monrovia, California, of tuberculosis at age 67. I found a reference that stated that a Jerome Quiroga, age 11, crossed the border from Mexico to the United States at Laredo, Texas, on December 3, 1913. This indicates that Carlos (Jerome) joined his mother and sister in San Antonio about one month after the siege of Monterrey.

Carlos had a very successful career as a performer and also as a dance director. He choreographed such films as *Hollywood Party in Technicolor* (1937), *Thrill of a Lifetime* (1937), *He's My Guy* (1943), *Hi Buddy* (1943), *Hi Ya Chum* (1943), *Hi Ya Sailor* (1943), *Larceny with Music* (1943), *Never a Dull Moment* (1943), *Sing a Jingle* (1943), *Wintertime* (1943), *Bowery to Broadway* (1944), *Hat Check Honey* (1944), *The Merry Monahans* (1944), *Murder in the Blue Room* (1944), *Take It Big* (1944), *Men in Her Diary* (1945), *Song of the Sarong* (1945), and *That's the Spirit* (1945), among others. He also staged many Fanchon and Marco revues, several editions of Shipstad and Johnson's "Ice Follies," "Roller Skating Vanities," and the "Pan Pacific Aquacade." He served as the choreographer at the Roxy Theatre in New York for five years, the Fox Theatre in Brooklyn for two years, and the Paramount Theatres in Brooklyn and Los Angeles for seven and a half years. He also staged several Las Vegas shows, including Mae West's act. At the height of his financial success, Carlos and his wife Malvina owned three homes, but as work lessened he struggled to make ends meet. As an avid gardener, he began to sell flowers that he had grown himself.

e. Juan Quiroga aka John Quiroga, John Romero, Johnny Romero

John was born January 16, 1901 (his son said he was born in 1903), and died on March 14, 1990 (his son said he died in 1989), of pneumonia. There is a listing for a border crossing on December 2, 1913, for Juan Quiroga, age 10, which also indicates he came to join his family shortly after the siege of Monterrey.

John performed for many years with his brothers and also as a solo act. He was known for his great comic timing and his stage combat skills. He was also an accomplished juggler. As part of his solo act he mimed eating a peanut butter sandwich. He was billed in various shows as "The Juggling Jester," "The Mexican Pantomime," and "the man who does everything." Alex remembered hearing him say, "These gringos don't like us so I'm going to defend us and become a fighter." John did eventually become a professional boxer.

The Salt Lake Tribune, April 1, 1949, p. 25, states:

Johnny Romero, versatile comedian, formerly appeared at Chicago's Palmer House with Hildegarde. His name is well known at the Sherman hotel of that city, at the Last Frontier in Las Vegas, in New York and San Francisco, as well as leading entertainment spots in Europe. He has headlined at Monte Carlo, and his last appearance in motion pictures was in the Cisco Kid series. He comes from the famous Romero family troupe, which played the Orpheum Circuit for three years and was booked 10 years straight in Europe.

In his later years John went into the real estate business, and when he retired, became an avid golfer. Alex said that John kept a bottle of whiskey in his golf bag. Alex also mentioned that the first time he played golf with his brother John, Alex hit a hole in one.

f. Oscar Quiroga aka Oscar Romero

Oscar was born March 26, 1908, in Monterrey. According to Alex, Oscar became a heavy drinker and quite a ladies' man. Often he nearly missed trains when traveling with his brothers in the act because he was still with the woman he had picked up in that town. When he left the vaudeville act in Paris in the mid–1930s, he remained there during World War II,

167

Notes—Chapter 2

serving in the French underground. He contracted tuberculosis and, after the war, he traveled to Los Angeles to see his mother before he died. Oscar died from tuberculosis on May 23, 1947, in Los Angeles at City of Hope.

g. Judith Quiroga aka Judith (Judy) Romero
Judith was born around 1911 in Mexico, and died circa 1929 in Los Angeles. Alex said his sister died of tuberculosis and recalled vividly the day of her death when his mother went crazy with grief. John's wife Sydney once told him that Judith had died of a heart attack. Alex once told me that Judith was in love with cowboy film actor Hoot Gibson and that the two planned to marry. There is a photo in the family files autographed from someone named "Hoot," but I was unable to confirm whether or not it was Hoot Gibson.

h. Mario Quiroga
Mario was born around 1912 in Mexico. He died of tuberculosis some time in the early 1920s in Los Angeles at age ten or eleven. According to Alex, Mario was the darkest-skinned of all of the brothers and looked the most Mexican. He was often the brunt of prejudice because of this. He and Alex were very close and even as an old man Alex spoke fondly of his brother Mario.

10. Malvina Polo was a trained concert pianist as well as an actor and dancer. She came from a show business family. Her mother was film actress Alice Finch and her father was Eddie Polo, who was reputed to be Queen Mary's favorite movie star. He lost his career as a leading man in films with the advent of talking pictures. Eddie Polo was also a stunt man and acrobat and was the first man to parachute off the Eiffel Tower. After giving up performing, Malvina supported her husband Carlos between his choreography work by sewing sequins on costumes for the *Ice Follies*.

11. Eichenbaum, Rose. *Masters of Movement: Portraits of America's Great Choreographers*. Washington: Smithsonian Book, 2004, p. 165, quoting Alex Romero.

12. In 1925, Carlos was cast as one of three dancing boys performing behind the leads in the silent MGM film *The Merry Widow*. The first day of filming, he was told to just watch the number. After the two stars had finished their rehearsal, he was taught the routine. Carlos was a fast study and mastered his part easily, but during breaks continued to practice. The star of the picture, Mae Murray, was watching him and, after a while, snapped her fingers and called over the film's director. She pointed to the leading man she had been dancing with and said, "Fire that man." Then she pointed at Carlos and said, "I want to dance with him." Carlos became principal dancer on the film. Later, Murray also demanded that Carlos partner with her in an Apache dance for her next film, *The Masked Bride*. The two became good friends and Carlos was the steady dance partner of the silent film star. He also coached Murray for her solo dances. Carlos coached and trained many other film stars: Ramon Novarro, Vilma Banky, Nancy Carroll, Erik Rhodes, Alice White, Betty Grable, and more.

13. This particular quote by Alex was made during an interview recorded on July 20, 2004, at the Motion Picture Home in Woodland Hills, California. The interview was conducted by three students from Auckland University of Technology in New Zealand. The students, Aimee Harvey, Caroline Rattray, and Grace Crawford, interviewed Alex as part of their Senior Research Project for the Faculty of Health, Bachelor of Dance degree. The project supervisors were Dr. Alice Knappstein, Dora Krannig, and Jennifer Nikolai. The editing was done by Dr. Pasquale Moscatello.

14. Alex told me that he got no further than fourth grade. Although he was a well-informed, intelligent man, he was always embarrassed that he had not had more formal schooling. Whenever he wrote me a birthday or Christmas card, it usually included an apology for his spelling.

15. *Ogden Standard-Examiner* from June 10, 1928, p. 6.

16. "New Thrill Film With 'Artsists' [sic] Next at Capitol," *The Salt Lake Tribune*, Salt Lake City, UT, December 9, 1928, p. 58.

17. Sydney Marcene Allen met John in 1928 when she was 19 and they were both working in a show in Culver City, California. John and his brother Oscar were performing their staircase tap dancing routine and Sydney was one of a group of six dancing girls. The two married shortly afterward in Riverside, California, and Sydney joined the Romeros' vaudeville act, being billed as one of the sisters. In 1929, she gave birth to John S. Quiroga, Jr., also called John Romero, Jr. When John and Sydney toured Asia and

Europe in vaudeville, they left John Jr. with Sydney's parents in Fort Worth, Texas.

18. "Lively Program Hold[s] Capitol Theater Stage," *The Salt Lake Tribune*, Salt Lake City, UT, December 10, 1928, p. 9.

19. Alex said that if anyone had known that Judith had tuberculosis while she was touring in vaudeville "they would have been put in jail because it was so contagious."

20. Alex told me that this coach had a great bearing upon his life but could not remember the man's name.

Chapter 3

1. According to Alex, the nickname "Pup" was given to him by Carlos, who told him he looked like a puppy dog. The name stuck and all his brothers began to call him that.

2. *The Idea* "Venetian Nights Depicted on Stage in Gondoliers Setting." Published by Fanchon & Marco, LA: December 27, 1930, p. 1, Presented as Part II of The Last Word, Prepared by the F & M Publicity Staff, Vol. 4, No. 51.

3. In his interview for the Auckland University of Technology, Faculty of Health, Bachelor of Dance — Senior Research Project by Aimee Harvey, Caroline Rattray, and Grace Crawford (recorded on July 20, 2004), Alex was somewhat befuddled at times, but at one point launched into a story about his first performing job. It was a story that I had not heard before but he went into a bit of detail, and so I wondered if it was indeed true. Alex explained that his first performing job happened when he was only six years old.

> I started as an extra. You know what that is? It doesn't pay you nothing, but you've got to start somewhere. And then when I was an extra, a fellow noticed me, and I was a little kid then, see. I was about six years old.

Alex explained how as a little boy he came upon a group of American boys. "And here they were, and I can't speak their language, and I'm looking at them like that and now, all of a sudden I know what they say..." Alex said that he saw the kids rub their fingers together and he realized they were talking about money, so he followed them. The boys led him to a movie shoot where filming was going on with an old-fashioned crank camera. When they arrived, the director told the kids to "get outta there" because they were making too much noise. The kids ran away but Alex stayed. The director asked Alex, "Why don't you go with them?" Alex smiled and shrugged. The director smiled back and as filming continued he gestured to Alex to stay quiet.

Alex said that in the movie scene there was a fighter being watched by two young boys. The director looked at Alex, smiled, and said to him, "You know, I need one more guy. Why don't you go in there?" When he was relating the story, Alex laughed, "And you know I couldn't say anything in English." He said that he joined the scene and started talking gibberish and everyone laughed and the director said, "Hey that's great." Alex giggled at the memory and concluded the story by saying, "And that was my first time as an actor!"

4. *The Idea* "Venetian Nights Depicted on Stage in Gondoliers Setting" Published by Fanchon & Marco, LA: December 27, 1930, p. 1, Presented as Part II of The Last Word, Prepared by the F & M Publicity Staff, Vol. 4, No. 51.

5. *Ibid.*

6. Alex often slipped out between shows where his family was performing and went to nearby theaters to see various vaudeville acts. In one city Alex witnessed a demonstration of Bill Robinson's ability to run backwards when the famous tapper challenged the Princeton track team to a race. Robinson ran backwards as the runners from the university ran forwards. Bojangles beat them all.

7. Eichenbaum, Rose. *Masters of Movement: Portraits of America's Great Choreographers*. Washington: Smithsonian Book, 2004, pp. 165–66, quoting Alex Romero. King, King and King were considered one the top tap acts in the world, specializing in synchronized tapping. The brothers hailed from Philadelphia. Sometimes they dressed in convict outfits and chained themselves together. Their style of tap was close to the floor and utilized a lot of toe stands.

8. In an earlier interview Alex said that he forgot to put on his underclothes and that Oscar pulled down his pants on stage as a joke.

9. This quote and story about Alex falling through the stage came from John Romero, Jr., in a letter date October 4, 2001.

10. Alex's companions at the club were his best pals Ernie Kearney and Sam Gormley. Alex had met Kearney when he and his mother moved to Tujunga to care for Judith, and Kearney introduced him to Gormley. Gormley (Frances Driscoll's cousin) brought Faun along that night.

Notes—Chapter 3

11. An Irish girl, Frances Fleury Driscoll, known as Faun to her friends and called Faunie by Alex, was born October 7, 1915, and died April 28, 1997. Faun's father was Dennis O. Driscoll, who worked in the oil business. In the 1920s, he had invented a fishing appliance that was used in drilling operations, but sold the patent. Faun's father was often gone for a number of months on business, and due to marital problems, he and his wife lived separately. Faun's mother was Valentine F. Clarke from Pennsylvania, who kept the Driscolls' daughters with her in Covina, California. Faun had three sisters, Denise, Mary Kate (called Kate) and Edna, who was about three years older than Faun. Edna, an opera singer, died before she could fulfill her dreams of singing in New York. Her death was the result of an accident in which a car she was in was struck by a train. Miraculously she survived unharmed, except for a cut on her forehead. They cleansed the wound, but Edna got a bacterial infection and died as a result. Denise married and had two sons, Chuck and Phil, and Kate had three children, Bart, Butch, and Alix. Butch lived with Alex and Faun for a few years and Alix (sometimes known in the family as Little Alix) later married Alex's nephew, Carlos Romero, Jr. Alex and Faun were married for almost 62 years. After their children were born, they called each other Mudder and Dadder.

12. In one interview, Alex's daughter Melinda said with a laugh that she would never forget the name of her mother's first fiancé. She said, "I heard about Gordie Jenkins every time she was mad at Dad!"

13. John Romero, Jr., sent me information that his father and mother went to Asia and Europe in 1933. I assume that it was in the fall of that year since I found the following review of John in the US in August of 1933: "John Romero presents a novelty tap different from the usual run of dancers. He does an imitation of a colored boy, which brings many laughs. Romero formerly headed several Fanchon and Marco units." (From the *Ogden Standard-Examiner*, Ogden, Utah, August 10, 1933, p. 12.)

14. John Romero told his son that he joined Mussolini's Fascist Party during this period because it was easier to move around in the country if one belonged to the Party.

15. I was unable to determine the touring itinerary of the Romeros' European act. Alex did have his old passports, but they were too confusing to interpret. I do know that the act was in Holland, Germany, and Norway in 1936, Belgium, Italy, Hungary, Romania, Poland, and Germany in 1937, and Luxembourg, France, Germany, and Poland in 1938.

16. Alex told me that when he arrived in Norway his trunks were stolen. Later, after he married, he and Faun were at an outdoor bistro when he saw a young man wearing one of his double-breasted jackets. Alex remembered that the man was taller and fatter than Alex so the jacket wouldn't close. Alex approached the man, who ran away. Alex chased after him, shouting at Faun to stay at the restaurant. Alex eventually jumped on the running board of a passing taxi and caught up with the man. With gestures, he said to the man, "This tie is mine! This jacket is mine!" The man then started to go after Alex. Alex turned and easily outran the overweight man. When the man gave up chasing Alex, Alex turned and followed the man. This continued until Alex was able to get a detective's notice. When questioned, the man said that Alex was the thief. The detective then asked Alex how he could prove the clothes were his. Neither of the parties would relent and so the detective put both Alex and the man in his car to take them down to the station when the young man finally confessed he had stolen the clothes and thrown Alex's trunk in the river. The detective made the young man's parents replace the trunk, which they did. According to Alex, the replacement was even better than the original. When the matter was resolved, Alex invited the detective to come to see the act.

17. In a letter from Faun to her mother (written during her voyage to Europe to marry Alex). Faun talks about flirting with the male passengers on board the ocean liner, especially the handsome radio operator. When I asked Alex's daughter Melinda about this, she said that a lot of fellows liked Faun and that she was quite a flirt.

18. Alex's mother also traveled with them for a short while.

19. According to family stories, Oscar's Mexican citizenship and involvement in the theater world kept him hidden as part of the French resistance for a good part of the war. He escaped on foot from Paris when the Germans invaded the city and went to the mountains where he lived on black bread and water. He contracted tuberculosis there and his health deteriorated rapidly. After the war he came to the United States to see his mother before he died. Oscar was eventually awarded

a medal of honor for his service to the Free French Forces.

Chapter 4

1. Alex remembered the director LeRoy Prinz as short and husky. He talked about how he had heard that Prinz had a metal plate in his head, a result of being injured when he served as a flyer. At age 15, Prinz had run away from home and joined the French Foreign Legion. During World War I he served in the French Aviation Corps with the 94th Aero Squadron. Prinz was shot down 15 times during the War.

2. I have not been able to confirm which film marked Alex's debut. He remembered that the dance was only about 12 bars long; that Prinz was the dance director and that the audition was at Warner Brothers. Some possibilities are *The Hard Way* (1943), *Mission to Moscow* (1943), and *The Desert Song* (1943).

3. I have not been able to identify the Universal movie in which he did the air tours. He remembered that the choreographer was Lester Horton, but could not remember the name of the movie. Some possibilities are *White Savage* (1943), *Gypsy Wildcat* (1944), and *The Climax* (1944).

4. Alexander Goudavich (also spelled Goudovich, or Goudevitch), whom everyone called Sasha, became a great friend of Alex's. He was born of aristocratic Russian parents in Monte Carlo. He was trained in ballet in France and became a member of the Ballet Russe. Later Alex and Sasha worked together again as specialty dancers in *Texas Carnival*. Alex also hired Sasha to be one of the dancers in the "Jailhouse Rock" number.

5. MGM's Gene Kelly was loaned out to Universal for a non-musical role in a film called *Christmas Holiday* with Deanna Durbin. This was the film he was shooting when he met Alex for the first time. Kelly had completed *Cover Girl* before coming to Universal and a sneak preview of *Cover Girl* premiered in Pasadena while he was still working on *Christmas Holiday*.

Chapter 5

1. The Ziegfeld Follies was also known as *Ziegfeld Follies of 1946*. The costly and elaborate film began production in 1944 and was not released until two years later.

2. Alex bought it from an old lady who kept the car up on blocks. The car had a wooden bottom, and a top lined in silk. The tires were good, but the right door wouldn't work and was wired shut. He used the car to go to the studios for auditions and work.

3. After Alex passed the audition and was hired by Cole, he worked with Rod Alexander and Charles Lunard, the two boys he had taken to the audition. He asked them again and again if it had been a coincidence or if they knew what the actual Cole audition combination would be. They never told him.

4. In his book *Unsung Genius: The Passion of Dancer-Choreographer Jack Cole* (New York: Franklin Watts, 1984, p. 133), Glenn Loney states that the three new men chosen at the audition were Rod Alexander, Alex, and Bob Hamilton. Alex insisted that it was not Bob Hamilton, but Charles Lunard. Alexander and Lunard were both in *The Ziegfeld Follies* and Hamilton was not. This seems to confirm Alex's story about driving the dancers to the audition and then all three having to put off working with Cole for a week because of their commitments at MGM. Before this audition for Cole's troupe at Columbia, other dancers had already been hired by Cole such as George and Ethel Martin and Francine Ames.

5. Alex was then making $62.75 a week before taxes at MGM. When I asked Alex to give me a short quote about what it was like working for Cole, he responded with a chuckle, "The money was great," before he launched into his praises of the man.

6. According to an article in the *Los Angeles Times* entitled "Jack Cole made Marilyn Monroe move" (August 9, 2009, p. 4), "For four years, Cole ran a resident dance group at Columbia, where innumerable dancers ruined their knees perfecting the master's diabolical floor slides." Alex said that because Cole hated blood so much, he eventually had his dancers wear kneepads, but only when they started rehearsing to go on the road with the act. They were also allowed to use them on the road.

7. Loney, Glenn. *Unsung Genius: The Passion of Dancer-Choreographer Jack Cole.* New York: Franklin Watts, 1984, p. 133.

In an article in *Dance Magazine* entitled "All That's Jazz — The Art of Jazz Dance" (August 1999), Bob Boross wrote:
From 1944 to 1948, as a choreographer at Columbia Pictures in Hollywood, Cole was permitted to train a group of dancers under contract for studio film assignments. Some of those dancers in his daily classes were

Notes—Chapter 5

Gwen Verdon, Carol Haney, George and Ethel Martin, and Bob [sic] Alexander. It was, in effect, a Jack Cole dance company, with technical training that included classes in Cecchetti ballet; Humphrey-Weidman modern dance; gymnastics; and East Indian, Cuban, and flamenco ethnic forms. Although there has never been a codification of this technique, his extraordinary standard became synonymous with the highest level of modern jazz dance training. During the 2004 interview Alex gave for the three students from Auckland University of Technology, he explained that Cole's approach to jazz dance was totally new: "It took us about a half a year just to learn what he was doing."

8. Loney, p. 133. Alex also talked about Cole doing this.

9. Alex recalled, "During all my years there, I think we had tap shoes on once ... for a number that Nick Castle came and did for him because [Cole] wasn't a tap dancer. And we did 'Sing, Sing, Sing' with tennis shoes on. Otherwise, all the other numbers were barefooted.

Cole also asked his dancers to take class in the nude at one point. The women of the company refused, but the men did rehearse naked, until the head office at Columbia found out about it and demanded that Cole stop the practice. Cole then designed outfits for the men consisting of tiny shorts. He forbade them to wear dance belts or other undergarments for support, telling them that it prevented them from strengthening the loins.

In the Jack Cole Collection of his papers at UCLA (J.C. Box 4 Folder 4) there is a reference to this in one of the interviews:

The women would not dance nude in Jack's Columbia classes, but he did have a nude class for the men—"During one squatting exercise, one dancer had a laughing fit. Cole fired him on the spot, saying, 'This is serious!' Cole rehired him the next day, possibly realizing how it must have looked, from the back of the studio, to see all those genitalia waving about."

Alex mentioned this incident. The dancer who laughed was Rod Alexander.

10. After Carol Haney joined the company, she once made a mistake and Cole threw a chair at her and fired her on the spot, shouting, "I don't ever want to see you again." Haney was rehired the next day after Cole's blowup. Haney was usually Alex's partner when the company danced on the road.

After Alex began assisting Gene Kelly, Alex was responsible for getting Haney in as an assistant working in the movies.

11. When I first worked for Alex as a dancer, he was one of the kindest choreographers I had ever met. After we became friends, I asked him about his style of teaching in rehearsal, and he told me that after all the abuse he saw Cole heap on his dancers, he had made a conscious decision not to act like that ever. He said,

I think that working for Jack ... although I didn't mind the roughness and the attitude and he was really mad at us sometimes ... but I think that it was that... [that made me think], "I will never talk to dancers like that. They get it if you are nice to them, encourage them..."

That is not to say that he didn't idolize Cole. When I asked him what it was like to work for Cole, he responded, "I never saw anything like it and never had anyone else. I felt he was a dancing god."

12. Loney, p. 134, points out that Cole's troupe was important to Cole for a variety of reasons. "Not only did it give him a nucleus of highly trained dancers, but it also gave him a ready pool of assistants who could help teach the steps and routines to other dancers, engaged from film to film for large-scale numbers..." In a July 2, 2012, interview, Ted Klein explained how Alex's training with Cole helped turn him into the kind of dancer and assistant that could do almost anything. It not only developed amazing technical prowess and ability to move from style to style easily, but also built seemingly unheard-of physical strength. Klein said, "Alex was an extraordinary person to have assist you because he could do damn near anything!" He added that working with Cole also toughened Alex up emotionally. He added, "Alex did dance for Jack Cole and never lost his job!" The training that Alex Romero received from Cole was also vital in his development as a choreographer because he had a chance to observe firsthand Cole's innovative approach to dance on film.

13. Ann Miller was pregnant during the filming of *The Thrill of Brazil*. In her autobiography *Miller's High Life*, p. 141, she states that the most challenging dancing was during the finale: She writes, "For this, I had to climb way up high on this big platform to dance. Ordinarily this wouldn't have bothered me but because of my pregnancy I was frightened that I would get dizzy and fall. I was so nerv-

Notes — Chapter 5

ous about it that we had to do the scene over and over." After that day, Miller returned home and her new husband Reese Milner beat her so badly that filming on the movie had to be halted for two weeks until her bruises healed enough to be covered by makeup. During another fight with her husband, Miller fell down a flight of stairs and was in such pain, she thought her back was broken. She was rushed to the hospital, went into labor, and gave birth to a baby girl, who died three hours later. While Miller was recuperating in the hospital, she filed for divorce from Milner.

14. Alex's skin was lighter than Mario's and he said that everyone thought Alex looked "like an Anglo." According to Alex, Mario's skin was the darkest of all of his brothers: "Mario was the only one who looked like a Mexican." When the pool officials denied Mario access to the facility that day, Alex also refused to swim. He said he threw a quarter at the guard and shouted, "I'm a Mexican, too!" After the two boys left, Alex came up with the idea of picking up big clods of dirt which he threw over the wall into the pool before running away.

15. Alex described the *Down to Earth* costumes by saying, "[We had] things around our arms and just half, little shorts, that looked like leather ... and we had funny hair. [Cole] made that himself. He took wire ... big thick wire and wound it around and painted it. He told the department what to do..."

16. Loney, p 148, describes another of Cole's dangerous stunts on *Down to Earth*. Originally a platform was supposed to lower from the top of the stage carrying nine women who played the Muses, with Rod Alexander as an escort. During a rehearsal, a hitch on one of the cables suspending the platform slipped and it rapidly crashed down to the stage floor. Alexander was able to jump off but the women were not and hit the floor. No one was hurt, but it was decided that the effect should be cut.

17. As Alex got busier with his work in the movies, Lunard took over most of the teaching at the Dance Art Studio. Alex eventually closed the studio as he became more and more involved with his work as a staff assistant at MGM and then as a choreographer.

18. Alex's daughters remembered this as a time of real conflict between their mother and father. After Oscar was moved to the sanitarium, Madame Gobri, sometimes called Sammy Belle, continued to live with the family. In exchange for her room and board, the Parisian ballerina offered dancing lessons to Alex's daughters. She also taught ballet at Alex's dance studio for a while. Gobri lived with Alex and his family for almost two years. When her visa was running out, Alex and Faun tried to arrange a marriage for her to dancer Frank Magrin, later one of the inmates in *Jailhouse Rock*. Magrin took classes and also taught at Alex's dance studio. Gobri was several years older than Magrin and wore a monocle. According to Alex's daughter Melinda, Gobri was "not too attractive, and that is putting it generously." Magrin would not marry her and Gobri eventually had to return to Paris.

19. Alex remembered how tight money was. "The first night I stayed in a good hotel. It cost about seven dollars a day. Then I used to go to a cheaper hotel and I'd eat in hamburger joints because I couldn't afford it." In the 2004 interview he gave to the three students from Auckland University of Technology, Alex said that the family's financial difficulties at this time were compounded because Faun had seen a doctor for some reason and need to buy some medicine.

20. Source unknown. Clipping taken from the Jack Cole Papers—UCLA—Coll. 172 Chez Paree (night club) Box 2 Folder: 3. Another review from the same collection states,
So wonderful are the Jack Cole Dancers, they both open and close the Chez Paree revue, sandwiching the songs of pretty Connie Haines and the comedy of Jackie Green between generous bits of Terpsichore. The Cole troupe fascinates the stay-up-lates—and small wonder! The twist of a wrist, the raising of an eyebrow, the turn of a head being so significant in the Cole interpretation of East Indian folk dance, this act constitutes one of the most diverting and entertaining in show business.

21. *Chicago-Herald American*, February 6, 1947, p. 24. Review by Nate Gross.

22. Unidentified and undated newspaper article written some time in 1947 by Bert McCord for a column called "Dining and Dancing" on p. 24. Found in Alex's mementoes.

23. Slapsie Maxie's was located at 5655 Wilshire Boulevard in Los Angeles's Miracle Mile. It was originally a restaurant called the Wilshire Bowl, but boxer-actor Max "Slapsie Maxie" Rosenbloom converted the art deco building into a nightclub in 1943. The spelling of the name of the club varies from reference to reference—Slapsy Maxie, Slapsie Maxie,

Notes—Chapter 6

Slapsie Maxie's, Slapsies' Maxie... According to Alex, Cole's act originally had been booked to play in Cuba, but *Slapsie Maxie's* came up with more money and Cole decided to take his troupe there instead.

24. Oliver, W.E. *Los Angeles Herald-Express*, "Potpourri at Slapsy's—Jack Cole Dance Group Stops Show." June 4, 1947, p. B-4, col. 3.

25. Mesmer, Marie. *Stage Review:* "Cole Dancers at Slapsy Maxie's." Jack Cole Papers—UCLA—Coll. 172 SLAPSIE MAXIE (night club) Box 3 Folder: 3.

26. Laurents, Arthur. *Original Story by Arthur Laurents: A Memoir of Broadway and Hollywood*. New York: Applause, 2000, p. 93.

27. This quote by Alex came from the 2004 Auckland University of Technology interview.

28. According to Alex, Cole liked Faun a lot. Once, when the couple was invited to Cole's house with the other cast members, Cole left all his other guests and went off with Faun by himself to talk with her for hours.

29. During the Auckland University of Technology interview, Alex said that when he first quit Cole's Troupe in Los Angeles, he forgot to take his costumes back.

Chapter 6

1. During a Kelly interview conducted by Lane Fuller for *Interview Magazine* in 1994, he stated,

I had a great assistant, Alex Romero, and we took turns lifting Vera-Ellen; she was great at that. Finally, we saw that we had some high spots but we had lost our story. So we threw practically all of them out and went into the story of the girl vamping the guy, and the bad guy coming in trying to get the girl and shooting her. It was interesting to do, and less trouble than doing a thing where you start with an idea in your head.

2. At the end of Vera-Ellen's dance in "Slaughter on Tenth Avenue" she is shot and falls down a flight of stairs. According to Yudkoff, *Gene Kelly: A Life in Dance and Dreams*, p. 193,

The talented cinematographer Harry Stradling proposed the use of a 28-millimeter lens that would distort Vera-Ellen's face in a monstrous closeup for a shocking finale. Here again Gene was risking the wrath of Mayer.... Mayer's mandate over the years had always been: "The ladies have to look pretty at all times, no matter what." By this time Freed had so much faith in Gene's constant reaching for moments to spark the film, he gave the special lens choice a go-ahead. "If worse comes to worst," he said, "We can always shoot again." They never shot it again.

3. During *Words and Music*, June Allyson gave Alex a picture inscribed, "For Alex, bless your sweet soul for being so wonderful—Always, Junie."

4. In the Auckland University of Technology interview, Alex mentioned that his starting salary as an MGM staff assistant was about $140 a week.

5. Alex's mother was a strong, volatile woman, but his wife Faun could also be strong-willed. Alex recalled that when they were first married, his mother cooked for them but that Faun wanted to try cooking herself. She said, "Alex, I want to be the cook now." Alex's mother heard the request and said to Faun, "No, Faunie! No, no! You're no good!" Faun replied, "I don't care and I'm gonna do this." Alex recalled that Mamacita was so upset, she took a bottle of wine and hit herself over the head with such force that the bottle actually broke and wine splattered everywhere.

6. Charles Walters was called in to replace the original director of the film, Vincente Minnelli, the husband of Judy Garland. The change came at the recommendation of Garland's psychiatrist because the couple was having marital troubles at the time. Walters was director and choreographer of the movie although Fred Astaire choreographed his own numbers. According to some sources, Robert Alton also worked on the "Drum Crazy" number.

7. In his book *Judy Garland: The Secret Life of an American Legend*, p. 219, David Shipman says that Garland used to kid Irving Berlin. "When, in rehearsal, he offered some advice on her interpretation of one of his songs, she backed him against a wall and waved a forefinger at him: 'Listen, buster, you write 'em. *I* sing 'em.' Berlin howled with laughter." Garland also kidded the director Charles Walters who had recently directed *Good News* with June Allyson. Shipman writes, p. 219,

When, after hearing of the assignment, Walters first approached Garland, she was rehearsing "A Couple of Swells" with Kelly. "Look sweetie," she greeted him, "I'm no June Allyson, you know. Don't get cute

Notes — Chapter 6

with me. None of that batting-the-eyelids bit, or the fluffing of the hair routine for me, buddy! I'm Judy Garland and just you watch it!" As he said: "Judy loved to growl, loved to *pretend*."

8. *Easter Parade* overlapped *Words and Music*. Alex began working on *Easter Parade* after Gene Kelly was injured and Fred Astaire replaced him.

9. The part played by Ann Miller in *Easter Parade* was originally slated to go to Cyd Charisse, but Charisse strained a tendon and Miller was called in to replace her. Miller was still recuperating from the fall and loss of her baby that occurred shortly after *The Thrill of Brazil*. Because of the accident, Miller still had to wear a back brace much of the time and also spend time in traction. When she started the movie she had not been able to dance for several months. In her autobiography, p. 149, Miller writes, "I was in excruciating pain with my back all during the shooting of *Easter Parade*. I couldn't dance in a steel brace so I had to be taped up every day, from just under my bust to a little below the navel." Each night after filming, Miller had to put on her back brace and go back into traction.

Fred Astaire was initially hesitant to work with Miller because of her height, but agreed to do the picture with her if she wore ballet shoes when they danced together. Miller was also made to wear her hair flatter to make her appear shorter.

10. There are varying reports of how Kelly broke his ankle. Some books state that he did it playing volleyball with children, others say that it occurred during a game of touch football with adults at his home, others simply state that he just fell. In Alvin Yudkoff's biography *Gene Kelly: A Life of Dance and Dreams*, p. 165, the author states that Kelly was playing volleyball against some college athletes from UCLA and USC:

A giant on the opposite side of the net spiked a shot down at a player on Gene's team. The ball caromed off a hapless hand and was arcing up out of reach of everybody, a sure point for the other side. But Gene raced to make a save. He slipped on a patch of wet grass and a foot slid out from under him, simultaneously with a severe twinge in his ankle. The pain was unbearable. He sprawled on the ground, and when he got to his feet it was even worse.

In an interview held on July 2, 2012, Gregory Gast said,

Alex told me that the way Gene Kelly broke his ankle, which prevented him from doing *Easter Parade*, was that he was playing, I remember it as volleyball, and that he was such a tough competitor. Everyone else wanted to have fun and Gene could pitch a fit if he thought they shouldn't have lost, and they lost that round or that match, and there was a break in the action and he went inside to get a drink or something, and he kicked the door jamb so hard out of frustration and anger, that he broke his ankle.

In the book *Gene Kelly*, p. 132, author Clive Hirschhorn writes that after Kelly broke his ankle, Louis B. Mayer came to visit him and Kelly told the studio head that he had broken his ankle "rehearsing a rather complicated dance step" because he was afraid Mayer wouldn't "respond too well to the truth." Some sources say Kelly suggested to Mayer that he call Fred Astaire to replace him in *Easter Parade*, others say that when Astaire heard of the accident he contacted Kelly to express his sympathy, but that the idea to use Astaire as a replacement came from Arthur Freed.

11. In *Fred Astaire: The Man, the Dancer*, p. 203, Bob Thomas states that before his accident, "Gene Kelly rehearsed for a month on his numbers, including 'Drum Crazy' and the tramp song with Judy, 'A Couple of Swells.'"

12. Thomas, Bob. *Fred Astaire: The Man, The Dancer*. New York: St Martin's, 1984, p. 204.

13. Astaire, Fred. *Steps in Time*. New York: Harper & Brothers, 1959, p. 292.

14. Stanley Donen was the official choreographer on *The Kissing Bandit*, but Alton was brought in to do the "The Dance of Fury" number. Alex was hired to assist Alton for that number only.

15. Garland rehearsed for two weeks on *The Barkleys of Broadway*. Then her behavior became erratic and she began missing rehearsals. Arthur Freed consulted Garland's doctor and decided to replace her. After she was suspended Garland refused to give up the movie. Ginger Rogers was already hired and rehearsing, when Garland showed up one day on the set. In his book *Judy Garland: The Secret Life of an American Legend*, p. 227, David Shipman relates the story:

She arrived on the set in full makeup and costume. No one from either of those departments had had the forethought to warn anyone on the set, and the cast and crew

Notes—Chapter 6

watched incredulously as Garland went up to Ginger Rogers and gave her a withering look obviously taking in the down on Rogers' cheeks. To make sure Rogers would not forget what she meant Garland sent her a shaving mug. According to Oscar Levant, who was playing the part of a friend of the principals in the film, Garland "was presenting herself and parading around the set having a gala ball. She was very friendly with the operating cameraman, but when she posed herself behind [Levant presumably meant before] the camera it was unnerving. Ginger, a woman not given to quarrels, became overwrought and retired to her dressing room." The crew members were delighted to see Garland and, because she was Judy Garland, no one dared to ask her to leave; but the longer she remained, the less could be accomplished that day. Finally Charles Walters, as kindly as possible, asked her to go. She refused, so he took her by the arm and led her to the door. As they disappeared, Garland was still shouting abuse about Rogers.

16. *Take Me Out to the Ball Game* was released in the United Kingdom under the title *Everybody's Cheering*.

17. During filming of *Take Me Out to the Ball Game*, Alex developed a deep and lasting friendship with Betty Garrett, who he remembered as "a very nice lady... a wonderful lady." I met Garrett a few times at Alex's birthday parties and other social events. She was indeed a wonderful lady, and it was clear that she and Alex had a special affection for each other. Alex once told me with a twinkle in his eye, "She says bad words." Alex never swore.

18. This quote was said in different forms in various interviews. In the 2004 Auckland University interview, Alex said that when Kelly first approached him about doing *Take Me Out to the Ball Game* he specifically asked if Alex knew anything about baseball. Even though he didn't, Alex answered, "Oh, yeah!"

19. Alex said that he was used to stars treating him very well when they were on the set, but after the film was completed, they would sometimes snub him on the backlot or in the commissary. He said that Sinatra wasn't like that. Sinatra always called out and greeted Alex if he passed him walking on the backlot. Some time around 1949 or 1950, the star came up to Alex and said, "You've been so good to us. What would you like?" Alex couldn't think of anything. Sinatra indicated he'd like to do something nice for Alex's daughters, so he bought them a grand piano. The thing was huge and it took four men to get it up the stairs to Alex's apartment. Melinda was in seventh grade at the time, about 12 years old, and the piano was so big, it was hard to play. Melinda didn't like it, so the family eventually sold it. Years later Melinda wondered if that huge piano really had come from Sinatra. She said, "I would have been terribly impressed if it did." In an interview held on 7/2/12, Gregory Gast said, "[Alex] liked talking about the difference[s] between stars that he worked with whether it was about their generosity or their openness to talk about his creative involvement, and he said that Frank Sinatra bought him a giant, hi-fi television-stereo one Christmas as a thank you for working on a picture, and Fred Astaire gave him a little pair of Fred Astaire-brand taps."

20. Quote from Alex's July 20, 2004, Auckland University of Technology interview.

21. In speaking of the conflicts and problems on the set of *Take Me Out to the Ball Game*, Yudkoff, p. 194, writes, "Through the sweltering summer of 1948, Sinatra, too, was cause for front-office headaches. He continued to fight the need for rehearsals and would simply attend when the mood struck him."

22. Busby Berkeley called Alex into his office during the early days of pre-production and told him, "I'm the director, but I don't want to go down and sit in on all the rehearsals. But I have to know what the hell's going on." Berkeley was in essence asking Alex to spy on Kelly for him. Alex nodded and smiled back at Berkeley, but never reported what was going on in rehearsals, refusing to go behind Kelly's back. Berkeley eventually stopped asking.

23. In her autobiography *Betty Garrett and Other Songs*, p. 108, Garrett tells of a similar incident:

Busby had long been famous for his high "dolly" shots of huge chorus lines dancing in kaleidoscope patterns. In *Ball Game*, he was determined to get the entire ballpark in one shot. The camera was mounted high on a crane so it could shoot down on the action below and Busby kept shouting, "Back! Back! Farther back!" to the cameraman. Gene Kelly, who stood there taking this in, muttered, "Yeah, back to 1930."

In the book *Dancing on the Ceiling: Stanley Donen and His Movies*, p. 92, author Stephen M. Silverman quotes Stanley Donen as saying, "Berkeley turned out to be impossible on

Notes — Chapter 6

the picture. He didn't know what he was doing. He couldn't remember anyone's name. He'd been to jail. He had no talent by then. It was sad." On p. 94, Donen adds, "I thought Busby Berkeley was contemptible, his work, not the man. I thought what he did was just stupid, with no feeling toward people. It was everything I didn't want to do at the time. I thought it stunk."

Berkeley eventually quit as the director of *Take Me Out to the Ball Game*, the official line being that he was suffering from exhaustion. It was his last directorial assignment. Kelly and Donen took over the direction of the film and finished it.

24. According to Esther Williams' autobiography *The Million Dollar Mermaid*, p. 167, when Kelly and Donen came up with the idea for the movie they originally had Kathryn Grayson in mind for the lead, but producer Arthur Freed wanted Garland. On p. 163, Williams states that June Allyson was first slated to replace Garland when Garland was unable to do *Take Me Out to the Ball Game*, but Allyson was pregnant at the time and turned down the role. It was then offered to Williams. According to Yudkoff, p, 194, when Kelly heard that Esther Williams was cast he said, "Wet she's a star, dry she ain't."

25. Williams, Esther, with Diehl, Digby. *The Million Dollar Mermaid*. New York: Simon & Schuster, 1999, pp. 168–69. Williams says that her *Take Me Out to the Ball Game* experience was "pure misery" (p. 166). She shares a story that in one scene the two were sitting on a loveseat when she responded to Kelly's rudeness. Williams writes,

Just as we were about to say our lines, [Kelly] looked at me, then looked out at Stanley Donen behind the camera and said, "You know something? This sonofabitch even *sits* tall." "Gene," I said, "I was born with long legs and a long waistline. Swimming gave me broad shoulders. I have perfect proportions in a swimsuit, and that's why I'm here making movies at MGM. I'm sorry that my physique doesn't fit in with your plans—you'd like me to be petite, with short little legs and narrow shoulders, but there's nothing I can do about it. I can't make myself five-two, and I can't make you six-three, either. For this scene it would help a lot if you'd just sit up straight. If that's not enough, try tucking one foot under your ass."

26. In addition to her shabby treatment by Kelly, Williams also had to deal with Kelly's best friend Donen. According to Yudkoff, p. 195,

[Williams] was convinced that Stanley Donen, of all people, "didn't respect her acting." She complained to Freed, who immediately ordered him to make a public denial. But Donen took a deep breath and refused, saying: "I can't do that Arthur. She's absolutely right."

In his book *Dancing on the Ceiling: Stanley Donen and His Movies*, p. 89, author Stephen M. Silverman writes about how Donen was bothered by the swimming star's eyesight. He quotes Donen, "She was extremely nearsighted. She was practically blind. She'd rehearse her scenes wearing her glasses, and everything would be fine, but then, come time to shoot, she'd take off her glasses and she would crash into the set."

27. Alex remembered that Freed came in to the rehearsal studio and decided to cut the number. But according to Williams' autobiography, the number was shot, but cut when problems with shooting it developed during filming. She writes on p. 171,

The song was obviously written for five-foot-two-inch June or Judy, not for Esther, who was nobody's "baby." At the end of the number, both Gene and I were to lose our balance and fall in the fountain. Somehow I got through the number, but as we were shooting, something wonderful—disastrously wonderful—happened. The camera operator did about the worst thing you could do while filming: He froze about a third of the way through the song. He got behind in the moves and captured nothing on film from a point early in the song. He never told us to stop before we fell in the water, and of course our costumes were now dripping wet. In order to keep the film on schedule and on budget, they decided to cut the number rather than reshoot.

28. Alex attributed this quote to Busby Berkeley during the July 20, 2004, Auckland University of Technology interview.

29. According to the Internet Movie Database, the idea to shoot on location was first suggested by Ann Miller, who begged Louis B. Mayer to shoot scenes in New York City because she had never been there. Garrett writes in her book *Betty Garrett and Other Songs*, p. 111,

When we started making *On the Town*, only Frank, Gene and Jules Munshin were actually supposed to go to New York for filming. They were the ones running around town while all the other scenes with the women were shot in the studio. But Ann Miller was so unhappy when she learned we weren't going that she went to Arthur Freed, the producer of the movie, and cried real tears and said it wasn't fair. He relented so we all went and stayed at the Waldorf for a week. While the boys were working, we went shopping and to Broadway shows, saw friends, and had a ball.

Yudkoff writes, p. 197,

From his first moments on the assignment, Gene was determined to create a film wrenched free of the limitations of the Hollywood studio. He said: "It was only in *On the Town* that we tried something entirely new in the musical film. Live people get off a real ship in the Brooklyn Navy Yard [a dock Gene knew well from his own naval service]... We did a lot of quick cutting — we'd be on top of Radio City and then on the bottom — we'd cut from Mulberry Street to Third Avenue — and so the dissolve went out of style. This was one of the things that changed the history of musicals more than anything.

30. The filming of *On the Town* began on March 5, 1949. The film's principals went to New York City for locations shots on May 23.

31. Alvin Yudkoff. *Gene Kelly: A Life in Dance and Dreams*, p. 199.

32. Jeanne Coyne, who had been a pupil of Gene Kelly's when he taught classes in Pittsburgh, was married to Kelly's friend Stanley Donen. The couple had married during the pre-production of *Take Me Out to the Ball Game*. They divorced in 1951 and Coyne became Kelly's second wife in 1960. They had two children together, Bridget and Timothy. Coyne died of leukemia on May 10, 1973, at age 50.

Chapter 7

1. Janet Leigh was actually 22 during the filming of *The Red Danube*. She had been in *Words and Music* playing the role of the wife of Richard Rodgers, but Alex had no contact with her then.

2. In a Turner Classics Movie Film article on the web, Lisa Mateas wrote:

In order to convincingly play a ballerina, Janet Leigh began ballet lessons with MGM choreographer Alex Romero, who was charged with getting the actress into toe shoes so she could confidently execute a few steps. During one rehearsal Leigh's toe shoe became jammed between the floorboards and she suffered a severe knee strain, but she did manage to get the ballet steps right on screen.

Alex never mentioned the knee sprain in any of the interviews I did with him; however, a backstage shot from the movie that Alex had on the wall of his home, Leigh is wearing a brace on her left knee. Leigh writes about the accident in her autobiography.

3. Leigh, Janet. *There Really Was a Hollywood*. Garden City, NJ: Doubleday, 1984, p. 88.

4. When Leigh was hired by Howard Hughes to do a movie, she begged to have Alex as her choreographer. She arranged a meeting between Alex and Hughes to discuss the particulars. At the meeting Hughes told Alex that he couldn't use him because he had already contracted Marge and Gower Champion. Hughes eventually scrapped the picture entirely.

5. Charles Walters was originally slated to direct *Annie Get Your Gun* but when Arthur Freed asked him to renew his contract, the salary offered was the same as what he had been getting as a choreographer, not taking into account that he was now director. Walters refused the offer, but had his agent enter into negotiations. Freed accused Walters of being greedy and gave the film to Busby Berkeley. However, the relationship between Judy Garland and Berkeley proved to be so volatile, that Freed again approached Walters and asked him to take over the project. After Garland was fired from the project and Betty Hutton was hired, Walters left the movie and was replaced by George Sidney.

6. Shooting on *Annie Get Your Gun* began on April 4, 1949. On April 5 Keel fell off his horse when it was spooked by Busby Berkeley's yelling. The horse rolled onto Keel and broke Keel's ankle. Keel was unable to work on the film for the next six weeks as he recovered.

7. Shipman, David. *Judy Garland: The Secret Life of an American Legend*. New York: Hyperion, 1993, p. 238.

8. By the time the "I'm an Indian Too" number was being filmed, Busby Berkeley had been replaced with Charles Walters.

9. According to Shipman, pp. 239–41, Garland's contract was suspended by letter. The first arrived on May 10, 1949, from the vice-president of the studio, L.K. Sidney, the father of director George Sidney who eventually took over the directing of the film. The letter warned Garland that the studio had the

Notes — Chapter 7

right to replace her. A second letter arrived that same afternoon firing Garland. According to Shipman, "[T]he studio aide who delivered the letter, remembered Garland throwing herself on the floor in anguish, crying, 'No! No! No!,' but another version of the story has her saying to him: 'You can't do this to me. With this makeup on, I don't even know what tribe I belong to. What reservation do I go to?'" Alex repeated several times the story of Freed screaming at Garland on the set at the end of the number, and Garland not saying a word. The star's firing might have consisted of a combination of scenarios.

10. According to her autobiography, Hutton had originally tried to get her studio, Paramount, to buy the rights to *Annie Get Your Gun* so she could do the film version. But Freed at MGM secured the rights first, planning the musical as a vehicle for Judy Garland. (Ginger Rogers had also expressed interest in doing the part, but was told she was too elegant for the role.) After Garland was fired, Betty Garrett was told by studio head Dory Schary that she would be Garland's replacement. Garrett was thrilled by the offer, but she was hesitant to sign a seven-year contract with MGM and her lawyer had her hold out as negotiations were going on. In addition, her agent at William Morris also told her to hold out for more money. What Garrett didn't know at the time was that William Morris also represented Betty Hutton and their commission on Hutton was higher than on Garrett, so they were really pushing for Hutton. In the end, Garrett lost the opportunity to Hutton. Shipman, p. 245, states that after Hutton replaced Garland, Garland "visited the set of *Annie Get Your Gun* and responded to Betty Hutton's cheery greeting by calling her a 'goddamn son of a bitch.'"

11. Hutton, Betty. *Backstage, You Can Have: My Own Story.* p. 232.

In writing about the difficulties on the set after Hutton was hired, Mick LaSalle (SFGate.com website) said that he had spoken with director Sidney by phone and Sidney had told him, "Everybody had a wonderful time. [Hutton] and I had the greatest nonsexual relationship ever between an actress and a director. It was so much fun. As for the technicians being mean to her — the technicians couldn't give a damn. They hammer a nail on a set. They pan this light along. If it's Garbo saying, 'I love you, I love you'—they couldn't care about that. It was a job."

12. Calhern played Buffalo Bill after Frank Morgan, who was originally cast in the part, died during filming.

13. In Keel's autobiography *Only Make Believe: My Life in Show Business*, pp. 119–20, the actor relates the story:

One day late in the picture, Betty and I had a scene on a staircase where I could upstage her, and she couldn't do anything about it. She kept stopping the scene. Finally George Sidney said, "What's the matter, Betty?" "I'm being upstaged," she said. She moved me up and down the stairs, and I played it big and dumb. After 35 takes, George said, "That's a wrap."

Alex said that Keel always came over to Alex in between takes and asked him how he did. Alex always encouraged him, but warned him about upstaging himself. He told Keel, "You got to look where the camera is and stay even with her or even slightly in front but not back here because we aren't getting your face." As Alex remembered, "He got wise." Alex said that after working with Keel on *Annie Get Your Gun*, Keel "took him everywhere." He added, "I was his best friend from then on."

14. According to Esther Williams' autobiography *The Million Dollar Mermaid*, p. 185–86, *Pagan Love Song* was originally offered to Stanley Donen to direct. When Williams heard about this, she immediately went to the head of the studio, Dory Schary, to protest. After her horrible treatment by Donen and Gene Kelly on *Take Me Out to the Ball Game*, she demanded that Donen be replaced with another director. The film was offered to Alton as a compromise.

15. Williams also writes, pp. 184 and 189, that the film was originally intended to star Cyd Charisse; however, Charisse was pregnant at the time and the movie was re-scripted for Williams. During filming on Kauai, Williams discovered that she was also pregnant. The shooting schedule was redone to accommodate Williams so that her more athletic scenes could be shot first; the interior scenes, to be shot in Hollywood, could be helped with "movie magic" to disguise her expanding stomach, such as putting her "behind palm fronds and bunches of bananas." (Williams, p. 193.)

16. During the filming of underwater scenes in Hollywood, swimming star Williams almost drowned during a shot.

17. Moreno and Alex became very close and she frequently came to Alex's house to visit him and Faun after the movie. Also in

Notes—Chapter 8

Pagan Love Song was Charles Maau, a Polynesian prince whose father had been a chief. During the film, he also became good friends with Alex and often visited Alex's family. Alex's daughters remember that he always brought his ukulele and sang Polynesian songs to them.

18. On February 18, 2006, a year and a half before he passed away, Alex told me he assisted on *Three Little Words*. He had never mentioned the film before in previous interviews, but told me this information when we were looking through a coffee table book that had photos of movie musicals. He saw one from *Three Little Words* and said he had worked on the film. He had no other specific stories about the film, only saying that he liked working with Vera-Ellen and Fred Astaire.

19. Alex also mentioned *The Toast of New Orleans* during our time together on February 18, 2006. Originally he couldn't remember the title of the movie, but he talked quite a while about working with Mario Lanza. When I suggested the film might have been *The Toast of New Orleans*, he said, "Yes, that was it. And can you believe we did a Spanish dance."

20. According to Wikipedia, Lanza repeatedly tried to French kiss Grayson during the filming of their "Madama Butterfly" scene in *The Toast of New Orleans*. Grayson was put off by this, especially because Lanza's breathe always smelled of garlic. She asked costume designer Helen Rose to sew pieces of brass in her opera gloves so she could slap Lanza and prevent his unwanted advances.

21. According to the Internet Movie Database, the hotel set used in *Two Weeks with Love* was the same hotel used in *Annie Get Your Gun*. Costumes were also reused.

22. Reynolds, Debbie, with Columbia, David Patrick. *Debbie: My Life*. New York: William Morrow, 1988, p. 56.

Chapter 8

1. In the biography *Gene Kelly* by Clive Hirschhorn, p. 174, it states:
The *American in Paris* ballet turned out to be the most expensive production number ever filmed up to that point. The scene in the Place de la Concorde alone required a backdrop over 300 feet long and 40 feet high. Gene Kelly recalled how Fanny Brice used to come to the studio each morning and sit for hours watching the set designers painting the backdrops. Over 500 costumes were designed for the ballet before a final selection was made, and the whole thing took six weeks to rehearse and a month to shoot. The total cost was $450,000.

2. Sennett, Ted. *Hollywood Musicals*. New York: Harry N. Abrams, Inc., 1981, p. 240.

3. When watching this scene from *The Strip* Alex said at one point, "I choreographed that part." As with many pieces of choreography, dancers often contribute steps. Alex gave full credit for this number to Nick Castle, but it is interesting to know he made a contribution to the final product.

4. Ava Gardner played the role of Julie in *Show Boat*. The part was originally intended to go to Judy Garland, but Garland was not fully recovered after being fired for her erratic behavior during *Annie Get Your Gun*.

5. *Across the Wide Missouri* was narrated by Alex's close friend Howard Keel.

6. Alex said that he used the research department at MGM for the sword dance because William Wellman asked him to make sure it was authentic. However, after doing his research, Alex recalled that he "got the standards and then went a little wild myself."

7. Bruce "Butch" Noel Brainbridge was born on May 24, 1931, and died on June 5, 1988. He moved in with Alex's family when he was in high school, and, while living with them, he worked digging swimming pools, a profession he had learned from his English father Barton, who owned the Paddock Pool Business. A successful businessman and a heavy drinker, Butch's father had left his family to marry movie star Evelyn Keyes in 1938, shortly before she appeared as Scarlett O'Hara's younger sister in *Gone with the Wind*. Keyes left Brainbridge for director Charles Vidor within about one year and Barton committed suicide by shooting himself. Butch was nine or ten at the time. According to Alex's daughter Melinda, Butch was "very, very bright, well spoken, and good-looking. He was a hard-working guy, whose dyslexia, especially in those days, made it too difficult for him to consider going to college... Everyone loved him, but you wouldn't want to start a fight with him; he was strong as an ox and fast with his fists." Butch eventually moved to Cocoa Beach, Florida, to work with a swimming pool company and through that job, met a doctor who suggested he go to South Africa to start a pool company there. Butch went, and the company was successful, but the doctor never kept his promise of giv-

Notes — Chapter 8

ing Butch an actual share in the business. Butch quit and started his own business, and eventually became quite wealthy. In his thirties he became ill, gave up his business and moved back to the United States. He went to live with his brother Bart, who cared for him until his death.

8. Alex told me an interesting story about Kirk Douglas that did not necessarily relate to working on *The Bad and The Beautiful*, but occurred around the same time. Alex said he was rehearsing for a different film in one of the soundstages at MGM when Douglas came in and asked what he was doing. Alex answered, "Working out stuff." Douglas said, "Well, you look strong, could you come with me? I don't know where stage 6 is." Alex told him, "Oh, it's right around the corner." Douglas insisted that Alex come with him and when they got to stage 6, there were trapeze artists in there practicing. Douglas suggested that Alex go up on the trapeze. Alex did, and did a few simple tricks where he was caught by the professional catcher on the other trapeze. He remembered, "I was beginning to like it!" Kirk Douglas then did the same tricks and afterwards, as they were leaving the soundstage, Douglas jumped on Alex's back and said, "Alex, we did it!" There is a likelihood that this occurred in 1952 or 1953 when Douglas was doing MGM's *The Story of Three Loves*, in which he portrayed a trapeze artist.

9. Marilyn Christine also assisted Alton on *The Belle of New York*. Christine had danced in the *Ziegfeld Follies* movie, as Alex had. She also was the assistant choreographer on *Royal Wedding*.

10. This story was also related in Peter Levinson's book *Puttin' on the Ritz: Fred Astaire and the Fine Art of Panache*. New York: St. Martin's Press, 2009, p. 180:

I spoke to Alex Romero, then a dancer, and a friend of Astaire's, who watched him rehearse the "Dancin' Man" number. Finding himself stuck, Fred asked Romero, "What am I going to do, Alex?" Romero suggested, "Fred, we can do it this way... and then that way." Arthur Freed walked in so Fred asked me to show Arthur what I had come up with. Then he said, "That's perfect, Alex. Now teach it to me."

Alex spoke very highly of Astaire and of how willing the star was to give credit to others for their ideas. Although Alex highly respected Gene Kelly and considered him a close friend, he was confused that Kelly was not as quick to acknowledge Alex's contributions and would work out steps with Alex but make him sit down or leave the studio if the director or producer came in to see things.

11. Alex said that he did not work on *Singin' in the Rain*, but one day we were talking about how he had done a lot of things for Cyd Charisse. For example, he mentioned going to her home one Sunday and staging her in every room of the house for a photo shoot. During this conversation he mentioned that he had also helped her once at MGM on this dance with a very long scarf. I showed him pictures of Charisse in the "Broadway" ballet, and he confirmed that it was indeed the dance that he had helped on. When I told him that the number was from *Singin' in the Rain*, Alex told me that he was not officially on the film, he just came in to help his friends. Gene Kelly called this dance the "Crazy Veil" dance. In Clive Hirschhorn's book *Gene Kelly*, p. 188, Kelly talks about the experience of creating the number.

It started off as a sort of scarf dance, something that Isadora Duncan might have done. But there was nothing especially new about that, and my concern was to devise a scarf dance that was new, and that could only work in the cinema. So, first of all, I decided an ordinary scarf wasn't any good. Mine would have to be at least 50 feet long — and it would be part of Cyd's costume. Well, the only thing you can do with a piece of material that size without tripping over it, is to keep it moving. But how? The answer seemed to be to use a wind machine. But the normal wind machine wasn't powerful enough to control the veil the way we wanted it controlled, so I finished up using three aeroplane motors. That's when our problems really began because how to use them without blowing Cyd clean off the set? We had to experiment for days before we discovered that by pointing the machines down on the ground, we could make the veil shoot up, or by pointing them straight at Cyd and lowering the velocity, we could get it to fly back or ruffle slightly. I can honestly say that the shooting of that particular dance was about as complicated as anything I've ever done...

12. Ann Miller sometimes invited friends in to watch rehearsals and always introduced Alex as her choreographer. While working on *Small Town Girl*, Alex also helped create Bobby Van's big dance number in the emporium. He was called away to work on another movie and so did not help with Ann Miller's

181

Notes—Chapter 8

"Shaking the Blues Away" for the film. For that number, Alex explained that Busby Berkeley came up with the concept and then tap dancer Willie Covan was called in to work with Miller on creating steps.

13. Quote taken from a personal note written to Alex by Miller on the occasion of the Jazz Dance LA "Tribute to Alex Romero," held on October 13, 2001, at the Harriet and Charles Luckman Fine Arts Complex at California State University, Los Angeles.

14. Alex was especially attracted by the thought of working with Debbie Reynolds, whom he knew from *Two Weeks with Love* and *Skirts Ahoy*, and also from choreographing numbers for her for a charity called the Thalians. They were already close friends. In one conversation, Alex mentioned that Arthur Lowe, Jr., the producer of *Dobie Gillis*, told him that Debbie requested that Alex choreograph the film.

15. Because of the budget on *Dobie Gillis*, Alex had no assistant and also had to do some on-camera dancing himself.

16. Eichenbaum, Rose. *Masters of Movement: Portraits of America's Great Choreographers*. Washington: Smithsonian Book, 2004, p. 176. In other interviews Alex repeated, "[Fosse] never used a hat before, and after that he did in his own work."

17. According to Alex, Pan was going to be a priest. A devout Catholic, he frequently donated money to Loyola. He asked Alex to work with kids at the school on a show to teach the students some Jack Cole style. Both Pan and Alex donated their time. Alex remembered all the priests and nuns coming in to watch rehearsals. Alex brought in Carol Haney to help, and it was during this time that Pan met her, eventually asking her to also assist on *Kiss Me Kate*.

18. Carol Haney and Jeanne Coyne were also assistants to Hermes Pan on *Kiss Me Kate*. Haney worked with Alex on the suitors' big jazz number, creating the Jack Cole-like moves, in particular working out floor steps while Pan oversaw the number. When he was called away to work with Keel on "Where Is the Life That Late I Led," Haney finished and set the number with Pan, although Fosse often received credit for doing the choreography.

19. Keel, Howard, with Spizer, Joyce. *Only Make Believe: My Life in Show Business*. Fort Lee, NJ: Barricade, 2005, p. 151.

20. 1987 Howard Keel interview http://www.talkabouttheatre.com/group/rec.arts.theatre.musicals/messages/501275.html

21. Keel, p. 152.

22. The working title of *The Band Wagon* was *I Love Louisa*. This was the title of a song performed in a revue by Fred Astaire and his sister Adele on Broadway in a production also called *The Band Wagon*. The revue opened on June 3, 1931. Adele Astaire retired after the critically successful show, leaving show business to marry Lord Charles Cavendish. The movie *The Band Wagon* had a new script written by Betty Comden and Adolph Green.

23. Minnelli was notoriously slow and *The Band Wagon* ended up far behind schedule. In his autobiography *Steps in Time*, pp. 302–3, Astaire relates that in one scene, he became so exasperated with Minnelli that he stormed off the set. Arthur Freed calmed Astaire down and when he returned to the set Astaire apologized to Minnelli. Minnelli responded, "Oh, that's perfectly all right, Fred, I drive everybody crazy."

24. The dance-in for Cyd Charisse was Pat Denise, who also served as an assistant choreographer on *The Band Wagon*. Denise later assisted Michael Kidd on *Seven Brides for Seven Brothers*, as did Alex.

25. Alex said that Daniels' full routine with the brushes and rags was so wonderful that Astaire eventually decided to cut Daniels' part in the number down because he was afraid it would steal too much focus. After finishing *The Band Wagon*, Alex called Daniels to tell him, "He [Astaire] was so tickled with you." When asked how his business was doing, Daniels told Alex, "I don't do that no more. I'm going into show business." Daniels formed a nightclub act and according to Alex, "he packed 'em in." Daniels once invited Alex and Faun see his act. The couple went to the club in South Central LA. In the middle of the first number, Daniels stopped and announced to the audience, "Ladies and gentlemen, I want you to meet the man that's responsible for me working with Fred Astaire." Alex and Daniels stayed in touch and remained friends. Alex recalled, "He had a great smile— 680 teeth!" Daniels was born Wilbur Leroy Daniels but was nicknamed Sloppy. He made $350 for his work on *The Band Wagon* for the period of one week, but the movie changed his life. He continued successfully in show business after the film, and eventually became a regular on the television series *Sanford and Son*. He died in 1993 at the age of 65. Daniels was the inspiration for Red Foley's 1950 hit song "Chattanoogie Shoe Shine Boy."

In *Jet Magazine* (October 1952), an article

entitled "Bootblack Lands Movie Role with Astaire" appeared. It offers a slightly different version of the story:

Leroy, the bebop bootblack, landed in the movies, and the burlesque dancers, shooting gallery owners, and "winos" on Skid Row, in Los Angeles, now have a celebrity in their circle.

Leroy Daniels, who has been mixing shoeshining and bebop at Sixth and Main for 10 years, got his movie break after dancing star Fred Astaire decided he wanted another dancer to do a specialty number called "Shine Your Shoes" [Shine on Your Shoes] in the Metro-Goldwyn-Mayer musical, *The Band Wagon*. A talent scout suggested Daniels. Astaire went downtown, watched Leroy dance and make hot rhythm with his rags and brushes, then signed him on the spot.

At first rehearsal, Daniels didn't miss a step. "I never had any training," he explained proudly. "Dancing just comes natural, I guess."

Daniels was a curiosity at Sixth and Main from the first, an achievement in view of surrounding attractions. Up and down the street were burlesque houses and risqué attractions, bars with sexily dressed "B" girls, pawn shops, and numberless bold shoeshine boys who literally reached out and grabbed customers for their rag-popping "shine-'em-up" routines.

When Daniels added the bebop touch, however, he became the No. 1 shine boy on the street. He danced a jig and attracted passersby, some of whom became paying customers. The crowds attracted more passersby, more paying guests. Soldiers and sailors from all over the country paused to enjoy his performances before shipping out to other points. If someone put a nickel in the jukebox alongside the stand, Leroy really got hot, added extra licks to his clever rhythms. The boys on the street smiled and clapped, but not many thought anything would come of his dancing. But, Leroy did. He once took a leave of absence and danced in Mexican nightclubs. Ever so often, he'd hustle over to a theater and win a few dollars on amateur programs.

Then came the break.

It hit the shoeshine boy with surprise, undreamed-of opportunity.

Leroy hopes the stint with Astaire will lead to other movie roles, but he has no desire to give up his bebop shoeshine job.

"I'll keep my regular stand," he said. "I couldn't disappoint my regular customers. They come down here expecting to get a dance and a shine for 20 cents, and I wouldn't let them down."

The customers somehow feel the same way, look to Leroy as one bright spot in their day.

Chapter 9

1. On June 12, 2002, the Los Angeles Conservancy presented a screening of *Seven Brides for Seven Brothers* for the 16th Annual "Last Remaining Seats" program at the Orpheum Theatre (a downtown Los Angeles theater that Alex had performed in when he was a young man in vaudeville). Gregory Gast recalled, "I took him there in the hopes that I could reunite him or re-introduce him to Michael Kidd. [Alex] always told me, "[Kidd] hated me!" Gast asked why and Alex explained that he was assigned to *Seven Brides* because he was the contract assistant at MGM, but Kidd wanted to use his own assistant from New York. Alex told Gast, "He didn't speak to me the entire picture." Gast continued his story, "We're at the event and there's a lot of milling about — in and out of the seats for about an hour before the movie starts and behind me in the row is Michael Kidd and his wife. Alex was up talking to some people. He wasn't seated at the moment and they hadn't seen each other, so I turned around and got his wife's attention and said, "Do you know this is Alex Romero?" And she said, "Oh! Oh!" and she whispered to her husband, "That's Alex Romero!" and he said "Alex! Alex!" and it began this slo-mo — two elderly warriors making their way to each other through the crowd." Gast explained how thrilled Kidd was to see Alex and then the two were joined by Howard Keel and Russ Tamblyn, who all began hugging each other. Gast remembered, "And Alex realized this man didn't hold a grudge against him."

2. This statement was made in a filmed tribute shown at Alex's memorial service. Kidd died shortly afterwards. Kidd's testimonial was filmed by Ted Klein. Klein later told me in a July 2, 2012, interview that Kidd elaborated off-camera about Alex's astounding dance abilities and how valuable he found Alex's contribution as his assistant on the film. Klein said,

[Kidd and Alex] worked together a lot on *Seven Brides*, and all the things that you saw in that big dance sequence — all of it — was

Notes—Chapter 9

worked out between the two of them on stage, all by themselves with whatever equipment they could get, but they assumed was part of what farmers would be using. And all the stuff that you saw, all the gymnastic stuff that Russ [Tamblyn] did and everything else, Alex did it and taught it to everybody else. And basically it worked out that Michael would say to him, "Alex, what do you think they can do?" and Alex would offer a suggestion. And it was eccentric stuff because Alex could do damn near anything. And they found guys who could basically replicate what Alex did.

3. On February 12, 2006, Alex told me by phone that Kidd had made this comment during a Professional Dancers Society gathering. He could not remember the date the comment was made.

4. The most enduring friendship Alex formed during *Seven Brides for Seven Brothers* was with Russ "Rusty" Tamblyn. Tamblyn maintained a true loyalty to Alex throughout his life, often came to Alex's home and even dated his niece Alix Bainbridge for a while.

5. Keel, Howard, with Spizer, Joyce. *Only Make Believe: My Life in Show Business*. Fort Lee, NJ: Barricade, 2005, p. 167.

6. Keel's act previewed in Hollywood two days before moving up to Las Vegas. It was presented one afternoon for an invited audience of friends at Ciro's nightclub on Sunset Boulevard.

7. The lead role of Ruth Etting in the film was sought by many actresses, including Ava Gardner and Jane Russell. MGM originally promised the role to Jane Powell, but then they grew concerned that Powell was too refined. James Cagney suggested Doris Day, and the studio brought her over from Warner Brothers where she had just completed a seven-year contract.

8. *The Bridgeport Telegram*, Bridgeport, CT, June 25, 1955, pp. 14–15.

9. When he was asked about Day and James Cagney in his July 20, 2004, Auckland University of Technology interview, Alex said, "It was just like heaven to me, working with people like that."

David Kaufman says in his book *Doris Day: The Untold Story of the Girl Next Door*, p. 186, that Day enjoyed making the film and played around with the cast and crew. He quotes Day, "I had a lot of glasses with a big nose attached in my dressing room. I drove [director Charles Vidor] crazy. I would get all dressed up in a beautiful dress and picture hat and come out with these glasses on. He would say, 'Get the hell out of here.' We were always hysterical in my dressing room."

10. After filming this number, Alex arranged for one of his female dancers, Patti Nestor (Patti Cox Mazer), to travel to Mountain Home Air Force Base in Idaho in December to perform it as a solo for the men of the 389th Squadron in a special Holiday show. Debbie Reynolds, Eddie Fisher, and Keenan Wynn also performed. This info was taken from an interview with Nestor held on March 20, 2012. She had a clipping from the *Los Angeles Herald and Express*, dated December 29, 1954, that described the event.

11. For the Ziegfeld Follies number in the movie, a pair of beautiful legs was painted on the backdrop. The legs belonged to Cyd Charisse.

12.) Kaufman pp. 189–90 says that several advertising tie-ins were created for the movie, including Doris Day paper dolls and coloring books.

13. "Cagney Hoofs to Keep Self Trim." *Oakland Tribune*, Oakland, CA, July 12, 1955, p. 24.

14. Patti Nestor Cox Maser, who danced in *Love Me or Leave Me*, said that Cagney was extremely friendly and often ate lunch at the commissary with the members of the ensemble. She said that on the way to eat, he would practice limping. Cagney played the part of racketeer Martin "The Gimp" Synder in the movie, and had to limp on screen.

15. *Love Me or Leave Me* was a critical and financial success and in later years Day said that it was her favorite of all her films.

16. Thorpe also directed *Jailhouse Rock*, and had been hired as director for *The Wizard of Oz* (and was fired off that project after two weeks). Alex said that Thorpe wasn't that good of a director, but he was fast, so the studio used him a lot. Thorpe could do as many as 32 setups a day, whereas Vincente Minnelli could only do one.

17. Jane Russell turned down the movie *Love Me or Leave Me* in order to do the lead in *I'll Cry Tomorrow*, which in the end she did not do. The role was eventually given to Susan Hayward.

18. Ballard made this comment when I asked her about *Pleasuredome* at an event at the American Academy of Dramatic Arts in Hollywood on March 5, 2012.

19. Despite developing a friendship with Moore during the making of *Diane*, Alex was disheartened when the very next day after

Notes — Chapter 10

completion of the film, Moore was cool to him on the lot.

The next day, I'm going to the commissary. And at the commissary, you line up, stars and all... it's so busy and crowded all the time. And as I walked up, Roger Moore's right there. He's talking to some people and I'm with a couple of dancers. And because we got along so well, I waited until he wasn't talking, and I tapped him like that and said, 'Hi Roger.' And he said, 'Oh, hi.' And that was it. I was so embarrassed. And that was the last I heard of him.

About four years later, when Alex was doing *tom thumb* in London, he discovered that Lana Turner was in the city and had the hotel room right next to his. He recalled, "And I didn't know she was there and I'm coming out the door and she sees me and says, 'Alex!' and she comes and she hugs me. And I tell her Russ [Tamblyn] is here. She knows Russ. She knows everybody. And we had lunch together that day." Turner told Alex about a party being held at Moore's place and the next day, they all went to the party and Moore and Alex reconnected.

20. Eichenbaum, Rose, and Hirt-Manheimer, Aron. *The Dancer Within: Intimate Conversations with Great Dancers.* Middletown, CT: Wesleyan University Press, 2008, pp 125–26, "Russ Tamblyn."

21. In his July 20, 2004, Auckland University of Technology interview, Alex explained that the producers of *Happy Hunting* called MGM asking for recommendations for a choreographer. MGM suggested Alex and he was hired for the show. When he left *Joyride*, Alex was replaced by Nick Castle who completed the show, although Alex's work on the two numbers was still used.

22. *Happy Hunting* opened at the Majestic Theatre on 44th Street on December 6, 1956, and closed on November 30, 1957, running for a total of 412 performances. The musical received four Tony nominations: Best Actor in a Musical—Fernando Lamas; Best Actress in a Musical—Ethel Merman; Best Supporting Actress in a Musical—Virginia Gibson; and Best Costume Design—Irene Sharaff. (Information from the Internet Broadway Database.)

23. Merman and Lamas did not get along at all according to Alex, who said that they were always trying to steal focus from each other. Alex related a story that has become theater lore. Lamas had costume designer Irene Sharaff create trousers in one outfit that clung to his body and emphasized his large endowment. During a tryout in Philadelphia, Lamas entered the stage in the costume and elicited gasps from the audience. Alex related that Merman was furious and demanded that the pants be altered. According to Merman's autobiography, pp. 198–99, Lamas tried charging the producers, of whom Merman was one, for luxury items he ordered for his dressing room, upstaged her in scenes, stepped on her lines, and even wiped off one of her stage kisses in full view of the audience. In the book *Brass Diva: The Life and Legends of Ethel Merman,* p. 283, Caryl Flinn relates a story of the two stars' first meeting (taken from the book *I've Got Rhythm! The Ethel Merman Story*, p. 138, by Bob Thomas):

The two stars greeted each other with a degree of formality and immediately began reading their first scene together. After ten minutes, Lamas held up his hand to halt the proceedings.

"Excuse me," he said in his mellow Argentine accent, "but I would like to ask a question. Is this the way it's going to be?"

"Is what the way it's going to be?" Burrows [the director] asked wearily.

"What I mean is, am I going to read my lines to Miss Merman and Miss Merman reads hers to the audience?"

Merman's eyes narrowed, her jaw tightened. "Mr. Lamas," she began, her voice growing edgy, "I want you to know that I have been playing scenes this way for 25 years on Broadway."

"That doesn't mean you're right," Lamas replied, "that just means you're old."

A witness to the exchange comments: "From that moment on, it was World War III."

24. One of the dancers Alex used in *Happy Hunting* was George Martin. Martin and his wife Ethel were both members of Jack Cole's Columbia dance troupe with Alex in the mid-1940s.

25. *Cedar Rapids Gazette,* Cedar Rapids, IA, September 9, 1956, p. 46.

26. When Alex first learned he was going to New York to choreograph *Happy Hunting*, he asked Patti Nestor if she would like to do the show with him. Nestor had just performed for Alex in the musical *Joyride* and had also danced for him in *Love Me or Leave Me* and *I'll Cry Tomorrow*. She was also in the movies *Oklahoma!* and *Carousel*, and despite having a good career in the movies, she agreed to go to New York "because of Alex. I loved him so much. He was the sweetest man

in the world." Nestor became Alex's unofficial assistant on *Happy Hunting*. One day while working out ideas, Alex said that he thought it might also be beneficial to have a male dancer in rehearsals in order to do partnering. Nestor suggested Eugene Louis Faccuito, better known as Luigi. Alex knew Luigi and agreed with the suggestion. Luigi had been in a devastating car accident at age 21, and doctors doubted he would ever walk again. Through extensive rehabilitation he was able to dance again. He had plastic surgery and worked as a dancer in films, but was unable to get featured parts in the movies because of the damage to his face. Alex had worked with Luigi during *On the Town, An American in Paris, Annie Get Your Gun,* and *The Band Wagon,* and took the dancer to New York for *Happy Hunting* as his other unofficial assistant. Luigi stayed in the city and became known as one of the most popular modern jazz teachers. Many well-known performers studied with him, including Alvin Ailey. Parts of his codified jazz warm-up are still used by teachers around the globe.

27. *Happy Hunting* tryouts began in Philadelphia on October 22, 1956, at the Shubert. It ran for three sell-out weeks, setting box office records. It then previewed in Boston for three weeks, with similar success. Because of his commitments in Hollywood, Alex had to leave the production after Philadelphia. In Boston, Bob Herget took over as musical stager. The majority of Alex's original choreography was kept intact according to Patti Nestor, who stayed with the production. Hergot changed a few things here and there, and both he and Alex are listed in the official New York opening night credits as musical stagers.

28. Alex's choreography for *Happy Hunting* was athletic and energetic as his choreography typically was. He did one number that took place on board a ship in which the female dancers pole-vaulted on shuffleboard sticks, while the men of the ensemble slid underneath them. In an interview with Patti Nestor held on March 20, 2012, she told me that Alex created one effect for the show that involved having her hit an offstage trampoline and then come flying through the air onto the stage disguised as Ethel Merman. She landed behind a rock, and Merman herself then crawled out from behind the rock to a huge audience response. One night Nestor's boot was loose and when she landed behind the rock, she broke her ankle. Merman continued on with the performance while Nestor writhed in pain. The injury was so severe that Nestor was forced to leave the show. After six months recovery, she joined the cast of the Broadway show *Li'l Abner*. She later danced for Agnes de Mille in the musical *Goldilocks*.

29. Kelly did return to MGM for the making of the *That's Entertainment* movies, but *Les Girls* was his last major musical and starring role for the studio.

30. The weekly *Eddie Fisher Show* alternated with *The George Gobel Show*. It ran for two years before being canceled.

Chapter 10

1. In one interview with Alex late in his life, he said that when he met Elvis for the first time Elvis said to him, "I don't want to see you." Alex asked, "Why don't you want to see me?" Elvis replied, "You're one of those boys." Alex asked, "What kind of boys?" Elvis said, "I think you're one of those sissy boys." Alex said, "I work with Gene Kelly and Fred Astaire." Elvis said, "I apologize." In all other interviews, he repeated the story that is told in the main text.

2. Brown, Peter Harry, and Broeske, Pat H. *Down at the End of Lonely Street: The Life and Death of Elvis Presley*, p. 123.

3. Guralnick, Peter. *Last Train to Memphis: The Rise of Elvis Presley*. Boston: Little, Brown and Company, 1994, p. 409. The quote continues:

"Elvis looked at me, and I looked at Elvis and Cliff," said George Klein, who had gone to the rehearsal room with the others, "and Alex Romero was a really nice guy, and he said, 'Elvis, will you please try it?' And Elvis got up to copy his steps, and, just from the first instant, you could tell it wasn't going to work. And Elvis said, 'Man, that's not me.' So Alex, being such a sharp guy, said, 'Have you got any of your records in your dressing room?' And we put records on, 'Don't Be Cruel' and 'Hound Dog' and 'All Shook Up.' And Alex said, 'Would you just show me what you do onstage?' Well, Elvis would go along if he thought you knew what you were doing, so he went through about three songs and Alex Romero said, 'I got it. See you later, Elvis.' And Elvis said, 'What do you mean you got it?' He said, 'Elvis, what I'm going to do is I'm going to go home tonight and I'm going to take what you do and work it into the routine, and it's

Notes — Chapter 10

going to be you, what you normally feel comfortable doing onstage, but I'm going to choreograph it.' The next day we came back to the same little rehearsal hall, and Alex Romero's choreographed the scene so it looks like you're watching Elvis. He put 'Jailhouse Rock' on and put little markings on the floor, and said, 'Elvis, just do what you feel comfortable doing.' So Elvis whipped through it, and, man, he had it. And he couldn't wait to do the dance sequence."

In George Klein's biography *Elvis: My Best Man. Radio Days, Rock 'n' Roll Nights and My Lifelong Friendship with Elvis Presley*, pp. 79–80, there is a similar version of the encounter:

Romero got right to work. He put on an acetate recording of "Jailhouse Rock" and went through the dance sequence, moving in a smooth, powerful style. When he finished, he looked to Elvis—who looked like his worst fears about dancing had come true.

"Alex," he said, "I can't do that. It's just not me. I'm a rock and roll guy—I can't move like Gene Kelly."

"Will you try it?" asked Alex.

"Sure, I can try, but I don't think it'll be worth a damn."

Alex cued up the record again and led Elvis through the steps. And Elvis was right: It wasn't worth a damn. He just couldn't make Alex's moves seem natural for him. It looked like all of Romero's work was going to have to be scrapped, leaving a hole where the dance sequence should be. Then the choreographer had a flash of inspiration.

"Elvis—do you have some of your records over in your dressing room?"

"Yeah."

Romero sent me to get the records, which included Elvis's latest number one, "All Shook Up." While I was on that errand, the choreographer called the MGM sound department and had a speaker system and a microphone sent over to the dance studio. When the gear was set up, Romero turned back to us.

"Okay, Elvis, here's what I want you to do. George is going to play the music, and you get up like you're onstage. Use the microphone, and show me what you do in concert."

I played "Don't Be Cruel" and "All Shook Up" and Elvis went through all the best moves he'd been using onstage while he was on tour—wind milling his arms, working his hips and shaking his legs, snapping into dramatic poses in time with the music, and cutting loose with some knee slides on the floor.

"I got it," said Romero, as the music came to an end. "Meet me back here tomorrow." Elvis and I went back to that dance studio the next day, and I know he was still nervous about what to expect. But when Romero cued up "Jailhouse Rock" again and went through a new dance sequence, what we saw was a stroke of brilliance. Romero had taken all of Elvis's natural stage moves and turned them into a routine that fit what needed to be done in the scene. Now when the choreographer stopped dancing, Elvis looked ready for action.

"That's me, man," he said. "I can do that all day long."

4. In all my interviews with Alex, he never strayed from his version of the story of how he met Elvis and showed him examples of rock and roll steps. I am unable to explain why other texts have differing accounts. Having seen the full range of Alex's work, I cannot imagine his ever approaching a rock and roll song, or a celebrity such as Elvis with the type of Hollywood leading man smooth moves that others have described. It was just not in his character to do that. Alex was extremely sensitive to the needs of each individual performer and each varying piece of material. He was viewed by those in the business as an innovator and considered to be someone who was creatively up to date. He was known at MGM as the rock and roll guy. Even as he grew older, up into his 80's and 90's, Alex was listening to the latest music and trying out the newest dance moves.

5. The original title of the movie was *The Hard Way*. The title was then changed to *The Jailhouse Kid*, and after Colonel Parker's objections in the production meeting, it was eventually changed to *Jailhouse Rock*. The female lead in the film was Judy Tyler. Tyler's birth name was Judith Hess. Her father was a trumpet player in the big band orchestras of Benny Goodman and Paul Whiteman. Tyler played Princess Summerfall Winterspring on *Howdy Doody* and had appeared in *Pipe Dreams* on Broadway. The young actress was killed in a car crash with her husband George Lafayette on July 3, 1957, three weeks after shooting *Jailhouse Rock*.

6. Romero rarely used assistants, preferring to work alone, but he established a great working relationship and friendship with

Notes—Chapter 10

Alex Ruiz, who went on to work with him on many projects. When asked if there was confusion on the set because they were both named Alex, Ruiz told me that he was called "Little Alex" and Alex Romero was called "Big Alex." Ruiz and his wife, ballet dancer Sally Whalen, often joined Alex and Faun at their home for Faun's home-cooked dinners. Whalen said, "Faun was a fabulous cook." The four then spent the evening playing Scrabble. When I interviewed Whalen, she said, "Alex was one of the most loving men I ever knew ... never said a cruel word to anybody ... and very, very clever ... very!" Ruiz, who was with Whalen at the time of the interview, added, "Everyone loves Alex." *Jailhouse Rock* was Ruiz's first film with Romero and he did not assist on the film. Romero did use a dancer named Betty Scott to help him for a short time when he was called away from the *Jailhouse* set to stage an incidental number on another film. He taught Scott the number and she rehearsed the dancers until he could return and take over again. I was unable to find out the title of that other film.

7. Magrin grew very close to Alex and worked with him on several projects. He frequently showed up at the house and was practically accepted as a member of the family. Magrin was a bit wild and crazy. Faun viewed him as her rebellious son, and spent a good deal of time trying to get him to behave. Magrin was unable to attend the tribute to Alex held by Jazz Dance LA, but on October 13, 2001, he wrote a letter to Alex that contained the following:

> Everyone knows that your dancing is superb, but it pales next to the man himself. I don't want to embarrass you Alex but you are truly the nicest person I have ever known. You have been my mentor, my teacher, my friend and if not for your patience, instruction and guidance, my life would not have been as full. My trips to Europe, the acts I've done, the shows we produced were all inspired by you. I don't think I have ever put a number together without thinking — what would Alex think of this?

8. Magrin and Elvis exchange taken from Brown and Broeske, p. 124. Magrin later said of Elvis's performance, "He was like an epileptic fit put to music. He had great rhythm, but he couldn't dance."

9. Quote taken from "Hey, Mr. Tamblyn Man." *Film Stew* by Pam Grady, December 8, 2005. http://www.filmstew.com/Content/Article.asp?ContentID=12929&Pg=2. A blog entitled *Elvis Presley's Movies: For Elvis Fans Only*, "Jailhouse Rock—MGM -1957," presents a slightly different version of how Elvis met Tamblyn.

> While Mr. Romero and Elvis were rehearsing, Elvis' friend, actor Nick Adams, introduced him to fellow actor and dancer Russ Tamblyn.... While visiting at the Tamblyn beach house that weekend before filming began, Elvis and Russ practiced dance movements and ways for Elvis to improve his performance.

Guralnick, *Last Train to Memphis*, pp. 410–11 quotes Tamblyn,

> I'll never forget it. I mean, no one could forget it. First, because Elvis was so big at the time. And second, when he came, they drove up in three limousines, and there was Elvis, and all his cousins and hangers-on and girls— it was like 15 or 20 people pouring out of these limos, and then they came in. It was nuts—I thought Nick [Adams] was just going to bring Elvis over, and it ended up being like 20 people came pouring into the room. They brought in soft drinks, and I had a record on, it was a Josh White record, that Elvis just flipped over. I can't remember the title, but it was a weird song, it was a good one with a real low, gutty guitar sound — I could never quite figure what it was about — and we played it about ten times in a row until Elvis finally asked if he could borrow it. Everybody else was sort of partying out on the porch, which was right out on the beach, and Elvis and I were over in front of the record player, and as he listened to the music, he started doing his dance with his knees like he does, and I said, "Great." I said, "Throw those knees." I guess just being a dancer, I could see where a couple of suggestions might help, so I said, "Throw those knees out more." So I showed him, and he said, "What did you do? Show me again." So the music was on, and we were standing there dancing in front of the record player, and I remember a girlfriend I had at the time was coming over that night and she told me later she came in and couldn't believe it, "There you were dancing with Elvis!" But he was really interested. It wasn't that I technically knew that much, but I was a street dancer, and I understood what he was doing, and I could see right away where with little exaggerated movements it would look better — it would put it on another

Notes — Chapter 10

level and make it stronger, and he got some of that in *Jailhouse Rock*.

On p 412, Guralnick states that Tamblyn saw Elvis again. According to Tamblyn,

I remember they were rehearsing, and I watched a little bit. When he got done with what he was doing, he came over to me and got me and said, "I want to show you something." And he took me back to his dressing room, and we went inside and he shut the door and said, "I've been working on this," and he started going into this dance, and sure enough he had really gotten his knees out further and gotten his elbows back and was doing more with his arms. He wanted to show me how he had been practicing, but he didn't want anybody else to know.

10. Ted Klein, who helped organize Alex's memorial service, surprised me during an informal interview on July 2, 2012, by revealing that as a young man, he had seen about a half-hour of the filming of the "Jailhouse Rock" number. He said,

I was there because I was working for the guys at Embassy [Films] and they were using MGM facilities to do some re-recording. I didn't meet [Alex], but I saw him working... I saw a bit of the filming of it. I saw basically, Alex standing there moving things around with his hands ... but this is a very inconspicuous guy on the set.

When I asked Klein how he happened to get onto a closed set, he explained that it was because of Gene Kelly. The Kleins owned the house next to the Kellys in Beverly Hills, and as a boy, Ted played with Gene Kelly's children. He continued;

He was still Uncle Gene to me ... in fact I think that's how I ended up going there. I saw Gene Kelly on the lot at MGM and I said, "Hello," and he was walking into the [soundstage] ... I guess he was on his way through, and they were having something—this musical thing was there ... it was one of those things where you stop and walk inside. You know, the light's not on so you could go in. And it was a big soundstage set, and it was all, you know...it's like a stage set, it wasn't like, you know, a movie set.

I asked Klein if he thought the number was special or unique. He said,

No I didn't, I really didn't, I just thought, "It's Hollywood." It was supposed to be a realistic thing but it clearly looked like a stage set with all these things set up and these guys are hanging off the things and this music is coming out of nowhere and Elvis is singing and these guys are dancing and it's like a fantasy.

11. Guralnick, p. 411. The quote in the text is from George Klein.

12. In his July 20, 2004, Auckland University of Technology interview, Alex said that after the filming of the "Jailhouse Rock" number, Elvis' manager, Colonel Tom Parker, also sought him out and said to him, "Alex, that's gonna make more money than [any of] the other ones."

13. Brown, p. 124–25.

14. Letter published in *Variety*, December 10, 1957, p 8.

Alex Romero's assistant on later films, Alex Ruiz, did not buy Berman's apology. When he read Berman's letter that Alex had framed and hung on his wall, Ruiz said, "That's all bullshit."

Alex asked, "What are you talking about? You know how much it cost that guy [to put the letter in *Variety*] and it did me a lot of good. It goes over the desk of almost every producer in the country and sometimes overseas too."

Ruiz explained, "No. I want to tell you what happened because I was in the number and the very next day after the opening, the *Reporter* and *Variety* both came out with it ... and the newspapers, about how great this number is and it's the best number that Elvis ever did and there's no credit for the choreographer..."

Alex asked, "So what's wrong with that?"

Ruiz said, "[Berman] saw that [the reviews] before he sent [the letter of apology] and you can see it on the date here, and he felt he better soothe you, before you [pointed it out]."

15. Goldman, Albert. *Elvis*. New York: McGraw-Hill, 1981, p. 241.

16. Guralnick, Peter, and Jorgensen, Ernst. *Elvis: Day by Day: The Definitive Record of His Life and Music*. New York: Ballantine Books, 1999, p. 106.

17. Travers, Peter. *People Magazine*, Vol. 23, No. 9, March 4, 1985, p. 6.

18. Suddath, Claire. *Time*. Top 10 Movie Dance Scenes—"The Prison dance in *Jailhouse Rock*," December 3, 2010. Accessed online at: http://entertainment.time.com/2010/12/03/top-10-movie-dance-scenes/slide/the-prison-dance-in-jailhouse-rock/#the-prison-dance-in-jailhouse-rock

Suddath comments, "Choreographer Alex Romero incorporated Elvis' signature hip shake and body-shimmying moves into this dance routine. The result? Only one of the best music videos ever — and created before music videos existed, no less!"

Chapter 11

1. Shortly after marrying in Olso, Norway, Alex and his new wife Faun went to Odense, Denmark, where the Romero brothers were performing. There the newlyweds met another performer, Erik Frederiksen, and his fiancé Edith. Erik was a musician who went on to play with such artists as Gene Krupa, Benny Goodman, and Nat King Cole. The two couples became dear friends. During World War II the four lost contact and did not re-establish it until 1955, when Edith saw Alex's name on the credits of *Love Me or Leave Me* when the Frederiksens saw it in Denmark. Contacting MGM offices in Copenhagen, they received help in forwarding a letter to Alex in Hollywood. Alex remembered that a studio mail boy on his bike delivered the letter one day while he was at work, and how overjoyed he was to hear from his Danish friends. Alex and Faun wrote back and the friendship was re-kindled. When Alex was going to London to choreograph *tom thumb*, he made a side trip to visit the Frederiksens for four days before starting his rehearsals. He recalled that as he was flying into London after his visit, the airport was fogged in and all flights were to be diverted, but the pilot saw one parting of the fogbank and made it into Heathrow. It was the last plane to land for several days, according to Alex. Although Erik and Edith were unable to travel to the US to visit Alex and Faun themselves, their sons Dan and Tom visited several times. When Alex and Faun met Erik and Edith in 1937, Alex gave them an American silver dollar. The Fredericksens' son Tom returned the dollar to Alex on his ninetieth birthday, when he surprised Alex and attended a party for him held at Alex's daughter Judy's home in Woodland Hills in 2003.

2. Alex had an inscribed picture from Sal Mineo, given to him during *A Private's Affair*. It read, "To Alex, a fine teacher and 'ditto' friend."

3. Bunch, Betty. "Time spent working on film with Gary Crosby was golden" *Las Vegas Review-Journal*. Posted July 6, 2011. http://www.lvrj.com/view/time-spent-working-on-film-with-gary-crosby-was-golden-1250 62123.html

4. *Ibid*. Alex said that Crosby had a horrible drinking problem and often drank during filming. In one number that Bunch described, Crosby kept teetering and falling over in the last pose when he was supposed to end kneeling. According to Alex, it took 96 takes before Crosby got it right. In the early days of filming, Alex admitted that he tried to cover for Crosby's inebriated behavior, but he finally got fed up with the actor.

5. Alex Ruiz, interview on May 19, 2000.

6. "*Say One for Me* at Colorado Thursday" *The Greeley Daily Tribune*, Greeley, CO, August 11, 1959, p. 16.

7. Alex Ruiz, interview on May 19, 2000. Despite the long hours, Ruiz enjoyed working with Romero. He commented, "He's easy to work with. I mean, there is nobody easier than Alex, nobody."

8. Parsons, Louella. *Los Angeles Examiner*, October 24, 1959, p. 9, Sec. 3. "TV Shows to Net Debbie Millions."

9. Alex did not enjoy working with Cantinflas at all. The Mexican comic, whose given name was Mario Moreno, was extremely rude to Alex on the set, even to the point of refusing to answer Alex's questions. Alex found out that Cantinflas was shunning him because he considered Alex a *pochos*, a Spanish word meaning a native-born Mexican who denies his heritage. Cantinflas' behavior was hurtful to Alex, who always maintained a fierce pride about his Mexican heritage.

10. The "Tequila" number that Alex set on Reynolds was also performed on a television show. Reynolds danced with both Alex Ruiz and Alex Romero as her back-up boys. Alex could not remember the name of the special, but Ruiz's ex-wife Sally Whalen said that she remembered that it was for a Donna Reed special. I was not able to confirm that.

11. During the filming of *Pepe*, Alex left Mexico briefly and flew to Las Vegas to do the number with Chevalier and a small section with Davis.

12. When Sidney informed Alex that, because the film was so far behind schedule, he would have to give a number to someone else to do, Alex remembered, "I didn't even ask who." He knew and respected Eugene Loring, but later would regret that he didn't get a chance to stage the dance himself. He said, "And wouldn't that be the hottest number of the bunch because it was so exciting. So I felt pretty bad about that, but I know it wasn't [Loring's] fault." On July 2, 2012, I interviewed Lysa Baugher Klein, who danced in *Pepe*, in the number that Loring set. She

Notes — Chapter 11

explained that during this time, the Screen Actors Guild was on strike. The production of *Pepe*, which had already started filming in Mexico, was allowed to continue there, but was not allowed to film anything new in Los Angeles until the strike was resolved. The producers decided to take advantage of the opportunity to continue in Mexico and kept Alex there to proceed with the production. Since Alex couldn't divide his time to be in both places, the producers brought in Loring, so that he could rehearse dancers in Los Angeles, since rehearsing was allowed. The plan was to get ahead so that when the strike was resolved, filming could proceed immediately in LA.

13. Also during the filming of *Pepe*, Sidney approached Alex and said, "Alex, I've been assigned to do a thing with Elvis called *Viva Las Vegas* and I want you to do it for me." Alex agreed, but lost the film because Ann-Margret wanted her own choreographer, David Winter.

14. The two men who danced with Shirley Jones in *Pepe* later came to Hollywood and ran out of money when they couldn't find steady work. To help them get home, Alex sold a gold Mexican dollar that was given to him by Joanne Woodward during the filming of *The Stripper* in 1963. The coin had Woodward's name engraved on the back, and Alex treasured it, but he wanted to help the broke dancers. The men returned to Hollywood some time later to try again to find work, but ended up broke a second time. They approached Alex, and despite Faun's protests, he again lent them money to return to Argentina.

15. Whitcomb, Jon. "All in a Day's Work," from *Cosmopolitan*, 1960. Article accessed online at: http://www.debbiereynoldsonline.com/articleboxofficedarling.htm

16. Ibid.

17. Alex Ruiz interview February 29, 2000.

18. Ray Danton sent Alex this note after the completion of *The George Raft Story*:

Dear Alex,
Thanks for lending me the benefit of your many years of experience in an art that I am totally unfamiliar with.
I am more than highly respectful of your profession, and I realize how inept I am. However, I take some pride in being able to accomplish the little I did, and I know that without your help it would have been impossible.
Thanks again for your kindness, your interest, and above all your enthusiasm. It meant a great deal to me.
Sincerely,
Ray Danton

19. "Danton Plays Raft." *Winnipeg Free Press*, November 4, 1961, Winnipeg, Manitoba, Canada, p. 43.

20. Alex was the one who originally introduced Chase to Astaire. He said,
[F]inally she met Fred and he wanted her to do the special... And I'm getting feedback because everybody is talking about it — she is arriving late. I mean, Fred, you know, is earlier than on time and rehearsing and she arrives at 11 o'clock in the morning and he's been there since nine. And everybody's beginning to hate her and Hermes can't do anything, you know Hermes is nice... I don't know what she thought. Maybe she thought, "Well, I got him now, he's got to do it." And she wound up doing all three of them [Astaire's TV specials]. And I heard all these wild stories and I couldn't quite believe it.

Alex said that for *The George Raft Story*, producer Arthur Swartz had been responsible for getting Chase her role. Swartz became increasingly frustrated with Chase's behavior on the set. Alex recalled, "Then Arthur Swartz tells me, 'Well, Alex, I fixed her red wagon. I called every producer in town and she's black balled by everybody. She's not going to do a movie here ever ... ever.' And she didn't. She didn't work for three years."

21. "Tango Revived in New Movie Drama." *Rocky Mountain Evening Telegram* Rocky Mountain, NC, March 4, 1962, p. 48.

22. Alex expressed great admiration for Cobb's work ethic: "This guy worked his tookus off, Lee J. Cobb. And he just couldn't get it. He said, 'That's pretty difficult.' ...Lee Cobb was so patient. He was sweating like a horse... And [finally] I said, 'You got it. You got it now.' And I said, that's all. That's it. You'll do it and then what we'll do is just turn it around and do it.... And he was just so great." For the close-ups of Cobb's dancing feet, Alex did the dancing himself.

23. For the gypsy dance, Alex remembered showing the number to Vincente Minnelli. "He came in and I ran it for him and he said, 'Alex, it's just wonderful, wonderful. It's just so exciting, it's just what I want.'" The movement in the routine was to the left, and Alex warned Minnelli about how the routine was directed, and Minnelli gave his approval. On

shooting day, however, Minnelli changed his mind and Alex had to reverse the dance and stop shooting while he re-taught the dancers. This same thing happened to Alex on *The Prodigal*. When he told this story, he shook his head and smiled, "The exact thing. It happened twice."

24. Clark, Roy. *Dance Magazine*, January 1962, p 44.

25. Alex especially enjoyed working with Yvette Mimieux, whose father was French and whose mother was Mexican. Mimieux spoke fluent Spanish, and Alex and she had long conversations together during rehearsals.

26. Alex Ruiz interview February 29, 2000.

27. This quote by Russ Tamblyn was made on a video that he, his wife Bonnie, and his daughter Amber shot for Alex's memorial, held on November 10, 2007. Tamblyn ended his story about dancing in the clouds by looking up and saying, "And maybe now, Alex, we can do that. Just hang in there and I'll see you in the clouds."

28. Clark, p.45.

29. Alex first choreographed for the Thalians in 1958 for a show held at the International Ballroom of the Beverly Hilton. The production, "Goodbye Gimp, Hello Bangkok," featured special lyrics written by Johnny Mercer, with music conducted by Elmer Bernstein. In the following years, the productions included a spoof of *The King and I* starring Donald O'Connor and the Crosby boys, and other elaborately staged shows. The Thalians moved to the Ambassador Hotel in 1964. In 1965, the "Cloak and Dagger Ball" was hosted by Rowan & Martin. In the foreword to Tom Lisanti and Louis Paul's book *Film Fatales: Women in Espionage Films and Television, 1962–1973*, p. 3, Eileen O'Neill describes dancing in one of the numbers Alex staged that year:

Each year we honored a celebrity with a star-studded fund raising gala. We also presented the honoree with our "Thalia" award, which Mr. Walt Disney designed for our exclusive use. Alex Romero, who choreographed many of Gene Kelly's wonderful dance sequences in MGM musicals, created our spy-oriented opening number. I can remember slinking onto the darkened stage to the now familiar James Bond theme while rhythmically shining flashlights over the audience's heads. As the stage lights brightened, it revealed our costumes of black trenchcoats...

The Thalians moved to the Century Plaza Hotel in 1966 with the show "The Vintage Years." The Walt Disney–designed award was given to Peter Ustinov. In 1968 the award was presented to Harold Lloyd and in 1968 to Jimmy Durante with a special concert given that year by Frank Sinatra. Alex took one year off from helping the Thalians in 1970, but rejoined them in 1971 with a tribute to Busby Berkeley. In 1972 the show honored Alex's long-time friend, Gene Kelly. The balls in 1973 honored Sammy Davis, Jr., in 1974, Lucille Ball, and for the Twentieth Anniversary of the organization in 1975, Debbie Reynolds.

30. Alex choreographed other nightclub acts, but could not remember all of them while I was interviewing him. He told me that Van Johnson's act at the Sands Hotel in the 1960's originally started out with Nick Castle as choreographer and Alex as Castle's assistant, but Alex eventually took over and staged the act himself. Alex also assisted Robert Alton choreographing Andy Williams' Las Vegas act.

31. "Goulash Not Food, New Dance Craze" *Lima News*, Lima, OH, April 17, 1962, p. 17.

Chapter 12

1. The sweater that Woodward gave to Alex was a bit oversized, so he eventually gave it to his nephew Carlos Jr., who was 6'3."

2. Alex learned to play jai-alai from Juan Lupe, a professional jai-alai player from Tijuana, Mexico, who dated his daughter Melinda. Alex used to take his family to Tijuana on weekends and they watched jai-alai matches and attended the bullfights. Lupe convinced Alex to try the game on the jai-alai court in Tijuana, and Alex loved it. He got some cestas and pellotas and taught the game to his nephews and their friends so he would have people to play against. The family garage under the house, provided a tall cement wall that was perfect for practicing the game. Alex Ruiz learned the game and the two often played at the studio when they had breaks.

3. *Something's Gotta Give* was Marilyn Monroe's last movie. On June 8, 1962, she was fired from the film for not showing up to work and often arriving late when she did come on the set. The swimming pool sequence is all that exists.

4. *Dance Magazine*, February 1967, p. unknown — taken from web article complied by Sue Cadman. *Gene Kelly, Creative Genius:*

Notes — Chapter 13

A Personal Celebration of His Life and Work—"Can't You See I'm Busy" http://www.freewebs.com/geneius/cantyouseeimbusy.htm

5. During an interview held on July 2, 2012, Suzanne Collins Kuller, whose husband Richard had put together the mini-documentary of Alex's life for his tribute, recalled a story that Alex had told her. He told me the same story. During the filming of one of Alex's later movies with Elvis, either *Clambake, Double Trouble,* or *Speedway,* the King of Rock and Roll told Alex that he still had not gotten over the death of his mother Gladys, who died in 1958 shortly after the release of *Jailhouse Rock.* Elvis said that he knew he was never going to live past the age his mother had lived. Gladys Presley died at age 42 and Elvis died in 1977 at age 42.

6. The original title for *Clambake* was *Too Big for Texas.*

7. *Clambake* completed shooting on April 27, 1967, and Elvis and Priscilla were married on May 1.

8. Lance LeGault met Elvis from having played the bass in a band that Elvis sometimes went to see. Legault danced in at least three Elvis films and sometimes helped coach Elvis on the dances that Alex had set. LeGault did not dance-in for Elvis on *Double Trouble* because the flamenco dance that Alex choreographed was too foreign to his style of movement.

9. Lance LeGault interview, March 8, 2000.

10. Ibid.

11. The working title of *Double Trouble* was *You're Killing Me.*

12. Filming on *Double Trouble* began June 11, 1966, and it finished the first week in September.

13. *Speedway* had several working titles before the final was settled upon. Among them were *Guitar City, So I'll Go Quietly,* and *Pot Luck.*

14. Nancy Sinatra's role in *Speedway* was originally offered to Petula Clark, who turned it down. Sonny and Cher also turned down roles in the film.

15. LeGault, March 8, 2000.

16. *Dance Magazine Annual 1968,* Dance Magazine, New York, p. 170.

17. Ibid.

18. "Alexandra's Eighty Thousand Dollar Strip Tease."

The Cumberland News, Cumberland, MD, September 6, 1969, p. 13.

Alex mentioned in one interview that he did at least 12 burlesque B movies that involved stripping sequences. He could not remember the names of the films. He also choreographed a strip at the famous Body Shop strip club on Sunset Boulevard in Hollywood. He credited his ability to choreograph women easily to his training with Jack Cole, who had his male dancers also learn the female parts of all his dances.

19. Alex mentioned in interviews that he choreographed at least five Academy Awards shows before they were televised. The Motion Picture Academy had no record of him as choreographer. There is a strong possibility, however, that he took over the staging of numbers from the choreographers who were hired for the job. He frequently did this when they needed help, or a star requested that he do their number.

20. In 1973, Kelly's second wife Jeanne Coyne died from leukemia. In an interview I had with Brian Byers on June 20, 2012, Byers said that Kelly took the show *Take Me Along* so that he could get his two children by Coyne, Bridget and Tim, out of Beverly Hills for a while after the death of their mother.

21. Gene Kelly, *Creative Genius: A Personal Celebration of His Life and Work* http://www.freewebs.com/geneius/readyforyourshow.htm

22. Quote from Brian Byers from interview on June 20, 2012.

Chapter 13

1. Chaplin was friends with Alex. The two had worked together years earlier when the producer was a pianist during the time Alex worked with Jack Cole.

2. Thalians program from 1977, exact date and page unknown; clipping ripped out and found in Alex's mementos.

3. After filming on *An American in Pasadena* was completed, producers Marty Pasetta and Buz Kohan sent Alex a thank you note. It was dated December 18, 1979, and included the following: "It was truly a pleasure working with you on the Gene Kelly Special. You are the most talented, cooperative, charming person to have around on any production."

4. *Variety* review from website by Sue Cadman: *Gene Kelly, Creative Genius: A Personal Celebration of His Life and Work*—"Ready for Your Show" http://www.freewebs.com/geneius/readyforyourshow.htm

Another review from the same website

Notes—Chapter 13

originally appeared in *The Philadelphia Bulletin* (page and date unknown). It read, Much of Kelly's own material was taken from his TV special broadcast earlier this year. The best of them was a precision tap executed in fine style with dancing partners Danny Daniels and Alex Romero....

5. Alex's assistant on *Love at First Bite* was a young woman by the name of Nancy Gregory. Alex brought her in while she was still in college. The two worked out the lifts that Alex later gave to Susan Saint James. Gregory said that the experience lit a spark within her to move permanently to Los Angeles and go into the business. She became an award-winning producer, director, choreographer, and writer. When I spoke with her by phone on June 27, 2012, and asked about Alex, she said, "He was wonderful to go to to find out what was happening ... a mentor to me ... a great guy, so caring."

6. Catherine Hicks later used the same choreography in part of an episode of her television series *7th Heaven*.

7. Lysa Baugher Klein was a part of Alex's regular group of dancers who did dubbing for him on several projects. She was also a dancer in *The Band Wagon*. A Charter Board Member, founder, and past president of the Professional Dancers Society, she had frequent contact with Alex through this organization. She and her husband Ted Klein were dear friends of Alex, and Ted was instrumental in helping to organize Alex's memorial.

When I interviewed her on July 2, 2012, and asked how she first knew about Alex, she began with a story about how as a little girl in the early 1930s, she lived in San Bernadino, California, and her mother would bring her down to Alhambra to take dance lessons. A favorite part of the weekly trip was to stop on the way home and eat at a restaurant that she thought was somewhere on the Foothill Freeway near Azusa. She said that the little café looked like a log cabin and was located far off the main road and that it was owned and run by the Romero family. She said she never saw the brothers there, but remembered hearing a lot about Carlos and the family of entertainers whenever she stopped in. She said that later in her life, when she was working with Alex, she mentioned the restaurant to him and he confirmed that the family was connected to the place. I asked Alex's oldest daughter Melinda and Carlos' daughter-in-law Alix if they had ever heard of the restaurant and both said they had not.

Melinda wrote to me about this on July 11, 2012:

I haven't spoken with Alix, but I did ask Judy [Alex's other daughter] about the restaurant and she came up with a very plausible theory, unless Alix can shed some more light on this. Dad would often misunderstand someone because of his hearing loss and, for many reasons, embarrassment, not wanting to hurt someone's feelings, agree with whatever it is they said. In fact, Judy said she had several conversations with him and after a fairly lengthy discussion, she would realize that he hadn't understood. She'd say, "Dad, you don't know what I'm talking about, do you?" She said he would look down and say, "No." I can just see him doing that ... the sweetest man to walk this planet. Still, some mysteries!

8. On the first day of filming on *City Heat*, Burt Reynolds was doing a fight scene and was accidentally hit in the face with a metal chair. The impact broke his jaw. As a result, he was unable to chew and was put on a liquid diet. The actor lost over 30 pounds. Tabloids speculated that his sudden loss of weight was a result of having AIDS.

9. The Professional Dancers Society Gypsy Robe grew out of a Broadway tradition in which a robe is passed to a member of a Broadway cast. The following explanation of the ritual was taken from the P.D.S. website at http://www.professionaldancerssociety.org/robe.html

It began in 1950 when Bill Bradley, in the chorus of *Gentlemen Prefer Blondes*, persuaded Florence Baum to let him have her tacky dressing room gown. He wrapped it elaborately and sent it to Arthur Parkington on opening night of *Call Me Madam*, telling him that it had been worn by all the Ziegfeld beauties. Arthur cut a rose off Ethel Merman's costume, sewed it on the robe and sent it to a friend opening in the next musical, *Guys and Dolls*. Since then it acquired rules and ceremony. It is presented on opening night at "half-hour" to the ensemble member who has done the most shows. Everyone must touch it for good luck. The recipient adds a memento of that show and passes it on to the next musical. When Carl Jablonski became a Board Member of the Professional Dancers Society, he suggested instituting the tradition of the Gypsy Robe to honor the Hollywood dancers. Ret Turner made the Robe. It is given once a year at the P.D.S. Fall Ball.

Notes — Chapter 13

10. Mann was nominated for an Emmy for Best Choreography for her work on the telethon.

11. Alex's daughter Melinda, Vicki Sabella (a volunteer at the Motion Picture Home), and I were in the room with Alex; I was holding his hand as he died. Debbie Bartlett arrived about an hour after Alex's death. A few hours later, we all gathered at Vicki and Paul Sabella's home in something of a wake, to celebrate Alex's life and reminisce about the man we all loved so much.

Alex is survived by his two daughters, Melinda Akard of Olveido, Florida, and Judy George of Woodland Hills, California; four grandchildren, Stephan Akard, Cathy Hurley and David and Jason George, and three great-grandchildren, Brandon Akard and Sean and Megan Hurley.

Two months after his death, a memorial service was held on Sunday, November 10, 2007, at 3:00 P.M. in the Dance Theater at Glendale Community College. Family, friends, and colleagues gathered to celebrate the life and legacy of this talented, gentle man. It was a tearful and yet joyous celebration of a life well-danced and well-lived.

Bibliography

Books

Astaire, Fred. *Steps in Time*. New York: Harper and Brothers, 1959.
Brown, Peter Harry, and Pat H. Broeske. *Down at the End of Lonely Street: The Life and Death of Elvis Presley*. New York: Dutton, 1997.
Casper, Joseph Andrew. *Stanley Donen*. Metuchen, NJ: Scarecrow, 1983.
Connor, Jim. *Ann Miller Tops in Taps: An Authorized Pictorial History*. New York: Franklin Watts, 1981.
Diccionario Histórico y Biográfico de la Revolución Mexicana. México: Instituto Nacional de Estudios Históricos de la Revolución Mexicana Secretaría de Gobernación, Tomo V, 1992, p. 222.
Eichenbaum, Rose. *Masters of Movement: Portraits of America's Great Choreographers*. Washington: Smithsonian, 2004.
_____, and Aron Hirt-Manheimer. "Russ Tamblyn" in *The Dancer Within: Intimate Conversations with Great Dancers*. Middletown, CT: Wesleyan University Press, 2008, pp. 125–126.
Flinn, Caryl. *Brass Diva: The Life and Legends of Ethel Merman*. Berkley: University of California Press, 2007.
Garrett, Betty, with Ron Rapoport. *Betty Garrett and Other Songs*. New York: Madison, 1998.
Giordano, Gus. *Anthology of American Jazz Dance*. Evanston, IL: Orion, 1978.
Goldman, Albert. *Elvis*. New York: McGraw-Hill, 1981.
Grider, Ann Sylvia, and Lou Halsell Rodenberger. *Texas Women Writers: A Tradition of Their Own*. College Station: Texas A&M University Press, 1997.
Guralnick, Peter. *Last Train to Memphis: The Rise of Elvis Presley*. Boston: Little, Brown, 1994.
_____, and Ernst Jorgensen. *Elvis: Day by Day: The Definitive Record of His Life and Music*. New York: Ballantine, 1999.
Harris, Charles H., and Louis R. Sadler. *The Texas Rangers and the Mexican Revolution: The Bloodiest Decade, 1910–1920*. Albuquerque: University of New Mexico Press, 2004.
Hirschhorn, Clive. *Gene Kelly: A Biography*. New York: St. Martin's, 1974.
Kaufman, David. *Doris Day: The Untold Story of the Girl Next Door*. New York: Virgin, 2008.

Bibliography

Keel, Howard, with Joyce Spizer. *Only Make Believe: My Life in Show Business.* Fort Lee, NJ: Barricade, 2005.
Klein, George, with Chuck Crisafulli. *Elvis, My Best Man: Radio Days, Rock 'n' Roll Nights and My Lifelong Friendship with Elvis Presley.* New York: Crown, 2010.
Leigh, Janet. *There Really Was a Hollywood.* Garden City, NJ: Doubleday, 1984.
Levinson, Peter. *Puttin' on the Ritz: Fred Astaire and the Fine Art of Panache.* New York: St. Martin's, 2009.
Lisanti, Tom, and Louis Paul. *Film Fatales: Women in Espionage Films and Television, 1962–1973.* Jefferson, NC: McFarland, 2002.
Loney, Glenn. *Unsung Genius: The Passion of Dancer-Choreographer Jack Cole.* New York: Franklin Watts, 1984.
Merman, Ethel, with George Eells. *Merman: An Autobiography.* New York: Simon and Schuster, 1978.
Miller, Ann, with Norma Lee Browning. *Miller's High Life.* Garden City, NJ: Doubleday, 1972.
Nash, Alanna. *Elvis Aaron Presley: Revelations from the Memphis Mafia.* New York: HarperCollins, 1995.
Reynolds, Debbie, with David Patrick Columbia. *Debbie: My Life.* New York: William Morrow, 1988.
Sennett, Ted. *The Art of Hanna-Barbera: Fifty Years of Creativity.* New York: Viking Studio, 1989.
_____. *Hollywood Musicals.* New York: Harry N. Abrams, 1981.
Shipman, David. *Judy Garland: The Secret Life of an American Legend.* New York: Hyperion, 1993.
Sidney, Robert. *With Malice Towards Some: Tales from a Life Dancing with Stars.* Bloomington, IN: 1st Books Library, 2003.
Silverman, Stephen M. *Dancing on the Ceiling: Stanley Donen and His Movies.* New York: Alfred A. Knopf, 1996.
Thomas, Bob. *Fred Astaire: The Man, the Dancer.* New York: St. Martin's, 1984.
Williams, Esther, with Digby Diehl. *The Million Dollar Mermaid.* New York: Simon and Schuster, 1999.
Worth, Fred L., and Steve D. Tamerius. *Elvis: His Life From A to Z.* New York: Wings, 1990.
Yudkoff, Alvin. *Gene Kelly: A Life in Dance and Dreams.* New York: Back Stage, 1999.

Articles and Other Sources

"Alexandra's Eighty Thousand Dollar Strip Tease" *The Cumberland News*, Cumberland, MD, September 6, 1969, p. 13.
"All Had a Chance at 'Hunting' Role." *Cedar Rapids Gazette*, Cedar Rapids, IA, September 9, 1956, p. 46.
Alton Evening Telegraph, Alton, IL, September 24, 1906, p. 1.
"Cagney Hoofs to Keep Self Trim." *Oakland Tribune*, Oakland, CA, July 12, 1955, p. 24.
Clark, Roy. *Dance Magazine*, January 1962, pp. 42–45.

Bibliography

"Danton Plays Raft." *Winnipeg Free Press*, Winnipeg, Manitoba, Canada, November 4, 1961, p. 43.

El Imparcial de Texas ("A Commercial Weekly Newspaper of General Information and Variety") Book IV, Number 160. San Antonio, Texas, October 30, 1913.

"Goulash Not Food, New Dance Craze." *Lima News*, Lima, OH, April 17, 1962, p. 17.

Gross, Nate. *Chicago-Herald American*, February 6, 1947, p. 24.

The Idea "Venetian Nights Depicted on Stage in Gondoliers Setting." Published by Fanchon & Marco, Los Angeles: December 27, 1930, p. 1. Presented as Part II of The Last Word, prepared by the F&M Publicity Staff, Vol. 4, No. 51.

Jack Cole Papers— UCLA — Coll. 172. Studio Dance Workshop comments; interviews about J.C. Box 4 Folder 4; Chez Paree (night club) Box 2 Folder: 3; SLAPSIE MAXIE (night club) Box 3 Folder: 3.

Laredo Times, Laredo, TX, March 25, 1917, p. 8.

"Lively Program Hold Capitol Theater Stage." *The Salt Lake Tribune*, Salt Lake City, UT, December 10, 1928, p. 9.

Long Beach Independent, Long Beach, CA, August 17, 1947, p. 62.

Los Angeles Times, September 18, 2007, Sec. B, p.9, col. 1. (Alex Romero's obituary.)

Mesmer, Marie. *Stage Review:* "Cole Dancers at Slapsy Maxie's." *Jet*, Vol. 22, No. 26, October 1952, pp. 60–61.

"New Thrill Film With 'Artsists' [sic] Next at Capitol." *The Salt Lake Tribune*, Salt Lake City, UT, December 9, 1928, p. 58.

Oakland Tribune, Oakland, CA, April 13, 1945, p. 12.

_____, April 29, 1950, p. 7.

Ogden Standard-Examiner Ogden, UT, June 10, 1928, p. 6.

_____, Ogden, UT, August 10, 1933, p. 12.

Oliver, W.E. "Potpourri at Slapsy's: Jack Cole Dance Group Stops Show." *Los Angeles Herald-Express*, June 4, 1947, p. B-4, col. 3.

Parsons, Louella. "TV Shows to Net Debbie Millions." *Los Angeles Examiner*, October 24, 1959, p. 9, Sec. 3.

Rice, Charles D. "Pepe Meets the Gang." *The Milwaukee Journal*, November 11, 1960, pp. 183–184.

"Ruth Etting Story Here." *The Bridgeport Telegram*, Bridgeport, CT, June 25, 1955, pp. 14–15.

Travers, Peter. *People Magazine*, Vol. 23, No. 9, March 4, 1985, p. 6.

Salt Lake Tribune, Salt Lake City, April 1, 1949, p. 25.

The San Antonio Light, San Antonio, TX, December 5, 1911, p.1.

_____, December 7, 1911, p.1.

_____, November 10, 1913, p.2.

"'Say One for Me' at Colorado Thursday." *The Greeley Daily Tribune*, Greeley, CO, August 11, 1959, p. 16.

"Tango Revived in New Movie Drama." *Rocky Mount Evening Telegram*, Rocky Mount, NC, March 4, 1962, p. 48.

"Venetian Nights Depicted on Stage in Gondoliers Setting," *The Idea*. Published by Fanchon & Marco, Inc., LA: Dec. 27, 1930, p. 1, Presented as Part II of The Last Word, Prepared by the F & M Publicity Staff, Vol. 4, No. 51.

Bibliography

Websites

Boross, Bob. "All That's Jazz: The Art of Jazz Dance." *Dance Magazine*, August 1999. http://findarticles.com/p/articles/mi_m1083/is_8_73/ai_55292586/?tag=content;coll.

Bunch, Betty. "Time Spent Working on Film with Gary Crosby Was Golden" *Las Vegas Review-Journal*, posted July 6, 2011. http://www.lvrj.com/view/time-spent-working-on-film-with-gary-crosby-was-golden-125062123.html.

Cadman, Sue. Gene Kelly, Creative Genius: A Personal Celebration of His Life and Work. http://www.freewebs.com/geneius/

Elvis Presley's Movies: For Elvis Fans Only, "Jailhouse Rock — MGM — 1957," July 22, 2004. http://movies.elvispresley.com.au/jailhouse_rock.shtml.

G.J. Demko's Landscapes of Crime:Mysteries in Mexico. http://www.dartmouth.edu/~gjdemko/mexico.htm.

Grady, Pam. "Hey, Mr. Tamblyn Man." *Film Stew* Interview, December 8, 2005. http://www.filmstew.com/Content/Article.asp?ContentID=12929&Pg=2.

"Howard Keel Interview, 1987." http://www.talkabouttheatre.com/group/rec.arts.theatre.muscials/messages/501275.html

Interview Magazine, May 1994. Gene Kelly interviewed by Lane Fuller. http://www.genekellyscene.com/Interview.htm.

"Jack Cole Made Marilyn Monroe Move." *Los Angeles Times*. August 9, 2009. p. 4. http://articles.latimes.com/2009/aug/09/entertainment/ca-marilyn-monroe9/4.

Kanellos, Nicolás. "Recovering and Re-constructing Early Twentieth-Century Hispanic Immigrant Print Culture in the US." *Oxford Journals: American Literary History,* http://alh.oxfordjournals.org/.

La Salle, Mike. "Time Has Changed 'Annie Get Your Gun' / Irving Berlin Musical Rereleased on DVD, VHS," November 12, 2000, SFGate.com. http://articles.sfgate.com/2000-11-12/entertainment/17666309_1_judy-garland-turner-classic-movies-hutton-extras.

Mateas, Lisa. "The Red Danube." Turner Classic Movies, http://www.tcm.com/this-month/article/189019%7C0/The-Red-Danube.html.

Pickens, J.N. Comet Over Hollywood: The Classic Movie Lover's Blog — You Can't Get a Role with a Gun: The Story Behind "Annie Get Your Gun." August 16, 2011. http://cometoverhollywood.com/2011/08/16/you-cant-get-a-role-with-a-gun-the-story-behind-annie-get-your-gun/.

Professional Dancers Society, Inc. http://www.professionaldancerssociety.org

Solomon, Sarah. "Western Military Academy." http://www.lib.niu.edu/1998/ihy981215.html

Suddath, Claire. "Top 10 Movie Dance Scenes—'The Prison Dance in Jailhouse Rock.'" *Time*, December 3, 2010. http://entertainment.time.com/2010/12/03/top-10-movie-dance-scenes/slide/the-prison-dance-in-jailhouse-rock/#the-prison-dance-in-jailhouse-rock.

Whitcomb, Jon. "All in a Day's Work." *Cosmopolitan*, 1960. http://www.debbiereynoldsonline.com/articleboxofficedarling.htm.

Index

Page numbers in **_bold italics_** indicate illustrations.

"Abba Dabba Honeymoon" 71
Across the Wide Missouri 75–6, 180*n*5
The Affairs of Dobie Gillis 78, 80–1, 182*n*14, 182*n*15
Akard, Melinda Maria Romero 3, 30, 32, 43–5, 92, 96, 126, 163*n*8, 164*n*9, 164*n*10, 165*n*1, 165*n*2, 170*n*12, 170*n*17, 173*n*18, 176*n*19, 180–1*n*7, 192*n*2, 194*n*7, 195*n*11
Akers, Karen 137
Aldrich, Robert 131–2
Alexander, Rod 40–1, 43, 47, 171*n*3, 171*n*4, 171–2*n*7, 172*n*9, 173*n*16
Ali Baba and the Forty Thieves 37
Allen, Sydney Marcene *see* Romero, Sydney
Allyson, June 51–3, **_53_**, 174*n*3, 174*n*7, 177*n*24
Alton, Robert 38, 50–1, 54–5, 66–7, 69, 73–6, 175*n*14, 181*n*9
Ames, Francine 41, 171*n*4
Ames Brothers 96
An American in Paris 72–3, 140, 185–6*n*26
"American in Paris Ballet" 72–3, 180*n*1
An American in Pasadena 134–5, **_134_**, 136, 139, 193–4*n*3
Annie 136
Annie Get Your Gun 66–9, 81, 178*n*5, 6, 179*n*10, 179*n*13, 180*n*21, 180*n*4, 185–6*n*26
"Arm Full of Sunshine" 136
Armstrong, Louis 73
Arnaz, Desi 47
"Arthur Godfrey in Hollywood" 122
Astaire, Fred 7, 38, 52, 54–6, 71, 77, 82, 99, 116, 133–4, 174*n*6, 175*n*8, 175*n*9, 175*n*10, 176*n*19, 180*n*18, 181*n*10, 182*n*22, 182*n*23, 182–3*n*25, 186*n*1, 191*n*20

"Baby Doll" 59, 177*n*27
The Bad and the Beautiful 76, 181*n*8
Bainbridge, Alix 165*n*4, 170*n*11, 184*n*4, 194*n*7
Bainbridge, Bart 76, 170*n*11, 180–1*n*7
Bainbridge, Bruce "Butch" Noel 76, 138, 180–1*n*7, 170*n*11

Ball, Lucille 125–6, 135, 192*n*29
Ballard, Kaye 91, 184*n*18
The Band Wagon 78, 82, 182*n*22, 182*n*23, 182*n*24, 182*n*25, 185–6*n*26, 194*n*7
The Barkleys of Broadway 54–6
Bartlett, Bill 2–3
Bartlett, Debbie 2–3, 195*n*11
Beaver, Anita 47
The Belle of New York 76–7, 181*n*9
Benny, Jack 125
Berkeley, Busby 58–9, 66, 71, 78–80, 86, 176*n*22, 176–7*n*23, 177*n*28, 178*n*5, 178*n*6, 178*n*8, 181–2*n*12, 192*n*29
Berle, Milton 130
Berlin, Irving 52, 66, 174*n*7
Berman, Pandro 97, 100, 106
Bieber, Nita 41
Blackburn Twins 51–3, **_53_**, 54
Blaine, Vivian 76
"Boulevard of Broken Dreams" 116
Brian, David 73
Brice, Fanny 180*n*1
Brigada Quiroga 7, 162*n*1
"Broadway Melody Ballet" 77, 181*n*11
Brown, Bryan 137
Buchanan, Jack 83
Burns, George 96
Buttons, Red 96
Byers, Brian 132, 193*n*20

Cagney, James 85, 87–8, 184*n*7, 184*n*9, 184*n*14
Calhern, Louis 69, 179*n*12
Cantinflas 113, 190*n*9
Cantor, Eddie 96
Caron, Leslie 110, 140
Carpenter, Carleton 71
Casa de Quiroga family home 7, **_9_**, 161*n*1, 162*n*3
Castle, Nick 43, 51, 71, 73, 76, 119, 172*n*9, 180*n*3, 185*n*21, 192*n*30
Chakiris, George 139
Champion, Gower 113, 178*n*4

201

Index

Chaplin, Charlie 14, 165n6
Chaplin, Saul 133
Charisse, Cyd 5, 54, 77, 83, 135, 175n9, 179n15, 181n11, 182n24, 184n11
Chase, Barrie 116, 191n20
Chevalier, Maurice 113, 190n11
Chez Paris 47, 173n20
"Chico's Choo-Choo" 112
Christine, Marilyn 181n9
City Heat 138, 194n8
Clambake 127–8, **128,** 193n5, 193n6
Clift, Montgomery 96
Cobb, Lee J. 117–8, 191n22
Cohn, Harry 40
Cole, Jack 1, 38–49, 51–2, 54, 86, 88, 94–6, 125, 129, 135, 140, 171n6, 171–2n7, 172n9, 172n10, 172n12, 182n17, 182n18, 193n18, 193n1
Cole's Columbia dance troupe 39–43, 45–6, 185n24
Cole's nightclub act and touring troupe 47–50, 173n20, 174n29
Collins, Janet 43
Colman, Ronald 14
Columbia Studios 35, 39, 40, 42, 46, 47, 140, 172n9
"A Couple of Swells" 174–5n7, 175n11
Covan, Willie 181–82n12
Cover Girl 36–7, 171n5
Coyne, Jeanne 61–2, 81, 178n32, 182n18, 193n20
Crain, Jeanne 91, 96
Crawford, Joan 119
Crocker, Dorothy 16
Crosby, Bing 111, 113
Crosby, Gary 110–1, 190n4
Cummings, Patricia 41
Curtis, Tony 113

Dahl, Arlene 66, 70–1, 73
Dailey, Dan 113
d'Amboise, Jacques 84
Dance Art Studio 46, 173n17
"The Dance of Fury" 54, 175n14
Dancing Cheat 14
Daniels, Danny 134–35, **134,** 136, 139–40, 193–4n4
Daniels, Leroy 82–3, 182–3n25
Danton, Ray 115–16, **117,** 191n18
Darin, Bobby 113
Davis, Bette 119
Davis, Sammy Jr. 113, 136, 190n11, 192n29
Day, Annette 128
Day, Doris 85–8, **87,** 106, 184n7, 184n9, 184n12, 184n15
"A Day in New York Ballet" **61,** 62
Dee, Sandra 96
Denise, Pat 182n24

Desilu Studios 126
"Diamonds Are a Girl's Best Friend" 135
Diane 91, 184–85n19
Donen, Stanley 56, 59, 61, 84, 175n14, 176–7n23, 177n24, 177n25, 177n26, 178n32, 179n14
Double Trouble 127–9, 193n5, 193n8, 193n11, 193n12
Douglas, Kirk 76, 181n8
Down to Earth 45–6, **45,** 47, 173n15, 173n16
"Drum Crazy" 77, 174n6, 175n11
Dunham, Katherine 43, 48, 91
Durante, Jimmy 96, 113, 192n29

Eadie Was a Lady 42
Easter Parade 52, 54, 175n8, 175n9, 175n10
Eastwood, Clint 138
The Eddie Fisher Show 96, 112, **112,** 186n30
Eddie Klein Productions 14
Eden, Barbara 110, 126
Elg, Taina 94
Ericson, John 126
Evans, Joan 76

F. Scott Fitzgerald in Hollywood 134
Fabares, Shelley 127
Faccuito, Eugene Louis *see* Luigi
Fanchon and Marco 16–7, 20–2, 165n6, 170n13
Fantasy Island 134
The Fastest Gun Alive 91–2
Faye, Alice 5, 119
Ferrer, Mel 78
Fisher, Eddie **112,** 184n11
"Five Foot Two, Eyes of Blue Has Anybody Seen My Gal" 86
Flipper 127
Follow the Boys 37–8
Fontaine, Joan 96
For Singles Only 130–1
Ford, Glenn 91–2, 114, 116–7
Forrest, Sally 73
Fosse, Bob 80–1, 182n16, 182n18
The Four Horsemen of the Apocalypse 116–9
Four Jills in a Jeep 37
Freed, Arthur 54–5, 57, 67–8, 77, 174n2, 175n15, 177n24, 177n27, 178n5, 178–9n9, 179n10, 181n10, 182n23

Gable, Clark 75–6
Gabor, Zsa Zsa 78, 113
Gardner, Ava 73–5, 78, 180n4, 184n7
Garland, Judy, aka Francis Gumm 7, 22, 38, 52, 54, 58, 66–8, **68,** 174n6, 174–5n7, 176n15, 178n5, 178–9n9, 179n10, 180n4
Garrett, Betty 3, 54–6, 60, 62, 135, 141, 176n17, 176n23, 177–8n28, 179n10
Garson, Greer 113

Index

Gast, Gregory 140, 176n19, 183n1
Gaynor, Mitzi 94
The Gazebo 114–5
George, Judy Ann Romero 33, 92, 96, 126, 164n9, 165n1, 173n18, 190n1, 194n7, 195n11
George, Sidney 63–5
The George Raft Story 115–6, **117**, 191n18, 191n20
Gigi 110, 140
"The Girl Most Likely to Succeed" 111–2
Les Girls 94–6, 186n29
Gobel, George 96
Godfrey, Ruth 41, 47
Golden, Ray 92
Gordon, Gale 126
Goudavich, Alexander "Sasha" 35–7, 73, **74**, 171n4
"The Goulash" 122
Gray, Margery 136
Grayson, Kathryn 54, 71, 81, 122, 135, 177n24, 180n20
"The Great Lady Has an Interview" 38
The Greatest Mother of 'Em All 131
Gregory, Nancy 194n5
Greene, Lorne 136
Greener, Dorothy 92
Grey, Joel 92
Griffith, Andy 125
The Grissom Gang 131

Hall, Huntz 122
Hamilton, Bob 41, 47, 171n4
Hamilton, George 135–7
Haney, Carol 47, **60**, 61, 81, 172n7, 182n17, 182n18
Hanna-Barbera 126, 136
Happy Hunting 92–4, **93**, 97, 185n21, 185n22, 185n24, 185–6n26, 186n27, 186n28
Hart to Hart 1, 137
Hartford, Huntington 92
Hay, Alexandra 131
Hayward, Susan 89–90, **90**
Hayworth, Rita 42, 45, 54
The Heat's On 35
Heidi's Song 136
Her Sister from Paris 14
Hicks, Catherine 135, 194n6
Hines, Earl 73
Hitler, Aldolf 29–30, 164n9
Hope, Bob 96, 126
Horne, Lena 47–8, 52
Horton, Lester 35, 171n3
Huerta, Victoriano 7, 161n1, 164n10
Hughes, Howard 73, 178n4
Hustle 132
Hutton, Betty 68–9, 178n5, 179n10, 179n11, 179n15

"I Guess I'll Have to Change My Plan" 83
"I Wanna Be a Dancin' Man" 77, 181n10
"I Wanna Be Loved By You" 71
I'll Cry Tomorrow 88–91, **90**, 100–1, 121, 184n17, 185–6n26
"I'm an Indian Too" 67–8, 178n8
"I'm Gonna See My Baby" 42
"I'm Writing a Letter to Daddy" 119
El Imparcial de Texas 161–2n1, 162n5
Ingels, Mary 130
Inside Straight 73

Jack and the Beanstalk 126
Jackson, Michael 110
Jailhouse Rock movie 11, 92, 96–108, 121, 184n16, 187n5, 187–8n6, 189n14, 193n5
"Jailhouse Rock" musical number 100–7, **102**, **105**, 140, 171n4, 186–7n3, 189n10, 189n12
James, Mitchell 71
Janis, Conrad 92
Jazz Dance LA "Tribute to Alex Romero" 66, 80, 139–41, 182n13, 188n7
Johnson, Van 54, 66, 122, 192n30
The Jolson Story 42
Jones, Shirley 113–4, 140, 191n14
Joyride 92, 185n21, 185n26
Jumping Jacks 76

Keaton, Buster 14
Keel, Howard 66–70, 73, 78, 81–2, 85, 122, 140–1, 178n6, 179n13, 180n5, 182n18, 183n1, 184n6
Kelly, Gene 7, 36–7, 48, 50–2, 54, 56–62, **60**, **61**, 71–3, 77, 82, 94, 99, 103, 126, 131–2, 133–6, 139, 171n5, 174n1, 174n2, 174–5n7, 175n8, 175n10, 175n11, 176n18, 176n22, 176–7n23, 177n24, 177n25, 177n26, 177n27, 177–8n29, 178n32, 179n14, 180n1, 181n10, 181n11, 186n29, 186n1, 186–7n3, 189n10, 192n29, 193n20, 193n3, 193–4n4
Kidd, Michael 82–3, 84–6, 182n24, 183n1, 183–4n2, 184n3
King, King, and King 22–3, 169n7
Kiss Me Kate 78, 81–2, 182n17, 182n18
The Kissing Bandit 54, 175n14
Klein, Lysa Baugher 4, 135–6, 190–1n12, 194n7
Klein, Ted 183–4n2, 189n10, 194n7
Knievel, Evel 134
Komack, Jimmie 91
Kuller, Richard 140, 193n5
Kuller, Suzanne Collins 193n5

"The Lady Is a Tramp" 52
Lamas, Fernando 92, 185n22, 185n23
Lane, Paula 122
Lanza, Mario 71, 180n19, 180n20
Laugh-In 126
Laurents, Arthur 48

203

Index

Laurie, Piper 96
Lawford, Peter 52, 113
Lee, Peggy 96
LeGault, Lance 127–29, *128*, 193*n*8
Leigh, Janet 54, 63–6, *64*, *65*, 113, 139–40, 178*n*1, 178*n*2, 178*n*4
Lemmon, Jack 113
Levant, Oscar 175–6*n*15
Lewis, Jerry 76, 96
Lewis, Sammy 122
Lights Out 14
Lili 78, *79*, 140
"Limehouse Blues" 38, 50
The Longest Yard 131
Loring, Eugene 51, 190–1*n*12
Love at First Bite 135, 194*n*5
Love Me or Leave Me 85–8, 91, 138, 184*n*14, 184*n*15, 184*n*17, 185–6*n*26, 190*n*1
Lowe, Arthur Jr. 80, 182*n*14
Lucille Ball Comedy Hour 126
Luigi 185–6*n*26
Lunard, Charles 40–1, 46, 171*n*3, 173*n*17

Maau, Charles 179–80*n*16
MacKenzie, Gisele 96
MacRae, Gordon 96
Madame Gobri 28, 47, 173*n*18
Maginetti, Gloria 41
Magrin, Frank 89–91, 101, *102*, 173*n*18, 188*n*7, 188*n*8
Mann, Anita 139, 195*n*10
Mann, Daniel 89
Manuela 122
Marilyn: The Untold Story 135
Martin, Dean 76, 113
Martin, Ethel 41, 47, 171–2*n*4, 172*n*7, 185*n*24
Martin, George 40–1, 47, 171*n*4, 171–2*n*7, 185*n*24
Maser, Patti Nestor Cox 4, 184*n*10, 185–6*n*26, 186*n*27
Mathis, Johnny 96
Mattis, Jack vi, 3
Mattox, Matt 84–5
May, Bert 73
McCrea, Joel 70–1
Medack, Peter 137
Meet Me on Broadway 42
Melcher, Marty 86, 88
Merman, Ethel 92, 94, 96, 185*n*22, 185*n*23, 186*n*28
The Merry Monahans 37
Mexican Revolution 7, 11–2
MGM Studios (Metro-Goldwin-Mayer) vi, 14, 22, 38–40, 49–50, 52, 54, 58, 60–1, 66, 68, 73, 77–8, 82, 84–5, 87, 91, 93–5, 97–9, 103, 108, 119, 126, 133, 135–6, 139–40, 174*n*4, 177*n*25, 178*n*2, 179*n*10, 180*n*6,

181*n*8, 181*n*11, 182–3*n*25, 185*n*21, 186*n*29, 186–7*n*3, 187*n*4, 189*n*10, 190*n*1, 192*n*29
Miller, Ann 42–3, *44*, 52, 54, 61–2, 73, *74*, 78, 80, 172–3*n*13, 175*n*9, 177–8*n*29, 181–2*n*12, 182*n*13, 183*n*1
Mimieux, Yvette 119–21, *120*, 192*n*25
Mineo, Sal 110–1, 190*n*2
Minnelli, Vincente 72, 82, 110, 116–9, 137, 174*n*6, 182*n*23, 184*n*16, 191–2*n*23
Mobley, Mary Ann 130
Monroe, Marilyn 125, 135, 192*n*3
Montalban, Ricardo 54, 71
Monterrey, Mexico 7, 8, 11, 161–2*n*1, 162*n*3, 163–3*n*5, 163*n*6, 163*n*8, 164*n*9, 164*n*10, 165*n*1, 167*n*9d, 167*n*9e, 167*n*9f
Moore, Garry 125
Moore, Mary Tyler 96
Moore, Roger 91, 184–5*n*19
Moreno, Rita 70–71, 179–80*n*16
Munshin, Jules 52, 62, 177–8*n*29

Nadel, Arthur 127
Newman, Paul 96, 123–4
"The Night They Invented Champagne" 110
Novak, Kim 113

O'Connor, Donald 22, 192*n*29
On the Town 54, 56, 60–2, *60*, *61*, 81, 177–78*n*29, 178*n*30, 185–86*n*26
Opening Night 125
Ortega, Alma 16, *17*
The Outriders 70

Pagan Love Song 69–70, *69*, 81, 179*n*14, 179–80*n*17
Pal, George 108–9, 126, 129–39
Palmer, Roy 3, 131
Pan, Hermes 55, 71, 81, 86, 182*n*17, 182*n*18, 191*n*20
Paramount Studios 14, 132, 136
Parker, Colonel Tom 99–100, *129*
Pasternak, Joe 86
Pathé Studios 14
Patricola, Tom 22
Pennies from Heaven 136
Pepe 113–4, 140, 190*n*11, 190–1*n*12, 191*n*13, 191*n*14
The Perry Como Special 125
Platt, Mark 84
Please Don't Eat the Daisies 126
Polo, Malvena *see* Romero, Malvena
Powell, Eleanor 92, 98
Powell, Jane 71, 85, 96
Powers, Stefanie 137
Premice, Josephine 91
Presley, Elvis vi, 11, 92, 96–107, *102*, *105*, 126–9, *129*, 186*n*1, 186–7*n*3, 187*n*4, 188*n*8, 188–9*n*9, 189*n*10, 189*n*12,

204

Index

189*n*14, 189–90*n*18, 191*n*13, 193*n*5, 193*n*7, 193*n*8
Presley, Priscilla Beaulieu 127, 193*n*7
Prinz, LeRoy 33–5, 171*n*1, 171*n*2
A Private's Affair 110–1, 190*n*2
The Prodigal 88–9, 103, 191–2*n*23
Professional Dancers' Society (PDS) 137–8, 184*n*3, 194*n*7, 194*n*9

Quinn, Anthony 78
Quiroga, Alfonso 12, 163*n*8, 166*n*9, 166*n*9b
Quiroga, Humberto, aka Hombert or Humbert Quiroga 12, 163*n*8, 166–8*n*9
Quiroga, Jeronimo, aka Jerome Quiroga, aka Carlos Quiroga *see* Romero, Carlos
Quiroga, Juan, aka John Quiroga, aka Johnny Quiroga *see* Romero, John
Quiroga, Judith *see* Romero, Judith
Quiroga, Mario 12–6, 43–4, 163*n*8, 166*n*9, 168*n*9h, 173*n*14
Quiroga, Miguel, brother 163*n*7, 163*n*8, 166*n*9a
Quiroga, Miguel, father 7–11, **8**, 161–2*n*1, 162*n*3, 163*n*4, 162–3*n*5, 163*n*6, 164*n*10, 165*n*1, 166*n*9
Quiroga, Norma, family maid 10–13, 165*n*11, 165*n*3, 165*n*8
Quiroga, Oscar, aka Ocky *see* Romero, Oscar
Quiroga, Soledad Chapa, aka Choli or Chole aka Mamacita 7–15, **8**, 18–9, 26, **29**, 52, 162*n*1, 163–4*n*9, 164*n*10, 165*n*11, 165*n*1, 165*n*2, 165*n*7, 167*n*9d, 174*n*5

Raft, George 37, 115
Raintree County 96
Rall, Tommy 81, 84–5
Randall, Tony 126
The Red Danube 54, 63–6, **64**, **65**, 139, 178*n*1
Reed, Donna 113, 190*n*10
Remington Steele 136
Reyes, General Bernardo 161*n*1, 163*n*5, 163–4*n*9, 166*n*9a
Reynolds, Burt 131–2, 138, 194*n*8
Reynolds, Debbie 7, 71, 76, 80–1, 96, 111–3, *111*, 114–5, 182*n*14, 184*n*11, 190*n*10, 192*n*29
Ride, Vaquero! 78, 81
Righteous Brothers 126
Riha, Bobby 126
Robinson, Bill "Bojangles" 169*n*6
Robinson, Edward G. 113
Rogers, Ginger 54–6, 175–6*n*15, 179*n*10
Romero, Carlos, brother 12–4, 16–7, **17**, 19–23, 37, 163*n*5, 8, 164*n*10, 165*n*1, 165*n*4, 165*n*6, 166*n*9, 167*n*9d, 168*n*10, 168*n*12, 169*n*1, 194*n*7
Romero, Carlos, Jr., nephew 164–5*n*10, 170*n*11, 192*n*1

Romero, Frances "Faun" Fleury Driscoll 24–6, **26**, 28, **29**, 30–2, 43, 46, 48–9, 75–6, 126, 138, 169*n*10, 170*n*11, 170*n*16, 170*n*17, 174*n*28, 179–80*n*16, 190*n*1, 191*n*14
Romero, John, brother 4, 12–3, 16, **17**, 19–27, **21**, **25**, **27**, 28–31, **29**, 37, 76, 126–7, 163*n*8, 165*n*1, 166*n*9, 167*n*9e, 169*n*1, 170*n*13, 170*n*14
Romero, John, Jr., nephew 163*n*8, 168–69*n*17, 169*n*9, 170*n*13, 170*n*14
Romero, Judith, sister 10, 12–3, 16–8, **17**, 33, 163*n*8, 166*n*9b, 167*n*9d, 168*n*9g, 169*n*19
Romero, Malvina 14, 16–7, **17**, 21–2, 163*n*8, 165*n*1, 167*n*9d, 168*n*10
Romero, Oscar 12–3, 16, **17**, 19, **21**, 21–2, **25**, 25–6, 28, 31, 46–7, 163*n*8, 166*n*9, 167*n*9f, 168*n*17, 169*n*8, 170–1*n*19, 173*n*18
Romero, Sydney 17, 20–2, **21**, **26**, 28, **29**, 30, 163*n*8, 168*n*9g, 168–9*n*17
Rooney, Pat 22
Rowan and Martin 126, 192*n*29
Rowland, Roy 70
Royal Wedding 181*n*9
Ruick, Barbara 80–1
Ruiz, Alex 3, 101, 111, *111*, 115–6, 121, 124, 187–8*n*6, 189*n*14, 190*n*7, 190*n*10, 192*n*2
Russell, Jane 184*n*7, 184*n*17

St. James, Susan 135, 194*n*5
Saxon, John 130
Say One For Me 111–3, *111*
Scene of the Crime 54, 66
Schaffner, Franklin 123
Scott, Betty 187–8*n*6
Scott, Lee **61**, 62, 73
Seven Brides for Seven Brothers 84–5, 182*n*24, 183*n*1, 183–4*n*2, 184*n*4
Seven Faces of Dr. Lao 126, 130
"Shakin' the Blues Away" 87, 181–2*n*12
SHARE, Self Help and Recovery Exchange 113, 121
"Shine on Your Shoes" 83, 182–3*n*25
Short, Bobby 122
Show Boat 73–5, 81, 180*n*4
Showalter, Max Gordon 92
Sidney, Bob 76
Sidney, George 113–4, 140, 178–9*n*9, 179*n*11, 179*n*13, 190–1*n*12
Silvers, Phil 125
Sinatra, Frank 54, 56–62, 113, 135, 176*n*18, 176*n*19, 176*n*21, 177–8*n*29, 192*n*29
Sinatra, Nancy 129, 193*n*14
"Sing, Sing, Sing" 47–8, 172*n*9
"Sing You Sinners" **90**
Singin' in the Rain 5, 77, 181*n*11
Skelton, Red 71
Skirts Ahoy 76, 182*n*14
Slapsie Maxie's 47–8, 173–74*n*23

205

Index

"Slaughter on Tenth Avenue" 50–2, 174n2
Small Town Girl 78–80, 81, 85, 181–82n12
Smith, Kate 96
Some Call It Loving 131
Something's Gotta Give 125, 192n3
Speedway 127–29, 193n5, 193n13, 193n14
State Fair 5, 119
Steffan, Paul 41
Stevens, Connie 131
The Strip 73, 180n3
The Stripper 96, 123–5, 191n14
Surfside 6 122
Swartz, Arthur 191n20

Take Me Along 131–32, 193n20
Take Me Out to the Ball Game 54, 56–60, 62, 176n16, 176n17, 176n18, 176n21, 176–7n23, 177n24, 177n25, 178n32, 179n14
Talmadge, Constance 14
Tamblyn, Russ 3–4, 23, 84, 92, 103, 106, 108–10, **109**, 121, 125–6, 140–1, 183n1, 183–4n2, 184n4, 184–5n19, 188–9n9, 192n27
Tars and Spars 42–3
Taurog, Norman 128
Taylor, Elizabeth 96
Taylor, Robert 78
Teagarden, Jack 73
Teatro Independencia 12
"Ten Cents a Dance" 86–7
"Tequila" 113, 190n10
Texas Carnival 73, **74**, 81, 171n4
The Thalians 113, 121–2, 134, 182n14, 192n29
That's Dancing 137–38
That's Entertainment 186n29
That's Entertainment, II 133
That's Entertainment, III 68
"These Boots Are Made for Walking" 129
Thief in Paradise 14
Thomas, Danny 125
The Thornbirds, Show Two 137
Thorpe, Richard 88–9, 103, 184n16
"Thou Swell" 51–3, **53**
Three Little Words 71, 180n18
The Thrill of Brazil 42–3, **44**, 172–3n13, 175n9
Thulin, Ingrid 116
"Tina Lina" 71
T.J. Hooker 136
The Toast of New Orleans 71, 180n19, 180n20
tom thumb 4, 106, 108–10, **109**, 126, 130, 138, 184–5n19, 190n1
Tonight and Every Night 42
The Tracy Ullman Show 138
Turner, Lana 76, 88, 91, 184–5n19
Twentieth Century–Fox 111–2, 123, 125
"The Two Californians," aka "The Californians" **27**, 28

Two Weeks with Love 71, 85, 180n21, 182n14
Tyler, Judy 187n5

Universal Studios 14, 35, 37–8, 171n3, 171n5
Until They Sail 96

Vallon, Ginette 13, 165n6
Van, Bobby 76, 80–1, 181–2n12
vaudeville 13, 16, 19–31, 167n9e, 169n6; see also Fanchon and Marco
Vera-Ellen 50, 61, 71, 77, 174n1, 174n2, 180n18
Verdon, Gwen 172n7
Vidor, Charles 184n9
Villa, Pancho 11, 13, 164n10
Viva Knievel! 134

Wagner, Robert 111–2, **111**, 137
Walsh, Raoul 110
Walters, Charles 52, 76, 78, 110, 174n6, 174n7, 178n5, 178n8
Ward, Rachel 137
Warner Brothers Studios 33, 122, 124, 137, 171n2
Weld, Tuesday 134
Wellman, William 75–6, 180n6
West, Bernie 92
West, Mae 35, 167n9d
What Ever Happened to Baby Jane 119
"Where Is the Life that Late I Led?" 82, 85, 182n18
"Who Tied the Can to Modern Man" 122
Williams, Andy 192n30
Williams, Esther 54, 56, 58–9, **69**, 69–70, 73, 76, 179n15, 179n16
Wilson, Don 125
Wise, Robert 96
A Woman of Paris 14, 165n6
A Woman Who Sinned 14
The Wonderful World of the Brothers Grimm 119–21, **120**, 126, 130
Wood, Lana 130
Woodward, Joanne 96, 123–5, 191n14, 192n1
Words and Music 51–3, **53**, 56, 174n3, 175n8, 178n1
Wynn, Keenan 71, 184n11

Xanadu 135–6

The Young Rip 129–30, **130**

The Ziegfeld Follies 38–40, 50, 171n1, 171n4, 181n9
Zorina, Vera 37
Zorro, the Gay Blade 136–37

www.ingramcontent.com/pod-product-compliance
Ingram Content Group UK Ltd.
Pitfield, Milton Keynes, MK11 3LW, UK
UKHW042000140426
5217IPUK00015B/895